Tecumseh & Brock

Tecumseh & Brock

The War of 1812

James Laxer

ANANSI

This edition published in 2012 by
House of Anansi Press Inc.
110 Spadina Avenue, Suite 801
Toronto, ON, M5V 2K4
Tel. 416-363-4343
Fax 416-363-1017
www.houseofanansi.com

Distributed in Canada by
HarperCollins Canada Ltd.
1995 Markham Road
Scarborough, ON, M1B 5M8
Toll free tel. 1-800-387-0117

Distributed in the United States by
Publishers Group Wes
1700 Fourth Street
Berkeley, CA 94710
Toll free tel. 1-800-788-3123

*Every reasonable effort has been made to trace ownership of copyright materials. The publisher
will gladly rectify any inadvertent errors or omissions in credits in future editions.*

House of Anansi Press is committed to protecting our natural environment.
As part of our efforts, the interior of this book is printed on paper that contains 100%
post-consumer recycled fibres, is acid-free, and is processed chlorine-free.

16 15 14 13 12   1 2 3 4 5

Library and Archives Canada Cataloguing in Publication

Laxer, James
Tecumseh and Brock / James Laxer.

Includes bibliographical references.
Issued also in electronic format.
ISBN 978-0-88784-261-0

1. Tecumseh, 1768?–1813. 2. Brock, Isaac, Sir, 1769–1812.
3. Canada—History—War of 1812. 4. United States—History—
War of 1812. 5. Canada—History—War of 1812—Participation,
Indian. I. Title.

FC442.L394   2012 971.03'4   C2011-908635-2

Library of Congress Control Number: 2011945361

Jacket and text design: Alysia Shewchuk
Typesetting: Sari Naworynski
Map adaptation: Alysia Shewchuk

 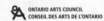

*We acknowledge for their financial support of our publishing program
the Canada Council for the Arts, the Ontario Arts Council, and the Government of Canada
through the Canada Book Fund.*

Printed and bound in Canada

To Sandy, Michael, Kate, Emily, and Jonathan

CONTENTS

AUTHOR'S NOTE

In this book, I have chosen to use the words "natives" and "native peoples" when discussing indigenous peoples in both the United States and British North America. The terms "First Nations" and "aboriginal peoples," while commonly used in Canada, are not regularly used in the United States. The usual reference today in the United States is either to "Native Americans" or to the specific group to which the author is referring, such as "Shawnees." The word "Indian" is used when it appears in a quote from the writings of the period.

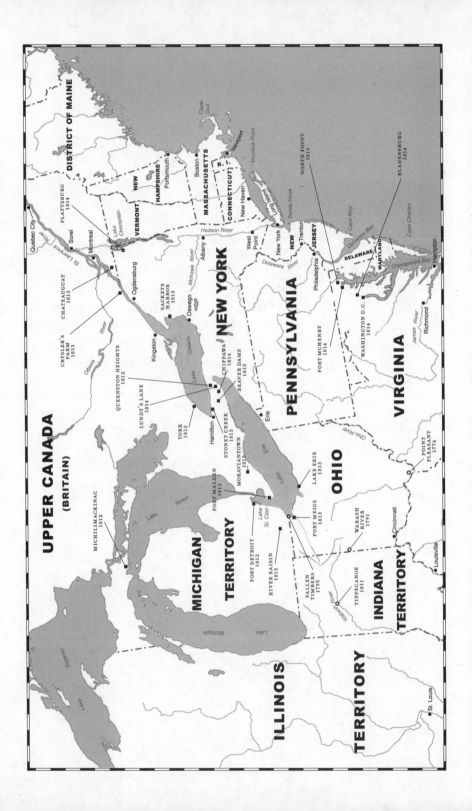

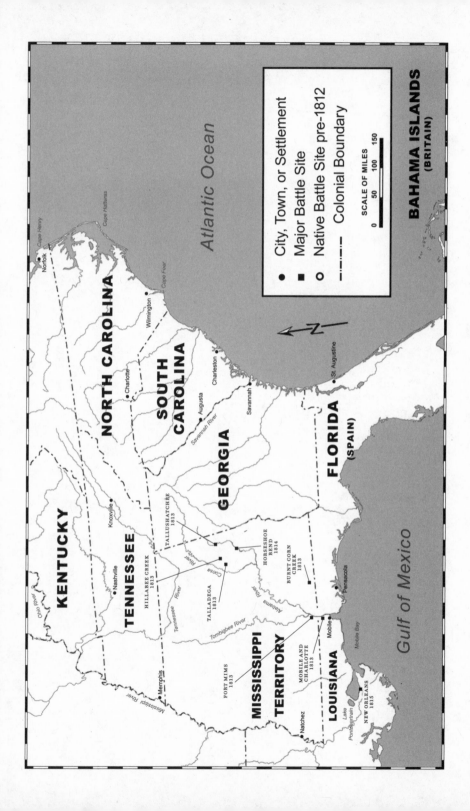

Introduction

Two Wars in One

"No tribe has the right to sell land, even to each other, much less to strangers . . . Sell a country! Why not sell the air, the great sea, as well as the earth? Didn't the Great Spirit make them all for the use of his children? . . . The only way to stop this evil [loss of land] is for the red man to unite in claiming a common and equal right in the land, as it was first, and should be now, for it was never divided."

TECUMSEH

Two bloody conflicts fused to become one during the War of 1812. The first was the American campaign to seize the land of native peoples along the western frontier. That can be called the Endless War. The second conflict, properly called the War of 1812, was the one the United States fought against Great Britain. The U.S. prevailed in the first war but failed to win the second one. As a consequence, the native peoples lost their lands to the Americans, while Canada avoided being conquered and annexed by the U.S.

Central to the drama are two men: Tecumseh and Isaac Brock. Although both fought and died on Canadian soil, neither had any particular attachment to Canada. Tecumseh was a Shawnee warrior, born near the Ohio River, whose consuming passion was the establishment of a native state on American territory. Brock was a career soldier in the British army who would have preferred a posting in Europe, where he could be involved in the war against Napoleon. Their backgrounds and life experience could not have been more different. But they were both warriors, and they recognized something in each other that drew them to unite their forces in the summer of 1812, thereby altering the history of the North American continent. The American heroes who emerged from the war — Andrew Jackson, Davy Crockett, William Henry Harrison, Commodore Oliver Perry, and Thomas Macdonough — were patriots, fighting for their country. Tecumseh and Brock were different. Neither was a patriotic Canadian. Neither was a Canadian at all. But without meaning to, they placed themselves among the founders of a country that one day would span the continent.

Though George Washington left office in 1797 with a warning to Americans to avoid "foreign entanglements," the United States could not avoid European power struggles. France and Britain were the principals in a titanic trial of strength, embroiled in a series of conflicts that can correctly be deemed the world war of the era. The wars began during the French Revolution, before the rise of Napoleon Bonaparte. From 1803 to 1815, during the Napoleonic Wars proper, Bonaparte's France ruled a continental empire that waged war against Britain's far-flung global empire.

Especially in the early years of the Napoleonic Wars, the French army was the world's most effective land-based military machine. The Royal Navy, however, was not only the supreme force on the seas, it was the world's largest and most advanced industrial organization. For the British, keeping the sea lanes open for the shipment of vital materials and preventing a French army from crossing the English Channel were matters of life and death. The Royal Navy was Britain's wooden wall.

In what the French and the British regarded as the lesser theatre of war, in North America, a showdown took shape that was intimately connected to the one in Europe. On June 18, 1812, when the fledgling United States of America declared war against Great Britain, the political and military leaders of President James Madison's administration had only one strategic plan of attack:

invade Canada. The abundant farmland of Upper Canada, wedged between the St. Lawrence–Great Lakes waterway and the rocky uplands of the Canadian Shield, was an inviting target for Americans who saw land as the means to wealth. This fitted well with the political urge to throw the British out of their last strongholds on the continent. Even American political leaders who did not aspire to the annexation of Canada felt sure that they could seize and hold Canadian territory as a bargaining chip, forcing the British to come to terms on a host of issues.

Two colonies stood out as objects of conquest: Lower and Upper Canada, the colonies that constitute present-day southern Quebec and southern Ontario, respectively. These great inland colonies, with their long and exposed borders with the United States and their populations living close to the frontier, provided American strategists with a plethora of possible invasion routes. U.S. forces could march north up the military pathway along Lake Champlain, cross the border, and close in on Montreal, or they could move down the St. Lawrence from their base at Sackets Harbor, on the eastern shore of Lake Ontario. Either of these routes would allow the Americans to seize both shores of the river and effectively choke off the British from moving soldiers and supplies farther west. Alternatively, the Americans could strike vulnerable Upper Canada with its population of less than one hundred thousand European settlers. They could send a flotilla across Lake Ontario to attack the major British base at Kingston or the less well defended capital of Upper Canada, York (now Toronto), or they could mount an assault at the mouth of the Niagara River. They could attack the British along the Niagara Frontier, dispatching troops in boats across the swift-flowing river. Or they could invade the vulnerable southwestern extremity of the colony with a crossing of the Detroit River. Over the course of the war, as it turned out, the Americans tried almost all of these invasion routes in their efforts to occupy Canada.

Several burning issues drove the Madison administration to declare war on Britain. Years of interference with American ships on the high seas by the Royal Navy had driven political leaders and commercial traders into a state of chronic exasperation. No less important was the hunger of Americans in the new states of the interior — Ohio, Kentucky, and Tennessee — to seize the land of native peoples.

Before the U.S. declaration of war against Britain, native peoples were already at war with the United States to halt the advance of American settlers onto their lands. The Endless War had smouldered for decades, since well before the American Revolution. During the first decade of the nineteenth century, the Shawnee chief Tecumseh made himself the pre-eminent leader of a great native confederacy, whose goal was to halt the settlers, keep land for the natives, and win back land already seized.

Tecumseh and his allies were fighting for a way of life that depended on the control of land. The clash between the native peoples and the Americans was a clash of civilizations. The settlers believed in individual ownership of land. On a plot, they could set up a homestead, start a farm, and raise animals. A settler family could produce the food it needed to feed itself. Or it could raise a crop or tend cattle or sheep to sell to nearby dwellers in towns. In the South, a family could acquire a vast stretch of land, move slaves onto it, and produce a tobacco or cotton crop to sell to a national or an international market.

Tecumseh and his brother Tenskwatawa, widely known as the Prophet, had an entirely different conception of land. For them, the land was not a private holding. It was the terrain on which villages and tribes could live, the women cultivating the fields to raise crops while the men fished and hunted. They did not want to give up their way of life and remake themselves as second-class American homesteaders. They carried a map of North America in their heads that was completely at variance with those of the Americans and the British. On their map were the territories of peoples who had lived on the land long before the white man.

Tecumseh's life spanned several critical episodes in the long narrative of the natives' struggles to protect their lands from the invasions of white settlers. That narrative began with the first arrivals of Europeans in the New World. By the early eighteenth century, virtually all of the native peoples in North America were caught in the web of relationships created by the French, British, and Spanish penetrations of the continent. The wars between the European powers drew native peoples into alliances with the French, the British, or the Spaniards, and against the natives who ended up on the other side. Native peoples fought one another for territory, sometimes carrying on traditional hostilities but often compelled to migrate — and therefore clash — by the encroachment of settlers and the waxing and waning of European imperial projects.

Tecumseh would find an unlikely comrade-in-arms in a British general named Isaac Brock. Born in 1769 into a prominent commercial family on the Island of Guernsey, off the north coast of France, Brock was a career British soldier who devoted himself heart and soul to the defence of Canada because it was a part of the British Empire. The stakes for Upper Canada were exceptionally high. Established by the British Parliament under the Constitutional Act of 1791, Upper Canada had a settler population of a mere one hundred thousand people by 1812. A frontier territory with only a few villages and towns, it had a fluid political culture at the outbreak of the war. Unlike Lower Canada's overwhelmingly French-speaking three hundred thousand inhabitants, whose society had existed for two centuries, Upper Canadians were mostly recent immigrants from south of the border and from Britain.

The genuine United Empire Loyalists who followed the British flag north arrived soon after the signing of the Treaty of Paris in 1783, which ended the American Revolutionary War. The Loyalists were strongly attached to the British Crown and were hostile to the new American Republic. However, immigrants from the United States who arrived over the following two decades, the so-called "Late Loyalists," came primarily for land. They exhibited no particular antagonism toward the U.S. and had no special attachment to Britain. The War of 1812 changed all that. Out of the war, the Upper Canadians took shape as a people alongside the long-established French Canadians. Farther east, the peoples of the Atlantic colonies, with the exception of newly founded New Brunswick, had developed identities over the course of their histories. In New Brunswick, which was carved out of the territory of Nova Scotia in 1784, thousands of Loyalists established new homes for themselves.

Brock did his duty in the colony, all the while longing for the day when he would be transferred from a backwoods corner of the imperial realm to participate in the "big show" in Europe against Napoleon. What distinguished Brock from the other leading British commanders in Lower and Upper Canada was that he understood the imperative of sustaining the alliance with the native peoples. And he knew that the alliance depended on an offensive war. Tecumseh's determination to go on the offensive against the Americans suited Brock strategically and temperamentally. Tecumseh and Brock understood each other. Together, they could do what neither could do alone.

Chapter 1

Tecumseh, the Shooting Star

IN THE MID-EIGHTEENTH CENTURY, the eastern half of North America entered an age of upheaval. The French Empire, whose territorial holdings extended from Île-Royale (Cape Breton Island) through eastern Canada and across the Great Lakes to the Mississippi River and New Orleans, was in the final phase of its unequal contest against the more populous and militarily superior British Empire in North America.

In 1755, under the command of Major General Edward Braddock, the commander-in-chief of British forces in North America, British and colonial troops set out from Virginia to assault French forces in the Ohio country at Fort Duquesne. Serving as a volunteer officer in the expedition was a Virginian by the name of George Washington. In July 1755, the French and their native allies routed Braddock's army, killing the British commander in the process. Washington presided at the burial service for the fallen general.

Later that year, the British, supported by colonial troops from New England, expelled the French-speaking Acadians from their homes along the Bay of Fundy, burning their settlements to the ground as ships carried the Acadians into exile. In September 1759, following a three-month siege, the British won the very brief but decisive Battle of the Plains of Abraham at Quebec, the engagement that tore the heart out of the French Empire in North America. In 1763, the Treaty of Paris handed New France, with the exception of the islands of Saint-Pierre and Miquelon, to Great Britain.

But that same year, the Ottawa leader Pontiac led an alliance of peoples, including the Senecas, Chippewas, and Delawares, in wide-ranging attacks on British posts in the Ohio country and the Great Lakes region, capturing all except Niagara, Detroit, and Fort Pitt.[1] Pontiac's mission was to restore the members of his native alliance to the position they had enjoyed in the days of the French Empire. Hundreds of settlers fled the territory where the attacks took place, and many more were killed or captured.

Though Pontiac and his allies won the battle, the war ultimately resulted in a stalemate with the British, who were forced to alter their policies and to establish a relationship with the native peoples of the region similar to the one that had existed with the French. In October 1763, the British government issued the Royal Proclamation, which recognized a vast "Indian Reserve" that stretched from the Appalachians to the Mississippi River and from the Floridas to Canada. The British were already moving toward the policies spelled out in the proclamation, but the armed struggle convinced them that white settlers and native peoples must be kept apart and that the settlers should not be permitted to encroach on native lands.

The inhabitants of the Thirteen Colonies — Delaware, Pennsylvania, New Jersey, Georgia, Connecticut, Massachusetts, Maryland, South Carolina, New Hampshire, Virginia, New York, North Carolina, and Rhode Island — deeply resented the Proclamation of 1763. Its denial of western lands to American settlers added to the growing list of grievances that would explode in the American Revolution in the following decade. The leading subjects in the much more populous and substantial British colonies along the American seaboard were developing their own ambitions, which would soon put them on a collision course with the mother country. Not only did they aspire to control their own taxation and compete with British commerce on the Atlantic, they had their sights set on acquiring native land that lay on the other side of the Appalachian Mountains. The native peoples along the East Coast had already lost their lands to colonists, whose population was rapidly increasing. Now the native peoples in the Ohio country and the future state of Kentucky had to face the aggressive colonists there, who were well on their way to becoming Americans.

Land was the chief form of wealth in the America of the day. Great landowners, notably those who ran the Virginia plantations, hungered for more property so that they could expand their operations when the soil on their existing plantations was depleted. And the American settlers' appetite for land could only be satisfied at the expense of native peoples. The war of the native peoples against the Europeans and later the settler invaders was an endless war. The conflict shifted from region to region over time as the British, the French, the Spaniards, and later the settler regimes took one piece of territory after another from the original inhabitants. Conventional maps of North America display national, provincial, and state boundaries. Another kind of map tells an equally important story: a map of the continent blocked off into regions and dated with the cessions of parcels of territory from native peoples to imperial and settler regimes.

Native peoples also fought one another for territory. Access to guns and horses played a major role in determining which native peoples won or lost particular struggles, as did the vagaries of epidemics. The winners periodically took the men, women, and children of the vanquished into slavery, sometimes using the slaves as currency with the whites to purchase guns, ammunition, and other goods.

In their struggles in the heart of the continent, French and British traders and soldiers fought to secure military and commercial alliances with particular tribes and to block their adversaries from achieving such alliances. For the whole of Tecumseh's life, the Ohio country was a theatre of nearly constant warfare, with brief stretches of peace punctuating long periods of conflict.

~

William Henry Harrison, the Indiana governor and future president of the United States, was Tecumseh's deadliest foe. He once described the great Shawnee leader as "one of those uncommon geniuses which spring up occasionally to produce revolutions and overturn the established order of things."[2]

Born in 1768 in one of two Shawnee settlements (either Chillicothe or Kispoko Town) along the Scioto, a tributary of the Ohio River, the legendary warrior chief Tecumseh entered a world engulfed by turmoil that extended from his village all the way to the other side of the Atlantic Ocean. There is some dispute about the date of his birth. His younger brother Lalawethika, who later changed his name to Tenskwatawa and became famous as the Prophet, claimed that Tecumseh was born in 1764 or 1765, but it seems more likely that he was born in 1768, based on the testimony of his childhood friend Stephen Ruddell, who played the twin roles of actor and commentator in Tecumseh's life.

According to Ruddell, on the evening of Tecumseh's birth his mother, Methoataaskee, looked into the heavens to see "a meteor shooting across the sky."[3] That was the origin of his name, Tecumethe, which in its abbreviated translation means "Shooting Star" or "Blazing Comet," but in a longer rendering means "I Cross the Way." (English-speakers have settled on the distorted form *Tecumseh*.) According to Shawnee custom, when a baby was six months old, his father would host a feast for friends and relatives to name the new member of the family. An older member of another clan would then select the baby's name and recite a prayer to promote his well-being. But in Tecumseh's case, the striking vision of the shooting star suggested the name.

Highly influential in Tecumseh's life were his eldest brother, Cheeseekau, and his sister, Tecumpease. Less influential was his older brother Sauawaseekau. Following Tecumseh came a brother, Nehaaseemoo, and then triplets, all boys, one of whom died at birth.[4] One of the two survivors was Lalawethika, who was to play an immense role in shaping Tecumseh's vision and politics.

Timing isn't everything for those whom history thrusts to the fore, but it does matter. Tecumseh was born the year before the arrival of Brock, Napoleon, and the Duke of Wellington, which put them all at the right age to play major roles in the interrelated conflicts of the era.

By the time Tecumseh was born, the Shawnees had long been a wandering people. Shawnee tradition claims that their tribe previously inhabited another land. According to the story, under the leadership of a member of the tribe's Turtle clan, the people congregated and marched to the seashore. As they walked into the sea, the waters instantly parted, allowing them to pass unharmed along the ocean bottom, until they reached the island where they would live.[5]

The Algonquian languages, of which Shawnee was one, were often found around the Great Lakes. The name *Shawnee*, which means "southerners," is one clue among others that indicates that the Shawnees dwelt in the South, possibly on the Savannah River in South Carolina. Mentions of the Shawnees show up in the stories of other tribes as well as in the records of the French and the English. French writers called them Chaouanons and sometimes Massawomees. The tribe's name has been written as Shawanos, Sawanos, Shawaneu, Shawanoes, and Shawnees.[6] By the 1660s and 1670s, when the Shawnees were featured in written records, they had settled on the Ohio and Cumberland Rivers. Not long after this date, however, Iroquois warriors attacked the Shawnees, who were dispersed to the east across the Appalachian Mountains, west to Illinois, and south to the Savannah.

In 1836, Albert Gallatin, who served as one of the U.S. commissioners appointed to negotiate peace with Britain during the War of 1812, published a study of the history of the native American tribes east of the Rocky Mountains, drawing on a host of earlier sources. Gallatin concluded that the Shawnees originally belonged to the Lenape tribes of the north and classified the Shawnee tongue as one of the Algonquian-Lenape languages. He conjectured that the Shawnees separated from other Lenape tribes and settled south of the Ohio River in what is now Kentucky. During the first half of the seventeenth century, wars with the Cherokees and Chickasaws drove a portion of the Shawnee people out of that territory as far east as the Susquehanna River. Then the Miamis invited the main body of the Shawnees to move to the Ohio country. There, in alliance with other tribes, the Shawnees went to war against the Iroquois, suffering a final defeat in that conflict in 1672. The vanquished Shawnees dispersed, some settling on the rivers of the Carolinas and many settling among the Muscogees (known to Americans as the Creeks) after being driven farther south. Other Shawnees settled in Pennsylvania and some stayed along the Ohio River.[7]

Five divisions composed the Shawnee tribe at the time of Tecumseh's birth: Mekoche, Hathawekela, Pekowi, Kispoko, and Chillicothe. A common language and culture bound the divisions together into the loosely constituted confederacy of the Shawnee tribe. The divisions appear to have emerged with the establishment of largely autonomous villages. In addition to belonging to one of the divisions, each Shawnee was a member of one of about a dozen clans. A Shawnee would choose a sexual partner from outside his or her own clan.

In Shawnee settlements, women and men did different jobs. Women built houses, made clothes, roasted meat, cooked stews, and baked bread cakes. They also worked in the fields to raise crops such as corn, beans, and pumpkins. In the spring, they tapped maple syrup from the trees. Men fished and hunted deer, rabbits, and buffalo. They also made weapons and trained to become warriors who could defend Shawnee settlements from attack.

Tecumseh's father, Pukeshinwau, meaning "Something That Falls," was an admired warrior who belonged to the Kispoko division and the Panther clan. Methoataaskee, Tecumseh's mother, belonged to the Pekowi division and was a member of the Turtle clan. Her name meant "A Turtle Laying Her Eggs in the Sand."[8]

Tecumseh's father and mother both lived among the Muscogees along the banks of the lower Tallapoosa River in present-day

Alabama, likely having arrived by different routes. The Tallapoosa Shawnees, among whom Pukeshinwau was probably born, frequently intermarried with neighbouring native peoples, and as well with French and British traders.

Whether Tecumseh had Muscogee and even English as well as Shawnee ancestry has always been a matter of speculation. According to one rumour, Tecumseh's mother was a Muscogee. Decades after Tecumseh's birth, John Prophet, the grandson of Methoataaskee, claimed that his grandmother had been of Muscogee ancestry. Evidence suggests that Tecumseh's father may have had Muscogee and English as well as Shawnee ancestors. Tecumseh's brother the Prophet claimed much later that their mother was their father's second wife. Shawnees were customarily polygamous, but if Tecumseh's father did have an earlier marriage, no children resulted, and he never married again after his union with Methoataaskee.

The couple moved north from Alabama to the Ohio country, most likely in 1759. Nine years later, when Tecumseh was born, representatives of the Six Nations Iroquois Confederacy signed the Treaty of Fort Stanwix (present-day Rome, New York). For a payment of 10,460 pounds, the Iroquois sold Kentucky and western Pennsylvania to the British, which allowed settlers to flood into Shawnee territory.[9] When they made the sale, the Iroquois claimed that the Shawnee and other native peoples who inhabited the land did so under the jurisdiction of the Six Nations Confederacy. The treaty robbed the Shawnee and other native peoples of their hunting grounds in Kentucky and threatened their settlements along the Ohio. Although the Shawnees did not accept the treaty, their views were swept aside.

A land rush brought an influx of settlers and profiteers. On April 3, 1769, a land office opened in Pittsburgh. On the first day of business, nearly three thousand applications for titles were filed, not just by individuals but also by the American colonies (still under British rule) themselves. In 1773, the governor of Virginia, John Murray, Earl of Dunmore, seized control of the region of Fort Pitt, elbowing

Pennsylvania aside. He planned to make Kentucky a colony of Virginia. The landed elites of Virginia, the most powerful and populous of the colonies, needed to expand to keep their plantations profitable.

In August 1774, two contingents of Virginia militiamen, one commanded by Colonel Andrew Lewis and the other by Governor John Murray, Lord Dunmore, pushed into the Ohio country. The expedition destroyed a few Shawnee villages on the Muskingum River. The Virginians — natives called them the Big Knives, a term they later extended to all Americans — headed toward the territory where Tecumseh's family lived. Although the Shawnees did not have nearly enough men to match the Virginians' numbers, the tribal council decided that the warriors must make a desperate attempt to defeat one of the advancing armies; a victory might draw other natives into the battle.

Tecumseh's father, Pukeshinwau, organized the Kispokos for the struggle and decided to take his eldest son, Cheeseekau, with him on the expedition. Six-year-old Tecumseh witnessed the war dances of the warriors and their ceremonies of purification as they readied themselves to confront the invaders. On the morning of October 10, 1774, at Point Pleasant at the mouth of the Kanawha River, the Shawnees attacked the contingent led by Colonel Lewis. Badly outnumbered, the Shawnees nonetheless inflicted significant casualties on the Virginians before being forced to withdraw. Having failed to stop the Big Knives, the warriors knew the enemy would press on to attack their villages.

The Mekoches and their chief, Cornstalk, who had led the fight at Point Pleasant, decided that the only viable course was to conciliate the Big Knives, a policy bitterly opposed by most of the Pekowis, Chillicothes, and Kispokos. Cornstalk agreed to give up Kentucky and surrender prisoners, including whites and blacks who had been taken as captives and white children who had been raised by Shawnees from a very early age. Despite intense opposition from the members of the other Shawnee divisions, Cornstalk went ahead with this offer of peace. In the Shawnee council, he stood and asked, "The Long Knives are coming upon us by two routes. Shall we turn out and fight them?" Hearing no reply, he declared, "Since you are not inclined to fight, I will go and make peace."[10]

Among the warriors who died at Point Pleasant was Pukeshinwau. During his final moments, he counselled Cheeseekau "to preserve unsullied the dignity and honour of his family and directed him in future to lead forth to battle his younger brothers," according to the account of Stephen Ruddell.[11]

For Tecumseh's family, the death of Pukeshinwau was followed by a one-year period of mourning that fell heavily on his widow, Methoataaskee, who was pregnant with the last of her children. It is hard to calculate how the loss of his father and the surrender of native land affected the young Tecumseh. What we do know is that he lived in a time of violence and war, that he witnessed the armies burn settlements and kill the inhabitants, and that he decided to devote his life to stopping the Big Knives from seizing native land.

When Tecumseh's father died in 1774, American colonists were embroiled in the political conflict that soon led to the American Revolutionary War. That same year, the British Parliament passed the Quebec Act, a measure that deeply alienated the colonists, just as the Royal Proclamation of 1763 had the previous decade. Under the Quebec Act, the British government vastly increased the territory of Quebec to include a portion of the Indian Reserve and much of what is now southern Ontario, in addition to the territories now included in Illinois, Indiana, Michigan, Ohio, Wisconsin, and portions of Minnesota. The act dropped any reference to the Protestant faith from the oath of allegiance in Quebec, which guaranteed the practice of Catholicism and restored the use of the French civil code to settle private disputes, while keeping the English common law for public administration, including criminal proceedings. The British government, already concerned about rising discontent in the

Thirteen Colonies, hoped the Quebec Act would bind the French Canadians to the British side in the event of conflict with the colonists.

The Quebec Act contributed to the rising fury of the mostly Protestant English-speaking colonists, who saw the territorial extension of Quebec as a barrier to their own expansion, opposed the new rights for Catholics, and feared an attack on their own powers of self-government. Delegates to the First Continental Congress, which assembled representatives of twelve of the Thirteen Colonies, met in Philadelphia in September and October 1774. The congress agreed to mount a boycott on British goods as a way of pressuring Britain to repeal the so-called Intolerable Acts, which imposed taxes on the colonies and asserted the right of the British Parliament to legislate for the colonies. The Quebec Act was included on this list. The congress agreed to call a Second Continental Congress to convene the following May. But on April 19, 1775, before the second congress was to meet, armed struggle broke out in Lexington and Concord, Massachusetts. The American Revolutionary War was underway.

The war between the British and the Thirteen Colonies exacerbated the political divisions among native peoples. Both sides in the conflict recognized native warriors as a force to be reckoned with, and they had an interest in recruiting them to their cause or at least neutralizing them. The British drew Mohawk leader Joseph Brant to their side. As a youth, Brant had attended a school in Connecticut, where he learned to speak, read, and write English. During the Revolutionary War, he mobilized Mohawk warriors and led colonial Loyalists in the struggle against the Patriots in the northern region of the Province of New York. In the summer of 1777, the Six Nations of the Iroquois Confederacy joined the struggle on the side of the British. In 1779, Sir Frederick Haldimand, the governor of Quebec, gave Brant the commission of captain of the Northern Confederated Indians.

Of the Shawnees along the Ohio, Cornstalk and the Mekoches agreed with some of the Delawares that neutrality was the best plan: it would not serve their interests to get involved in a white man's war.

But many of the Shawnees and the Mingoes, who had opposed Cornstalk's deal with the Virginians, saw the war as an opportunity to win back Kentucky. If they sided with the British, who were anxious to recruit them, they could expect to receive the arms and provisions they needed to take up the fight.

Neither side got what it wanted. In November 1777, Cornstalk, along with one of his sons, was gunned down by American militiamen incensed by a recent native ambush of two white men, one of whom had been killed.[12]

The newly founded United States, having declared its independence on July 4, 1776, after more than a year of war against Britain, proved incapable of outfitting its native allies with weapons and provisions, and was even unable to prevent attacks on them by white settlers. Formerly neutral Shawnees became antagonistic toward the Patriot side during the war.

But the more militant natives who had fought against the Patriots failed to recover their lost hunting grounds in Kentucky. In the chaotic conditions that prevailed, many Shawnees, including Tecumseh's mother and her family, moved farther west, abandoning their former settlements and establishing new ones. Nine-year-old Tecumseh's new home was the village of Pekowi. Not far west of present-day Springfield in Clark County, Ohio, the village was established on the northwestern bank of the Mad River, a tributary of the Great Miami River.[13] Bluffs dominated the north side of the water; farther along were woodlands and marsh. South of the river, a bountiful prairie invited the sowing of corn.

To the southeast of Pekowi, the Shawnees established the largest of their new settlements. Called Old Chillicothe, the town replaced the Chillicothe that had been abandoned farther east. It was located on the southeastern bank of the upper Little Miami River. Blackfish, the warrior leader of the Chillicothe division, was the dominant figure in the community. In 1777 and 1778, as part of their wartime struggle against the Patriots, the British backed Blackfish and the Shawnee armed expeditions into Kentucky. In February 1778, during a raid on the Licking River, Blackfish and his warriors captured twenty-eight settlers, including the legendary Daniel Boone. The captives were transported to the Shawnee settlements; some were adopted and the British paid a ransom to have others released. Boone and a few others managed to escape and return to Boonesborough, Kentucky, in time for an unsuccessful eleven-day siege of the settlement undertaken by three hundred native warriors and eleven whites.[14]

It's not certain whether the young Tecumseh met Blackfish, but he knew about the warrior's ultimate fate. In late May 1779, a party of three hundred whites from Kentucky carried out a raid on Old Chillicothe as a reprisal for the attacks on their settlements. Before the attackers managed to surround the town in stealth at night, their presence was discovered. Some warriors fled from the settlement, leaving only a small number to defend Old Chillicothe's women and children and the houses and council house. Blackfish led the warriors against the attackers, but he was severely wounded by a bullet that tore into his knee, splintering the bone and exiting through his thigh. His men were forced to retreat under fire. Throughout the night, the warriors kept up their defence from the council house and a few of the houses in the centre of the settlement. Although the Kentuckians put some dwellings to the torch, they eventually gave up the assault and withdrew, fearing that more warriors would arrive on the scene. While Old Chillicothe was not destroyed, seven natives were killed or mortally wounded. One of them was Blackfish.[15]

The Kentuckians launched further strikes against the Shawnee villages, bringing the war to where Tecumseh lived. George Rogers Clark, the highest-ranking Patriot military officer in the Northwest during the American Revolution, led a punishing mission in which a thousand men, outfitted with a 6-pounder artillery piece, burned down the town of Old Chillicothe. Although they lost many of their belongings and their crops, the inhabitants managed to evade the assault.

Clark then turned to Tecumseh's town of Pekowi. Alerted that the Americans were coming, the women and children — Tecumseh almost certainly among them — were dispatched to the bluffs near the town. The Shawnee warriors managed for a time to halt the advance of Clark's force when they unleashed a volley of musket fire on them. Outnumbered and outgunned, the warriors retreated into the town. But when the 6-pounder fired on them, they pulled out of the settlement and made their escape.

When Clark and his men withdrew two days later, Pekowi and the small nearby settlement of Kispoko were burned to the ground. During their rampage, members of the Clark expedition torched five towns, destroyed the ripening corn crops in the fields, and felled the fruit trees near the settlements. In their wake was a trail of desolation.[16]

Tecumseh, his family, the other inhabitants of his settlement, and those who lived in nearby settlements were driven out, forced to move northwest to establish new villages. By the following spring, the Kispokos, along with the other Shawnee divisions, were creating a cluster of new villages on the upper Mad River, not far from the present-day setting of Bellefontaine. This would not be the last time that the Shawnees, Tecumseh among them, would be forced to move during the Revolutionary War.

For the duration of the war, Shawnee, Mingo, Delaware, Wyandot, Potawatomi, Ottawa, and Ojibwa warriors fought alongside the British in attacks against the Americans in Kentucky and on the frontiers of Virginia.[17] In 1780, the British mounted a one-thousand-man incursion into Kentucky. The force combined British troops with natives from the Great Lakes and from the Ohio Valley, including Shawnees. In Kentucky, they forced the surrender of a couple of stations and captured about 350 men, women, and children — including Stephen Ruddell and his younger brother, Abraham, who were taken at Ruddell Station — and brought them back to the Shawnee settlements. Stephen and Tecumseh were both twelve years old when they first encountered each other. They soon were inseparable friends.*[18]

By the time the boys met, the course of the Revolutionary War was about to swing inexorably in favour of the Patriots. In 1781, with the crucial support of the French on land and at sea, the Americans won the decisive engagement at Yorktown, Virginia. Earlier that year, the thirteen founding states ratified the Articles of Confederation, the first U.S. Constitution. This gave the Continental Congress added legitimacy to oversee the war and to conduct diplomacy with European powers.

Having once more moved to be farther from the Big Knives, the Shawnees were still not safe from the attacks of the Kentuckians. In November 1782, George Rogers Clark led another mission against the new settlements, including the village of New Pekowi. Yet again, the settlement where Tecumseh lived was destroyed. This time the attack was late enough in the autumn that the crop had been harvested and most of the people had moved out to their hunting camps. While Shawnee warriors attempted to parry the attack, their numbers were no match for the one-thousand-man force assembled by Clark. The Shawnees were forced to move farther northwest to establish new settlements. Although the peace treaty between Britain and the newly created United States did not come into force until 1783, the effective end of the war pitting the Shawnees and their native allies against the Kentuckians came in 1782.

The struggle had been long and gruesome. Despite the defeats they had suffered and the rising military strength of the settlers, Shawnee warriors remained a formidable force. Some had fallen in

---

* Raised in a native family, Stephen and Abraham Ruddell became Shawnee warriors, fighting side by side with other members of the tribe when they were young men. Stephen, who was named Sinnamatha ("Big Fish") by his Shawnee family, later became a Baptist preacher and proselytized for the Kentucky Baptist Church. Abraham, who had been captured when he was only six, had a harder time adapting back into white society. He spoke broken English and was not socially comfortable. In Shawnee style, he wore ornaments that hung from the split rims of his ears.

battle and others had given up the fight and migrated south to live under American control, but many surviving warriors remained. And the Shawnees were successful in replenishing their ranks through the capture of young whites, who were brought into the tribe and trained as warriors. According to one estimate, over the course of the bloody conflict between 1776 and 1782, the natives killed 860 men who had been trained as soldiers in Kentucky. The Iroquois waged a similar struggle during these years against an influx of settlers.[19]

However, the Shawnee forays into Kentucky did not halt the migration of white settlers there. By 1782, Kentucky could arm and equip 1,300 men, a force that dwarfed the number of warriors the Shawnees and their allies could raise to counter them. By the time peace returned, the Shawnees had effectively lost the southern part of their territory; settler possession of Kentucky was irreversible.

In 1783, the United States was recognized by the British as an independent republic. The Treaty of Paris established the U.S. border along the line of the Great Lakes and extended its territory west to the Mississippi River. Spain held the territory west of the Mississippi and south of the U.S. in Florida. North of the new country were the British colonies that would one day become parts of Canada. The Treaty of Paris made no provision for the sovereignty of the native peoples. Under it, the Six Nations' lands were ceded by Britain to the United States. The U.S. government regarded the lands of the native peoples in the Ohio country and in western New York, Pennsylvania, Virginia, and Kentucky as theirs, won in a war and legitimized in a treaty. Even though the British held forts on the American side of the Great Lakes for years after the treaty came into effect, the Americans were determined to extend their effective sovereignty to the region, which put the Shawnees and the young Tecumseh directly in the line of the U.S. advance.

The end of the Revolutionary War and the Treaty of Paris transformed Quebec and the Atlantic colonies, Britain's remaining holdings on the continent. With the Patriots victorious, tens of thousands of British Loyalists left the United States. While many voyaged to Britain, others set out for British North America. Some Loyalists settled in the part of Nova Scotia that became the newly founded colony of New Brunswick. Others made their new homes in Quebec's Eastern Townships, or the north shore of the St. Lawrence River west of Montreal, or the northern shores of Lakes Ontario and Erie. In 1791, the British Parliament took note of the fact that tens of thousands of Loyalists were flooding into the province when it passed the Constitutional Act that divided Quebec into the colonies of Lower and Upper Canada.

The Treaty of Paris also had consequences for the Six Nations of the Iroquois Confederacy. Mohawk leader Joseph Brant convinced the governor of Quebec, Sir Frederick Haldimand, to grant land for a Mohawk settlement on the Grand River. In the fall of 1784, the Six Nations divided, with half of their people remaining in New York while the other half followed Brant to Quebec.

But the Treaty of Paris did not quash native resistance to the seizure of their land. Between 1783 and 1795, Brant returned to provide inspired direction to the native confederacy movement on the U.S. side of the frontier.[20] As a youth, Brant had believed that land negotiations between the Americans and individual tribes or small groups of native leaders were illegitimate. The confederacy as a whole had to agree to any sales of land, because the lands of native peoples were a common holding, a holding that included the territory on which their settlements were established as well as their hunting and fishing grounds.

In December 1786, Brant and the Shawnee war chief Blue Jacket participated in the formation of an alliance of northwestern tribes — Iroquois, Hurons, Delawares, Shawnees, Ottawas, Ojibwas, Potawatomis, Miamis, and Wabash River tribes — whose delegates assembled in a council at the mouth of the Detroit River. The common goal of this alliance was to hold on to native lands as agreed to in the Treaty of Fort Stanwix, negotiated with the British in 1768. In a message they sent to the United States Congress, the members of the confederacy insisted that any cession of native lands to the U.S. "should

be made in the most public manner, and by the united voice of the confederacy; holding all partial treaties as void and of no effect." While the
confederacy preferred a peaceful outcome, its members were ready to
use force to halt American expansion if they had to.[21]

Then, as later, the representatives of the U.S. government rejected
outright the concept that all native peoples held their land in common. The government's tactic was to divide the peoples from each
other, win over particular leaders, and make land deals with each of
them, insisting on the legitimacy of these undertakings. In 1784, U.S.
commissioners met with the Iroquois at Fort Stanwix — Brant was
not present — to bludgeon them into recognizing that they had been
conquered and giving up their claims to the Ohio country. The same
tactic was used in 1785 in talks with the Wyandots, Delawares,
Ottawas, and Ojibwas.

That same year, the representatives of the United States summoned
the Shawnees to a similar session at the mouth of the Great Miami
River, where the Americans had built Fort Finney. In January 1786, 230
Shawnees attended the meeting with the commissioners. Moluntha,
an elderly Mekoche who was the head civil chief, led the Shawnee delegation. The U.S. representatives were intent on forcing the Shawnees
to give up almost all of their territory. They insisted that the Shawnee
people had been conquered, and if they did not accede to the U.S. ultimatum, force would be used to compel acceptance. Many of the
younger warriors in the delegation were visibly angry.

Joseph Brant and Kekewepelethy, a Mekoche leader who strongly
supported the confederacy, pressed for resistance. When Brant had
heard about the agreements forced on other peoples by the Americans,
he had declared, as recorded by U.S. commissioners, that "all nations
of us of one colour were there and agreed as one man not to make
peace or war without the consent of the whole, and you likewise
know that one or two nations going to our brothers' council fire cannot do anything without the whole were there present." At Fort
Finney, Kekewepelethy rejected the American claim that the native
peoples had been defeated in battle and had therefore lost any claim

to their land. "We do not understand measuring out the lands. It is all ours," he insisted. The reply from one of the U.S. commissioners was just as clear: "We plainly tell you that this country belongs to the United States."

Threatened with force, the Shawnee chiefs yielded, and on January 31, 1786, they agreed to a treaty through which they gave up most of present-day eastern and southern Ohio, the lion's share of their territory. Instead of bringing peace, the deal drove those Shawnees who had not been present at Fort Finney to prepare for war. They were joined in their rejection of the U.S. position by local Mingoes, Cherokees, and Delawares. They also sought the support of the native peoples of the Wabash, dispatching riders with the message "to destroy all the men wearing hats . . . who seem to be leagued against us to drive us away from the lands which the Master of Life has given to us."[22]

In October 1786, eight hundred mounted militiamen from Kentucky crossed the Ohio River and assaulted the Mekoche town of Mackachack in a fight against the Shawnees who had rejected the Treaty of Fort Finney. Moluntha, the most important chief in the town, favoured peace with the Americans and had tried to restrain the younger warriors who wanted to take up the fight. The Kentuckians had no interest in the views of the chief or of the townspeople, who made an attempt to demonstrate their peaceful intentions by raising an American flag. Most of the town's warriors were away hunting when the attack occurred. The Kentuckians shot a few warriors and seized a number of prisoners, most of them women and children. The elderly Moluntha surrendered and was interrogated by Colonel Hugh McGary. The colonel concluded, almost certainly incorrectly, that in 1782 the old man had been involved in a native attack on Kentuckians. McGary struck Moluntha with a tomahawk, and when the chief tried to stand up, the colonel sank the blade of the weapon into the side of his head and proceeded to scalp him. McGary was later suspended from duty for one year for this atrocity.

The Kentucky force, taking their women and children captives along, looted and destroyed about half a dozen native towns. They put two hundred houses to the torch, slaughtered livestock, and destroyed about fifteen thousand bushels of corn. As a part of their haul, the Kentuckians took with them ten scalps. Shawnees were discovering that it made little difference whether you made peace or war with the Big Knives.

During these tempestuous years, Tecumseh learned an approach to land negotiations that relied on allegories for the commonality of native life. In one allegory, land was presented as a common meal consumed by all, "a dish with one spoon."[23] The young Tecumseh drew inspiration from the effort to form a common front among native peoples. Here was an attempt to do what had been tried a number of times before — to unite peoples who had different languages and ways of life and a long history of mutual hostility and warfare. In the late seventeenth century, Algonquin tribes had banded together to resist the aggression of the Iroquois. Early in the following century, the Iroquois peoples had cooperated to ensure their mutual security after deals were forced on them by the French and the native allies of the French. Shawnees, Delawares, and Mingoes in the Ohio country made common cause in the mid-eighteenth century to counter threats to their lands from both the British and the French. Another example occurred during Tecumseh's childhood, when his people allied themselves with other natives and with the British to fight the Kentucky settlers.

With their father gone, it fell to his older brother Cheeseekau to oversee Tecumseh's personal spiritual journey and groom him to become a warrior who would one day fight to defend native land.[24] He blackened his younger brother's face and sent him by himself into the woods to fast, meditate, and pray with the goal of finding his guardian spirit. It was customary for the spirit to appear to the young male in the form of a creature, often during a dream or trance. Having discovered his guardian spirit, the adolescent would never reveal it to anyone else. It was a source of power for him alone. The boy would normally repeat these journeys a number of times, the final journey lasting as long as three days.[25]

For Tecumseh, the transition from boyhood to early manhood was swift. He was acquiring the skills that would one day make him the greatest warrior and native leader of his time. Once, on a hunting expedition with Stephen Ruddell, Tecumseh reportedly felled sixteen buffalo with a bow and quiver of arrows. Years later, when Tecumseh had become a legendary figure, stories were often told about his prowess as a teenager. While some of them are no doubt exaggerations, he was clearly an accomplished hunter and therefore a valued provider to his community.

Those who knew him during these years have passed down accounts of Tecumseh as an athletic, attractive, friendly, and warm-hearted young man who drew many friends and admirers. "He was fond of creating his jokes," Stephen Ruddell wrote, "but his wit was never aimed to wound the feelings of his comrades." Young women found him appealing. While there were many opportunities for Tecumseh to develop relationships with women during games and hunting parties that involved both sexes, he tended to shun advances. A favourite activity was called the "bringing dance." The young men began the dance and then the young women would join in, each one selecting the man she wanted as a partner. The women often chose Tecumseh, but he usually laughed it off and didn't pursue these advances. "The women were very fond of him," Stephen Ruddell recalled, "much more so than he was of them."*[26]

Despite his good humour, Tecumseh had a serious goal that he pursued with unwavering dedication. He not only developed the skills he would need to be a superb hunter and warrior, he also learned lessons about his own and other native peoples that would

---

* Tecumseh "never evinced any great regard for the female sex," according to Ruddell. At different times over the course of his life he did live with a wife "whom he did not keep very long before he parted from her. He had a Cherokee squaw who lived with him the longest of any other." The custom among the Shawnees was for men to marry a number of women and to cohabit with them, usually one after the other.

prepare him to become a unique leader with a vision that could unite different tribes. The suffering he had experienced at the hands of the Big Knives — the death of his father, the destruction of villages in which he lived, and the loss of hunting grounds — had taught him that native peoples must stand together if they were to succeed in halting the usurpation of their lands by white settlers.

It is likely in a fight against the Kentuckians on the Mad River that eighteen-year-old Tecumseh found himself on a field of battle for the first time. To his shame, he learned that becoming a warrior was not easy. Tecumseh looked across the small, deadly space that separated him and his comrades from their foes, a moment for which he had long prepared. But when the soldiers unleashed volleys of musket fire, he panicked and turned tail. His brother and the others stayed and fought, until Cheeseekau was hit and fellow warriors carried him from the battlefield to safety.[27]

Late-eighteenth-century warfare required combatants to stand facing each other fifty or sixty metres apart, exchanging volleys of musket fire. It took nerve — and often not a little alcohol — to engage in such counterintuitive behaviour. The British regular army trained a soldier for three years to ready him for the battlefield.

Tecumseh had faced his first test as a warrior, and he had failed. He vowed never to show such cowardice again. It was a vow he kept.

Chapter 2

A Warrior's Odyssey

THE AMERICAN REVOLUTION opened the way for the citizens of the new republic to move west. In 1787, the U.S. Congress took a huge step toward exercising effective control over a vast stretch of territory on the northwestern margin of the new republic. It enacted the Northwest Ordinance to provide for the administration of the territory west of Pennsylvania and northwest of the Ohio River. Covering 673,000 square kilometres, the Northwest Territory comprised the present-day states of Ohio, Indiana, Illinois, Michigan, and Wisconsin, and the northeastern section of Minnesota. Thousands of American settlers surged into the lands. And at the mouth of the Muskingum River, the U.S. built Fort Harmar, a military post from which the passage of newcomers could be monitored.

That same year, delegates from the thirteen American states convened in Philadelphia, where they drafted a new constitution for the republic that gave the country a more centralized form of government than it had under the first American constitution, the Articles of Confederation of 1781. In 1788, George Washington, who had led the Patriot army to victory during the Revolution, was elected as the first president of the United States. Administratively, the nascent republic was much better equipped to collect taxes, raise an army, and launch a navy than the loosely connected states had been. For the native peoples, the new American government posed an existential threat. The Northwest Ordinance put the native peoples on notice that the U.S. intended, either through purchase and treaties or through force if necessary, to seize the land on which they lived.

While tribal chiefs made some efforts to negotiate peace with American representatives of the Northwest Territory, on the ground, militant Shawnees, Mingoes, Delawares, Cherokees, and Wabash warriors took matters into their own hands by mounting raids against the new settlers. Tecumseh's eldest brother, Cheeseekau, had a major role in these fights and grew in stature to become a minor war chief. On some occasions, his only companion in hit-and-run attacks was Tecumseh.[1]

Steeled by determination after his first failure in battle and groomed by his brother, Tecumseh also participated in ambushes on the flatboats that took settlers, along with their belongings and their livestock, down the Ohio River to Kentucky, where they planned to make their homes. The flatboats were obvious targets for native warriors — not only because their human cargo represented an immediate threat to the natives' villages and way of life, but also because they were a tempting source of weapons, clothing, furniture, and other possessions. About a hundred warriors — including Shawnees, Cherokees, and Mingoes — attacked the boats. Among the warriors were five whites, including Tecumseh's companion Stephen Ruddell, all of whom had been captured as children in Kentucky during the Revolutionary War.

In March 1788, the warriors established their camp on the Ohio River, just upstream from the mouth of the Great Miami River. Outfitted with a flatboat of their own, they set up their ambush around a point on the river where their prey would have little chance to avoid attack. The flatboats were lumbering craft that could not swiftly alter their course.

On the morning of March 21, a flatboat carrying five white men and a black woman sailed into the ambush point. About forty warriors pushed their own vessel out into the current and quickly boarded the settlers' boat. The victims did not resist. Two of the men were tied to a tree and had locks of their hair cut off, then were reunited with the others from their boat.

That same afternoon, the warriors attacked another vessel, this one with five men aboard. One of those captured was a sixty-year-old Baltimore merchant by the name of Samuel Purviance, who was travelling with his manservant.[2] Another was Thomas Ridout, an Englishman in his thirties who later became the surveyor-general of Upper Canada.[3]

The raiders stripped the travellers of many of their possessions and conveyed them to shore, where they joined the prisoners who had been captured that morning. The booty taken from Ridout, including clothes, a watch, cloth, a cane, two flutes, a writing desk, trunks, and a collection of books, was divided up among the natives. A third attack followed two days later. While many of those captured in the three attacks eventually made it home, others met a grisly fate.

On March 26, the warriors attacked two more boats on the Ohio, but those on board defended themselves and managed to escape. Later that same day, another flatboat rounded the bend in the river. Attacking from their own vessel, eight or ten natives quickly overcame three French scientists and their companion. One of the Frenchmen, offering his hand to help a native onto the flatboat, was struck with a tomahawk; another was shot and killed. The remaining two men jumped into the river and made good their escape, even though one of them had been seriously wounded.

Some of the warriors proceeded to kill prisoners — as many as five of them, including Purviance, the Baltimore merchant, who was either burned or battered to death. Purviance's manservant was beaten to death, and another man lost his life when he was burned alive.

As Stephen Ruddell later reported, Tecumseh distinguished himself during the attacks on the flatboats but was deeply distressed by the killing of prisoners, and he was especially appalled by the horrific torment endured when one of the captives was burned to death. Since the prisoners, as well as the booty, had been divided up among the warriors, Tecumseh was not in a position to halt the torture and the killing. According to Ruddell's account, "Tecumseh, who had been a spectator, expressed great abhorrence of the deed, and finally it was concluded among them not to burn any more prisoners that should afterwards be taken, which was ever after strictly adhered to by him."[4]

Whether Tecumseh, who was still a young warrior, was able to change the behaviour of the others is open to question. What is clear is that he was learning how to be a warrior without giving up his humanity. Ruddell wrote that the young Tecumseh "always expressed the greatest abhorrence when he heard of or saw acts of cruelty or barbarity practiced."[5] For the first twenty years of his life, Tecumseh was absorbing the world view of others. In his rejection of torture, he was beginning to shape his own responses to the disordered world around him, showing signs of the originality that would so distinguish him in the years to come.

By the autumn of 1788, Cheeseekau and a band of followers, tired of the endless and perhaps unwinnable fight against the Americans, decided to move to the other side of the Mississippi River. The territory there remained under the jurisdiction of Spain, a weak and tottering imperial power that exercised little effective control over the vast territory it supposedly ruled. A French merchant by the name of Louis Lorimier encouraged the move.

Lorimier had worked out an arrangement with the Spaniards to help them colonize territory along the Missouri River. The Spaniards favoured the idea of Shawnees and Delawares coming to the Missouri country, which would help ward off hostile native peoples to the west and strengthen Spanish defences against the Americans to the east. In the summer of 1787, word spread among the native peoples of the Ohio country that they could make a new life for themselves farther west. Tecumseh and his younger twin brothers, Lalawethika and

Kumskaukau, who were about fourteen years old, were to accompany Cheeseekau on the westward odyssey.*

With the harvest in hand, the party set out for several months to hunt so that they would be well supplied with meat for their odyssey on the other side of the Mississippi. They travelled down the Ohio River en route to the Mississippi. Below the mouth of the Tennessee River, they came upon a herd of buffalo and chased them at high speed. Tecumseh was thrown from his horse and lay on the ground in agony. He had broken a thigh bone.[6]

Cheeseekau and the others felt that Tecumseh could go no farther until his wound had healed. They found shelter for the winter and waited until spring to resume the journey. But when spring came, the broken bone had not set properly. Tecumseh feared the wound would never heal and that his hopes of becoming a warrior had come to an end.

Cheeseekau decided that the party needed to resume its journey west, so he counselled his brother to remain behind with a few warriors and catch up when he had recovered sufficiently. But Tecumseh refused to be left behind and fought off his feelings of depression and even thoughts of suicide. Although he could walk only with the aid of crutches, he set out with the party for the country west of the Mississippi.[7] Eventually the bone would heal, leaving Tecumseh with a slight limp for the rest of his life.

When the party crossed the Mississippi onto Spanish territory in the spring of 1789 — a pregnant historical moment when the new U.S. Constitution took effect and the French Revolution was about to erupt — things didn't turn out as Cheeseekau had hoped. Problems arose as a consequence of the ambitious plans of an American Indian agent and trader by the name of George Morgan, who wanted to establish a settlement to be populated by Americans on the western shore of the Mississippi River. Just below the point where the Ohio flowed into the Mississippi, Morgan planned to build a town he

---

* It is possible that Methoataaskee, their mother, may have joined the expedition. What is known is that she lived a long life and eventually died among the southern Cherokees.

called New Madrid, which he hoped would become the focal point of commerce for the Mississippi.

In February 1789, not long before the arrival of Cheeseekau and his party, seventy American settlers sailed down the Ohio and into the Mississippi to reach Morgan's new Mecca.* Cheeseekau and his party chose an odd historical moment to cross to the western shore of the Mississippi. The Spanish Empire, which nominally controlled the territory, was in steep decline against its British and French rivals. And the energetic and expansionist American Republic was already eyeing the lands west of the great river.

Although Cheeseekau and the others were not unwelcome west of the Mississippi, they soon abandoned the dream of a good life there and returned to the other side of the river. From there they

----

* New Madrid, it turned out, both figuratively and literally stood on shaky ground, and it failed to become a commercial hub. For Morgan's dream to come true, duties would have to be charged to commercial travellers in the name of Spain. In 1803, however, when the Jefferson administration purchased the vast Louisiana Territory from France, which had taken over the territory from Spain, New Madrid found itself on American soil. The entire route from settlements on the Ohio to New Orleans was now in the hands of the United States. Then, in December 1811, a colossal earthquake violently shook the region, destroying much of the new settlement and for a time even reversing the flow of the mighty Mississippi. To make matters worse, a technological revolution transformed travel on the Mississippi and its tributaries: the advent of the steamboat.

The first steamboat was actually cruising down the Ohio and into the Mississippi when the earthquake struck. Prior to the steamboat, the vessels that sailed down the Ohio and the Mississippi, some of them en route to New Orleans, were flatboats. They were constructed as cheaply as possible and each of them was destined to have one voyage only. Adding to the cost of the cargo that the flatboats transported to New Orleans was the cost of the disposable vessel itself and the high cost of getting the crew back upriver. The steamboat changed all that. It could sail downriver and then it could steam back up the Mississippi and into the Ohio. This new and revolutionary method of shipping and transportation changed the commerce of the whole region, inextricably tying the Ohio and the Mississippi together.

New Madrid did not factor into the new economy of the Ohio and the Mississippi, but there was no way that Cheeseekau could have known that when he crossed the Mississippi. As it turned out, Morgan returned to the East from New Madrid, giving up on the project he had started. Although there were some tensions between the Shawnees who arrived in the territory and the white settlers, the new settlements founded by the Shawnees had a promising beginning.

headed southeast to the rugged land located at the meeting point of the present-day states of Tennessee, Georgia, and Alabama. In late 1789 or early 1790, the party of Shawnees journeyed to that largely inaccessible country of plunging rivers, narrow gorges, and rocky heights. Its high point, Lookout Mountain, rises to an elevation of 729 metres above sea level, dominating the surrounding countryside and providing ideal cover for a defensive military force. Not far from the present-day city of Chattanooga, the territory was home to the Chickamauga Cherokees, who had been fighting a long battle of their own against the Americans. They had been pushed down the Tennessee River to this redoubt from which they could strike those unwise enough to travel through the area. The Shawnees, perceived by the warriors of the region as a similarly victimized people, were welcomed there.

Over the next half-decade, Tecumseh grew into manhood as a warrior in his own right and developed his own small following. Warriors became leaders not through formal promotion, as in the case of the British or American armies, but by winning the respect of their peers.

During his time near Lookout Mountain, Tecumseh and Cheeseekau and the other members of the Shawnee party, along with the Cherokees, took part in attacks on American vessels that navigated the swift rivers of the regions. Ugly, vicious fights ensued; travellers were robbed and killed and native warriors paid their own price in blood. It was vicious combat, the kind of warfare that had once been common along the frontier between the English and French colonies in eastern North America.

In the summer of 1791, Tecumseh left Cheeseekau at Lookout Mountain and returned to the Ohio country. Why he went is not clear; perhaps it was to play a role in the struggle in the North, where Joseph Brant's confederacy had disintegrated and the Americans were once again pressing for new cessions of land from native peoples.[8] By 1789 Brant's confederacy was in disarray, and some tribes signed a new treaty with the United States at Fort Harmar. Most tribes, disgusted by how they knew the negotiations would turn out, did not attend the meetings. Representatives of the Iroquois and some tribes from the Great Lakes did show up. There, in exchange for goods reckoned at nine thousand dollars in value and divided into two parts, they acknowledged the previous surrender of southern and eastern Ohio that dated all the way back to the Treaty of Fort Stanwix in 1768.[9]

The Shawnees, not prepared to accept the outcome at Fort Harmar, began to organize a new coalition of tribes, which included local Miamis, Delawares, Mingoes, and Cherokees, to resume the fight. In response to the renewed resistance, the United States dispatched a military force to the region, but the coalition warriors promptly routed the U.S. troops. The Shawnees were under no illusions that the U.S. would accept this single setback, and they expected a much more substantial expedition to be organized. In April 1791, Shawnee leaders sent dispatch riders far and wide, perhaps as far south as Lookout Mountain, urging warriors to come to the Ohio country to fight the Americans.

Tecumseh's journey north at the head of a party of eight warriors, which included his younger brothers Lalawethika and Kumskaukau, may have been in response to this call to arms. Back in the Ohio country where he had grown up, Tecumseh rekindled old friendships. No longer a promising young warrior from a family with a martial reputation, he was now a war chief, albeit a minor one.

As it turned out, Tecumseh missed out on the greatest military triumph ever won exclusively by native peoples against the Americans or the British. On November 4, 1791, one thousand warriors, led by Blue Jacket, an influential Shawnee chief; Little Turtle, a Miami chief[10]; and Buckongahelas, a Delaware leader (described by his people as their own George Washington), mounted a pre-emptive strike on the Wabash River (near present-day Fort Recovery, Ohio) against an American force commanded by Major General Arthur St. Clair, which was on its way to attack native towns. The warriors swept into the American encampment, killing and wounding a thousand U.S. troops and driving the survivors into flight.

The natives' triumph generated political shockwaves and inspired hope in the Ohio country that they might actually reverse the onslaught of settlement and take back some of the land they had lost. Impressed by the scale of the victory, the British briefly considered the idea of establishing a native buffer state between the Ohio River and the Great Lakes, a project that would come back to life almost two decades later, at the height of Tecumseh's career.

Defeat in the American Revolutionary War had not marked the end of British interest and ambition in the region that Americans called the Northwest Territory. For one thing, when the Treaty of Paris concluded the war in 1783, the British military still clung to many posts on the U.S. side of the new border. For another, the British retained a lively interest in the fur trade south of the Great Lakes. As far as the British were concerned, the Americans had not achieved unchallengeable control of this vital region. The British could recall a long series of changes in territorial arrangements in North America over the course of the eighteenth century. They had no reason to believe that the current boundaries were set in stone.

But the Americans did not see things that way. The administration of George Washington had no intention of accepting the stunning defeat on the Wabash as final. While the government was prepared to negotiate a temporary peace settlement with the native peoples in the region, its intention was to buy time until it could send a more effective military force into the territory to reassert U.S. control.[11]

In this urgent new conflict with the Americans, Tecumseh and his small band of followers skirmished with the enemy, sometimes on the attack and sometimes bearing the brunt of ambushes. Tecumseh learned how to give no ground when he found himself in a fight. He assessed a battleground with cool intelligence, discovered the enemy's weak point, and struck it with such force that he filled his adversaries with terror. It was over the course of these battles in which Tecumseh acted as a leader on his own that he developed a reputation as a formidable warrior.

Cheeseekau, still a more important leader than his younger brother, was also drawn into this new round of warfare farther south. Often his missions were launched against American settlements on the Cumberland River in Tennessee. Hit-and-run warfare against the settlers was a gruesome business. For a leader such as Cheeseekau, survival hung in the balance during each raid.

Tecumseh soon returned to Tennessee to fight at his brother's side. In late September 1792, Cheeseekau and his followers prepared to hit John Buchanan's Station, located six and a half kilometres south of Nashville. Stephen Ruddell records that before the attack commenced, Cheeseekau predicted that he would be killed. "Saying that his father had fell [sic] gloriously in battle," Ruddell wrote, "he considered it an honour to die in battle and that it was what he wished and did not wish to be buried at home like an old squaw to which he preferred that the fowls of the air should pick his bones."[12]

As in other episodes in this gruelling guerilla warfare, Cheeseekau and his allies positioned themselves around the station at midnight. They left their horses about a kilometre and a half away and stealthily approached the target on foot, under a clear full moon. They were only a few yards away from the gate when their footsteps spooked some cattle into flight. Alerted by the sound of the cattle and then by the approach of the warriors, an American soldier who was inside the blockhouse at the gate shoved his weapon through a porthole, fired, and shot Cheeseekau dead. For about an hour the assault against the station continued, but the Americans held a strong defensive position — they managed to kill and wound several warriors and escaped with no casualties.

The natives broke off the engagement and withdrew, carrying their dead and wounded on litters. Tecumseh took the body of Cheeseekau to honour him with a Shawnee burial. Since the death of their father when he was only thirteen, Cheeseekau had nurtured his younger brother and prepared him to become a warrior in the manner of those who had come before him. And now Tecumseh, shaped in large part by Cheeseekau, was ready to step into the void that had been left.

According to Shawnee custom, Tecumseh had to seek revenge for the death of his brother in order to allow his soul to rest. In the months that followed the disaster at Buchanan's Station, Tecumseh fought a couple of engagements against the Big Knives. In one battle in late November 1792, he led a small Shawnee band within a larger force of warriors to attack about forty American militiamen in central Tennessee. Some of the Americans were killed and most of the others fled. The leader of the American contingent, Captain Samuel Handley, was captured and threatened with death. In the end, his life was spared through the intervention of several warriors on his behalf. There is evidence, although not conclusive, that Tecumseh spoke up for the captive. The captain was later set free.[13] This was not the first time that Tecumseh had shown that he found the torture and execution of captives repugnant.

In a second firefight, Tecumseh and a small party, having set up a hunting camp near Big Rock while on their way to the Ohio Territory, were attacked by a much larger force of Americans. With his customary flair, Tecumseh managed to rally his small force, lead a counter-assault against the attackers, and drive them off, killing two of them in the process.[14]

Tecumseh had grown into a warrior of whom both his late brother and father would have been proud. Bravery and tactical brilliance were essential qualities that fuelled his rise to pre-eminence. His oratorical skills and his gift as a political leader would mark the next stage in his development.

At the end of 1792, unity among the tribes had been reinforced by the military victory on the Wabash, and there was hope among some natives that a robust alliance could be forged with the British. But as was repeatedly the case, political and military struggles between the great powers affected the fortunes of the native peoples in their campaigns to hold on to their land. While the war continued to simmer between the tribes and the United States, the French Revolution, which had erupted three years prior in 1789, had entered its most radical phase. In January 1793, France's deposed monarch, Louis XVI, went to the guillotine. The revolutionary French Republic transmitted waves of anxiety to monarchical regimes across Europe. The month after the execution of the king, France declared war on Britain. This was the latest chapter in the decades-long conflict for mastery in Europe between Britain and its continental rival, but now it took the entirely new form of an ideological struggle. The British joined the coalition of mostly monarchical European powers against France, which at times included Austria, Prussia, Spain, Portugal, and the Dutch Republic.

The British war against revolutionary France stoked fears that the struggle in Europe could soon spread to North America. Sir Guy Carleton, Lord Dorchester, who had been appointed governor of the Canadas, feared that the United States could be drawn into a military alliance with France. To aid in the defence of Canada, the British were suddenly much more interested in regenerating their alliance with the native peoples. One proponent of such an alliance was John Graves Simcoe, the lieutenant-governor of Upper Canada. In a visit to a new British post named Fort Miami, established not far from the southwestern shore of Lake Erie in April 1794, Simcoe informed native warriors of the contents of a speech in which Dorchester had asserted that the British planned to maintain their presence south of the Great Lakes. In his inflammatory address, Dorchester declared, "I shall not be surprised if we are at war with them [the Americans] in the course of the present year; and if so a Line [a new boundary] must be drawn by the Warriors' Children."[5]

While the natives looked to the British for support, the Americans geared up for another military expedition into the Ohio country to reverse the effects of their earlier defeat. Major General "Mad" Anthony Wayne, who was selected by President George Washington to lead the new force, planned to overwhelm the natives with a larger and better-trained army than the warriors had ever faced. By mid-1794, Wayne's men had constructed a string of posts that stretched 145 kilometres northwest from Fort Washington (present-day Cincinnati) into the heartland of native power.

In June 1794, an army of twelve hundred warriors under Blue Jacket's command, Tecumseh and his small band among them, embarked on a mission to cut Wayne's supply lines. Then they hoped to attack the isolated American forts one at a time. But the plan did not enjoy the support of all the groups of warriors who had been mobilized. This example highlights the recurring problem of native alliances. They were not top-down military organizations that did what they were told. They were coalitions, and those who did not agree with a set of tactics could simply pull out of the coalition. Confederacies waxed and waned as circumstances changed. For native peoples, politics at the village level always remained important, usually paramount. Confederacies that bound different peoples together arose only in response to threats that were perceived as immediate and dire. But these confederacies never amounted to states, federal or otherwise. They did not have an ongoing political structure, source of taxation, or military forces at the level of the confederacy. For common efforts, military forces were mobilized from below. These forces could as easily be removed from the central effort as added to it, so the confederacies were fluid.

The leaders of about half the native forces disagreed with Blue Jacket's plan and wanted instead to begin with an attack on Fort Recovery, the relatively weak post farthest north. They rejected Blue Jacket's more strategically daring plan to cut Wayne's supply lines to the south, which would allow them to deal with the posts one by one.

Blue Jacket had little choice but to go along with an initial assault on Fort Recovery. The attack on June 30, in which Tecumseh participated, began well enough, but following a rout of American soldiers outside the fort, the Ojibwas and Ottawas launched their own full-scale attack on the fort itself. This unwise tactic allowed the soldiers inside to take full advantage of their strong defensive position. With no cannon to reduce the stockade, the warriors were caught in long and futile exchanges of fire. The American post held out.[16]

Even after the arrival of reinforcements, Blue Jacket's force could not regain the initiative, which left the next move up to Major General Wayne. In August 1794, the natives received news that Wayne's troops were on their way. As they had in the past, the Shawnees, Tecumseh among them, were forced to abandon their settlements, leaving their crops in the fields, to retreat to new ground down the Maumee River. As they fell back, they passed Fort Miami, where they hoped to obtain British supplies and succour for their women, children, and elderly.

The native allies managed to mobilize about fifteen hundred warriors, including Wyandots, Ottawas, Ojibwas, and Potawatomis, as well as Shawnees, for the coming battle. More surprising was an unofficial British contingent among them, made up of a few French Canadians and fifty-two Canadian volunteers under the leadership of William Caldwell, a Scots-Irish immigrant to Pennsylvania who had fought on the side of the British during the American Revolution and afterward had joined the Loyalist migration to Canada.

Having set up Camp Defiance in abandoned native villages, on August 15 the Americans, numbering thirty-five hundred men, started their march down the Maumee River. The warriors set up a defensive line six and a half kilometres from Fort Miami to await the assault. On the morning of August 20, as few as five hundred warriors were on hand when Wayne's vastly superior force marched downstream and attacked at Fallen Timbers, a battlefield named for the trees uprooted by a recent tornado.

Although the first volleys from the warriors' muskets briefly panicked some of the Americans, numbers told. Wayne's force hit the warriors in a frontal assault as well as on their flank. Tecumseh and the Canadian volunteers maintained fierce islands of resistance, but the day was lost.

During their retreat along the Maumee, the defeated warriors reached the gates of Fort Miami. What happened in the following agonizing minutes left a stain on the relationship between the British and the natives for many years to come. The warriors cried out for the gates of the fort to be opened so that they could find safety inside. According to Blue Jacket, Major William Campbell, who was in command of the small British force there, shouted to the painted warriors below, "I cannot let you in! You are painted too much, my children."[17] Although Major Campbell understood the importance of the native alliance, he would not risk war with the United States.

The warriors continued their retreat, but they did not forget the betrayal by the British at Fort Miami.

The following summer, the United States negotiated peace with the native peoples. Among those who signed the Treaty of Greenville on August 3, 1795, was Blue Jacket. The treaty gave the Americans what they had already taken in the much-resented Treaty of Harmar, and more. The natives had ceded about two-thirds of today's state of Ohio. Although they were to be allowed to continue to hunt in the territories that had once been theirs, the United States claimed ownership. In exchange, the U.S. paid out twenty thousand dollars in goods and in perpetual annuities of one thousand dollars each to the Shawnees, Delawares, Miamis, Wyandots, Ottawas, Potawatomis, and Ojibwas. A few tribes from the Wabash and Illinois Rivers were to receive five hundred dollars a year. The Shawnees were particularly hard hit — they lost much of the land on which their settlements had been located.

Tecumseh had continued to grow in stature, and by 1795 he had attracted enough followers to set up his own village on either Buck Creek or Deer Creek, on land left to the Shawnees in Ohio. His village had a population of about 250, including his younger brother Lalawethika, the future prophet, and several other relatives. Shawnee civil chiefs who headed up village councils in peacetime sometimes inherited their positions and sometimes were selected for the office. War chiefs always achieved their position of leadership through their prowess. As the leader in his village, Tecumseh became both a war chief and a civil chief.[18]

For nearly three decades, Tecumseh served his apprenticeship. He learned the skills of the warrior, acquired the responsibilities of the chief, and knew the strategic lay of the land for the Shawnee and other native peoples. In the next phase of his life, the mantle of leadership in a great cause was placed on his shoulders. During the years following the Battle of Fallen Timbers in 1794, the tension between the Ohio and Indiana Territory settlers and the forces of native resistance moved inexorably toward a flashpoint. More than any other individual, Tecumseh would lead that resistance, not only in the region of the Great Lakes but also on a continental scale. Inevitably, the resistance movement was deeply influenced by the expansion of the United States, its rapid growth in population, and its transition from a series of states located along the Atlantic coast to a continental power that was pushing into the interior.

As for the Americans, their drive inland not only sharpened the conflict with native peoples, it inflamed tensions with the old imperial power. A new generation of American leaders was convinced that as long as the British remained a power on the continent, the United States could not achieve its territorial ambitions. As a new round of wars roiled Europe, influential Americans toyed with the idea of driving the British out of North America, and particularly the Canadas, whose territory thrust a dagger into the heart of the continent.

Chapter 3

A New Power

THOUGH GEORGE WASHINGTON, the first president of the fledgling United States, famously warned his fellow citizens against "foreign entanglements," the U.S. was hopelessly entangled with European power struggles. By the dawn of the new century, the French Revolution had been succeeded by the rise of Napoleon Bonaparte, who set himself up as first consul of France following a *coup d'état* in 1799.

Napoleon's ascent was based on the success of French armies that swept to victories against neighbouring powers, thus securing dominance for France in Europe. During his rise to the position of French emperor in December 1804, Napoleon consolidated his continental system, in which he and his relatives and military commanders took ruling positions in a host of satellite states. The sole major European power to hold out against domination by the French Empire was Great Britain.

Struggles for power on both sides of the Atlantic swirled around the central conflict between Britain and France. Although a rising power in its own right, the United States was continually buffeted by the effects of the Napoleonic Wars. The new republic was the world's largest "neutral" trader, and American seaports thrived or withered depending on how their access to the high seas was affected by the

combat between Britain and France. Despite the United States' recurring tendency throughout its history to withdraw from the world, the
new country was of and in the world whether its leaders liked it or not.

At home, with its population increasing and its commerce bur-
geoning, the United States was bursting at the seams on the Atlantic
seaboard and in the western interior. Just over five million Americans
resided in the nation's sixteen states (Vermont, Kentucky, and
Tennessee having been added to the original thirteen). About sixty
thousand American settlers lived in the country's frontier territories,
the Ohio Territory and the Indiana Territory. In future decades,
the states of Ohio, Indiana, Michigan, Illinois, Wisconsin, and
Minnesota would be established in this vital region, and the states of
Alabama and Mississippi would be created in the territories south of
Tennessee.

In the south, Spain exercised erratic control on the Gulf Coast,
while to the north, the United States butted against the British North
American colonies, the largest of which were the great inland colonies of Lower and Upper Canada.

American settlers were on the move westward to acquire land
from the native peoples, mainly in the Ohio and Indiana Territories
and in the territories south of Tennessee. In the first decade of the
nineteenth century, the population of the United States rose at a prodigious rate, soaring to over seven million, an addition of two million
people that was driven by immigration and natural increase.

Politically, the new country avoided the lapse into one-party rule
that so many had predicted for it. In 1801, the peaceful transition
from the Federalist administration of John Adams to Thomas
Jefferson's Democratic-Republican presidency tested the capacity of
the United States to allow rival political parties to function. In 1808,
James Madison, a member of Jefferson's party and a key figure in
drafting the U.S. Constitution, won the presidential election and succeeded Jefferson as chief executive. Constitutional government was
succeeding, but it was still in its early stages and required prosperity
and territorial expansion to sustain it.

In 1803, a one-year period of peace ended in Europe, and Britain and Napoleonic France plunged into war. The European conflict bestowed a glittering opportunity for the United States government to extend its borders. In 1800, Spain transferred the vast Louisiana Territory, comprising all or part of fifteen current U.S. states and covering 2.1 million square kilometres, to France under the secret Treaty of San Ildefonso. Spain had held the territory since 1762. (The actual transfer of authority was not completed until the end of November 1803.) In 1801, Napoleon dispatched a military unit to secure control of New Orleans, a move that shocked Americans and their political leaders. Jefferson's Federalist opponents accused the president of failing to defend American interests and called for war against France. Jefferson one-upped them not only by threatening war against France but also by touting the possibility of an alliance with Britain.

Jefferson did more than posture. He sent Robert R. Livingston, the U.S. minister to France, to Paris to negotiate the purchase of New Orleans. When the possibility of acquiring the entire Louisiana Territory was broached, Jefferson also sent James Monroe, the previous U.S. minister to France (and future secretary of state and U.S. president) to meet with French authorities. Having concluded that the Royal Navy would almost certainly seize New Orleans and that the Louisiana Territory would be lost to France in any event, the French emperor had already reconciled himself to the purchase. Napoleon had had enough of the western hemisphere by then: France had squandered an army of thirty-five thousand men during the Haitian revolution led by Toussaint Louverture.[1]

On April 30, 1803, Livingston and Monroe signed the Louisiana Purchase Agreement. Although Jefferson faced some domestic opposition for the purchase, he announced the deal to the American people on July 4, and on October 20, the U.S. Senate ratified the agreement. On December 20, the United States took possession of New Orleans; on March 10, 1804, the U.S. formally acquired ownership of the Louisiana Territory at a ceremony in St. Louis and organized its possession of the territory effective October 1.

For the paltry sum of approximately fifteen million dollars, the deal transformed the United States into a continental nation that now controlled the lands on both shores of the Mississippi and at New Orleans, the mouth of this essential corridor of commerce. By this time, the U.S. was already a nation pointed westward, with settlers flooding into Ohio, Kentucky, and Tennessee — a flow of settlement that confronted the native peoples of the region with a threat to their very survival.

Jefferson's brilliant coup in acquiring the Louisiana Territory gave the leaders of the new nation the assurance that the United States was destined to become a first-rank power. The purchase was bound to exacerbate hostilities with the native peoples in the interior. And this was happening at a time when the U.S. was being drawn into tense relations with both Britain and France as a result of the interference by the two powers with American commerce on the seas.

Throughout the French Revolutionary and the Napoleonic Wars from 1793 to 1815, strategists in Britain and France regarded economic warfare as an indispensable weapon. Both countries issued instructions to their navies to disrupt the commerce of the enemy, with dire consequences for American merchants. The U.S. government insisted that the goods on board "neutral" ships must be free from interference, a doctrine that the French and British stoutly rejected.

In July 1805, the British Admiralty Court issued a ruling that heightened tensions with the United States. The case involved the *Essex*, an American ship that loaded a cargo in Barcelona that was ultimately intended for Havana (in Spanish-ruled Cuba). Since Barcelona was within Napoleon's continental sphere, the vessel was liable to be seized by the Royal Navy. The American practice was to undertake what were called "broken" voyages to avoid British seizure, by landing en route at an American port, in this case Salem, Massachusetts. There the cargo was offloaded, and the ship was repaired and reloaded to set sail for Havana. It was then that the

British took possession of the vessel. The British court ruled that since Havana had been the intended destination all along, the seizure was legitimate.

The only way around such a seizure would have been for the shipper to pay an import duty when landing in the U.S., before the cargo was shipped elsewhere. The *Essex* decision gave the Royal Navy licence to take over U.S. vessels involved in the re-export trade.[2]

Britain reinforced this tough stance by blockading major portions of the European coast. To this provocation, Napoleon responded with the Berlin Decree, which banned all trade with Britain. In turn, Britain shot back with the Orders in Council, which stipulated that neutral ships en route for Europe, most of which were American, must first call at a British port to be inspected and licensed and to pay customs duties. Britain's foreign minister, George Canning, convinced the Tory government in London that a prohibition on the neutral carrying trade between the West Indies and Europe would be the surest way to retaliate against Napoleon. This edict was particularly resented by the United States because it hindered American commerce with Britain's competitors.[3]

In December 1807, Napoleon answered with the Milan Decree, which permitted France to seize ships that followed the rules set down by the British Orders in Council. This pair of duelling decrees, if fully implemented, would ban virtually all American trade with Europe.[4]

In 1807, even before learning of the Milan Decree, U.S. President Thomas Jefferson prompted Congress to pass the Embargo Act,[5] which made it illegal for American vessels to sail to any foreign port. The effect of the act was to call a halt to American exports. While foreign vessels remained free to carry imports to the United States, they too were barred from carrying American exports to foreign destinations on their return trips. Few foreign shippers were much interested in one-way trade. Through the Embargo Act, the U.S. was cutting off its nose to spite its face. The primary victims of the act were American ports, shippers, and commercial interests.

Jefferson hoped to teach both the British and the French the lesson that if they persisted in their ways, they would have to live without American goods. As a consequence, the value of American exports plunged from $108 million in 1807 to $22 million in 1808, while imports to the United States contracted from $138 million to $57 million. Not surprisingly, Jefferson's attempt to isolate the U.S. from Europe generated a sharp rise in smuggling, not least between British North America and the U.S. With their strong trading interests, New Englanders particularly loathed the Embargo Act. Their Federalist opposition to Jefferson's Republicans expressed the fury of the region.

Early in 1809, during its last days, the Jefferson administration pushed the Non-Intercourse Act through Congress to replace the reviled Embargo Act.[6] The new act banned trade only with Britain and France. Before the end of 1809, further legislation allowed American ships to trade anywhere but kept the ports of the United States closed to British and French ships.

British and French interference with American trade, combined with Jefferson's ineffective response, left Americans in a surly mood. But American rage was further provoked by an action undertaken by the British alone.

Throughout the presidency of Thomas Jefferson and in the early years of the Madison administration, American resentment mounted against the British for their actions on the seas and in the North American interior. Power brokers in federal politics were well aware that the United States was a sanctuary for British sailors looking for a better life than the one they had in the Royal Navy.

In 1805, an estimated eleven thousand sailors on American merchant ships were Royal Navy veterans or deserters. The United States allowed British deserters to become naturalized American citizens, but Britain did not respect the right of the U.S. to naturalize anyone born in the United Kingdom. The British claimed the right to halt

American ships on the seas and search for sailors who had deserted from the Royal Navy. On occasion, the Royal Navy executed men they seized from American ships; others were flogged, and most were "impressed" (forced back into service). This form of impressment infuriated Americans, who saw it as an assault on the sovereignty of the United States.

In June 1807, for example, a British naval squadron lay in wait on the waters of Chesapeake Bay, hoping to intercept two French ships in the vicinity. The presence of British warships in Chesapeake Bay, near the crucial ports of Baltimore and Annapolis and close to the republic's federal capital in Washington, D.C., infuriated the United States, but there was little they could do about it. In addition, the close proximity of the American coast proved too great a temptation to a number of sailors on the British ships. They deserted.

An incident on Chesapeake Bay brought Britain and the United States to the brink of war. The fifty-gun HMS *Leopard*,[7] commanded by the Royal Navy's Captain Salusbury Humphreys, pursued and intercepted the USS *Chesapeake*, an American frigate, off the coast of Norfolk, Virginia. U.S. Commodore James Barron refused the British demand to turn over British deserters to the Royal Navy. Operating under orders from Vice Admiral George Berkeley, the commander of the Royal Navy's North American station, Humphreys opened fire on the *Chesapeake*, killing three Americans, wounding eighteen others, and forcing the U.S. vessel to strike its colours. The British seized four members of the *Chesapeake*'s crew and carried them off. One of them, Jenkin Ratford, a well-known deserter, was later hanged from the yardarm of the HMS *Halifax*.

Two of the Americans seized had volunteered for service in the Royal Navy in 1806. They were both sentenced to receive five hundred lashes, but their sentences were later commuted. When the *Chesapeake* sailed back to Hampton Roads, the report of the incident provoked American fury and demands for retaliation. Realizing that its forces had gone too far, the British government decided to disavow Berkeley and issued an apology to the United States. By the autumn of 1807, the war fever had abated.[8] Although the *Chesapeake* incident did not lead to war, the Americans and the British remained deeply and bitterly divided over impressment.[*][9, 10]

The impressment of British sailors seized from U.S. ships was the sharpest wound endured by Americans before the War of 1812, the wound that would not heal. But in the interior, another struggle was underway, and this struggle also sharpened American antagonism toward Great Britain.

If embargo and impressment were front of mind for American states-men, a new group of American politicians with a different set of priorities came to the fore during this dangerous time. Land-hungry politicians exerted growing influence in the corridors of power of the United States. The goal of these new power brokers was the expansion of the American Republic. As the years passed, they whipped up sentiment in favour of a war that would drive the old imperial power out of its remaining holdings in North America. Deeply hostile to Britain, they became known as the War Hawks.

Henry Clay, the young politician from Kentucky nicknamed "the Western Star," personified the new breed. He spoke for the America

---

* The writings of two nineteenth-century authors illustrate the unbridgeable gap between the two countries on the subject. In his classic work on the history of Britain's naval power, written in the 1830s, British attorney-turned-naval-historian William James set forth the British position on why his country believed it had the right to retrieve its sailors from American vessels: "It is . . . an acknowledged maxim of public law . . . that no nation but the one he belongs to can release a subject from his natural allegiance, as that, provided the jurisdiction of another independent state be not infringed, every nation has a right to enforce the services of her subjects wherever they may be found. Nor has any neutral nation such a jurisdiction over her merchant vessels upon the high seas as to exclude a belligerent nation from the right of searching them for contraband of war or for the property or persons of her enemies. And if, in the exercise of that right, the belligerent should discover on board of the neutral vessel a subject who has withdrawn himself from his lawful allegiance, the neutral can have no fair ground for refusing to deliver him up; more especially if that subject is proved to be a deserter from the sea or land service of the former."

of the early nineteenth century, the America that had left the eastern seaboard behind in favour of the rising power of the West. His America pointed beyond the Appalachian Mountains to the Mississippi and west of the great river into the Louisiana Territory. Expansion west, south, and north was Clay's agenda for the future of his young country.

Henry Clay was born on the Clay family homestead in Hanover County, Virginia, on April 12, 1777. He studied law at the College of William and Mary, and in 1797 he was admitted to the bar. That same year, he relocated to Lexington, Kentucky, where he set up a law practice and soon became renowned for his courtroom oratory. Tall, gaunt, even cadaverous, the ambitious Clay married Lucretia Hart, the youngest daughter of the wealthy Colonel Thomas Hart, in 1799. This alliance connected him with the leading business elements in Kentucky.[11] He became a successful lawyer and a shrewd investor with a knack for speculating in land.

Clay soon developed political ambitions. In 1803, he won the election to become the representative of Fayette County in the Kentucky General Assembly. Three years later, the Kentucky legislature appointed him to complete the term of a U.S. senator who was forced to resign his seat. On his return to the state in 1807 after serving in the upper chamber in Washington, he was elected Speaker of the

---

In his rejoinder, written five decades later, U.S. President Theodore Roosevelt pointed out that "the United States maintained that any foreigner, after five years' residence within her territory, and after having complied with certain forms, became one of her citizens as completely as if he was native born." Roosevelt conceded that "the American blockade-runners were guilty of a great deal of fraud and more or less thinly veiled perjury [in swearing that the British sailors on their ships were not British]. But the wrongs done by the Americans were insignificant compared with those they received. Any innocent merchant vessel was liable to seizure at any moment; and when overhauled by a British cruiser short of men was sure to be stripped of most of her crew. The British officers were themselves the judges as to whether a seaman should be pronounced a native of America or of Britain, and there was no appeal from their judgment. If a captain lacked his full complement there was little doubt as to the view he would take of any man's nationality. The wrongs inflicted on our seafaring countrymen by their impressment into foreign ships formed the main cause of the war."

Kentucky House of Representatives. During these years he made himself the voice of Kentucky, whose population nearly doubled to four hundred thousand in the first decade of the century.

Clay was an economic nationalist who from the first days of his career set out to foster a national economic design that would forge ties of mutual interest between manufacturers in the East and agrarian interests in the West, and between the industrializing North and the frontier West. He later called this concept the American system.[12]

Clay made himself the leading spokesman of a band of young politicians from the West and the South whose belligerence toward Britain was a defining sentiment. With Henry Clay and others like him, the popular image of the United States morphs from the days of the American Revolution and the drafting of the U.S. Constitution to the age of the frontiersmen. The late-eighteenth-century figures seem antiquated in their fussy wigs and fancy garb; they appear in the guise of philosophers who are soberly and disinterestedly creating a new country based on a constitution intended to fashion a new beginning for mankind. From there, America bolts forward in the popular imagination as a land of plain-spoken individualists living on a vast continent and leaving the old ways behind them.

Both of these images are simplifications and distortions. They do contain a glimpse of the truth, however. Between the days of the Revolution and the drafting of the Constitution, on the one hand, and the epoch of migrants heading west on riverboats and horse-drawn wagons, America ceased to be an affair of the East Coast and instead became a continental project. The United States became markedly less European and more specifically American.

The Americans who led the Revolution were very much at home in both Europe and America. Although they regarded his clothing as odd, the French were happy to fete Benjamin Franklin as a philosopher cut from the same cloth as they were. Thomas Jefferson fitted in easily in Paris. He made sense of the world through the eyes of the European Enlightenment. Jefferson's Declaration of Independence was as much a product of European thought as it was of American thought. In fact, he wrote it for audiences on both sides of the Atlantic. While the document roused Americans to the righteousness of their cause, it explained the need for independence — "a decent respect to the opinions of mankind requires that they should declare the causes which impel them to the separation" — to a European audience.

The Revolution severed the link in political identity between America and Europe. After the Treaty of Paris of 1783, immigrants to America could no longer see themselves as transplanted Englishmen. They had to become Americans. A large part of the formative background of the Thirteen Colonies fell away with the Treaty of Paris, and those residents were already looking west while they fought for their independence from the mother country. Their future, revolutionary leaders such as George Washington believed, lay in the lands on the other side of the Appalachian Mountains.

Washington's appetite for new land could only be satisfied through the demolition of the barriers Britain placed in the way of western settlement. The War Hawks, in particular, had their eye on the desirable farmlands of Upper Canada. And those from Kentucky, Tennessee, and Ohio were intent on ending what they saw as the Indian menace along the frontier of American settlement. As a result, they detested the alliance between the native peoples and the British Crown, an alliance of convenience to be sure, but an alliance that still stood in the way of the movement of settlers onto native lands.

In the years immediately prior to the outbreak of the War of 1812, Henry Clay managed to make himself a key power broker in national politics. In 1810, the Kentucky legislature picked him to complete the term of a senator who had resigned to serve as a judge on the United States Circuit Court. In 1811, he was elected to the national House of Representatives, where he was chosen as Speaker of the House on the first day he sat in that body. Never had Washington seen such rapid elevation to the high office of Speaker, and it has never happened since.

Clay was a staunch adherent of the Republicanism of Thomas Jefferson and James Madison, and as Speaker of the House he learned how to wield immense influence. Despite Napoleon's interference with American shipping, Clay had not the slightest temptation to go to war with France. Instead, he saved his considerable bellicosity for the British. In Clay's mind, war with Britain would resolve a host of problems. For one thing, it would help resolve the economic downturn that for half a decade had plagued the regions of the United States west of the Appalachian Mountains. The British blockade of Europe had barred the farm produce of the Ohio Valley from the markets of the continent.[13] The disruption of the trade that flowed down the Mississippi to New Orleans and from there to Europe contributed to the strong anti-British sentiments of the West.

In addition, Clay and other western advocates of a showdown with Britain perceived that the British were constantly stirring up the native peoples against the settlers. In the minds of westerners and their political representatives in Congress, the best way to end the native threat was to drive the British out of Canada.

As Speaker of the House, Clay packed key committees with members who were equally antagonistic toward the British. One of them was John C. Calhoun, who was first elected to the House of Representatives in 1810, after having served as a member of the South Carolina legislature. He and Clay would be associated with each other for decades. Later in his career, Calhoun served as vice president of the United States, first under John Quincy Adams and then under Andrew Jackson.

Calhoun was born in 1782, into a family that owned a farm in the backcountry of South Carolina. When his father, a Scots-Irish immigrant from Ulster, fell ill, Calhoun quit school to devote himself to the family farm. Later, his brothers supported him financially so that he could resume his studies. In 1804, he graduated from Yale College, and then he studied law at the Tapping Reeve Law School in Litchfield, Connecticut. In 1807, he was called to the bar in South Carolina.

With a hawk-like countenance, piercing eyes, and, as the years passed, an ever more unruly head of hair that took on the appearance of ruffled feathers, Calhoun wielded an eloquence and sharp intelligence that made him more feared than loved. During the early years of his political career, Calhoun was a nationalist who promoted American expansion and the use of the power by the federal government to promote internal development. However, as the slavery issue became ever more prominent, Calhoun became a fierce proponent of states' rights, and he advanced the notion that slavery was a "positive good." Convinced of the self-evident supremacy of whites, he argued that slaves benefitted from the paternalism of their masters. In a speech in the United States Senate in 1837, Calhoun spelled out his case: "I may say with truth, that in few countries [other than the United States] so much is left to the share of the labourer, and so little exacted from him, or where there is more kind attention paid to him in sickness or infirmities of age. Compare his [the slave's] condition with the tenants of the poor houses in the more civilized portions of Europe — look at the sick and the old and infirm slave on the one hand, in the midst of his family and friends, under the kind superintending care of his master and mistress, and compare it with the forlorn and wretched condition of the pauper in the poorhouse."

Twenty-nine-year-old Calhoun voted for Henry Clay's elevation to the position of Speaker of the House of Representatives. He shared Clay's hostility to Britain and was convinced that the United States and the old mother country were on the path to war. To those who warned of the costs of such a war, Calhoun retorted: "We are next told of the expenses of war, and the people will not pay taxes. Why not? Is it from want of means? . . . No; it has the ability, that is admitted; and will it not have the disposition? Is not the cause a just and necessary one? Shall we then utter this libel on the people? If taxes should become necessary, I do not hesitate to say the people will pay cheerfully."⁴ For Southerners such as Calhoun, the alliance with the rising political power of the West was about land. While the lust for new land pointed west and north, it also pointed south. Although the Louisiana Purchase had carved out an empire for the United States west of the Mississippi, the Floridas remained in the hands of Spain.

Southerners believed support for war with Britain would lubricate their effort to possess the Floridas.

Clay backed the drive for the Floridas. In 1810, while still a senator, he defended the Madison administration's military occupation of a part of Spanish-ruled West Florida that had not been included in the Louisiana Purchase. Looking north, he declared ebulliently, "The conquest of Canada is in your power. I trust I shall not be deemed presumptuous when I state, what I verily believe, that the militia of Kentucky are alone competent to place Montreal and Upper Canada at your feet."[15]

It has often been said that money is the mother's milk of politics. In the early nineteenth century, land was the surest route to money and thereby to political influence. In turn, the state was the instrument of force and coercion through which more land could be obtained. The hunger for land was the appetite that bound the War Hawks together, whether they were southern slave owners or western settlers.

One man who understood the game and its objectives better than most was John Randolph, the maverick congressman from Virginia who coined the epithet "War Hawks" to describe Clay, Calhoun, and company.[16] Many believed Randolph was deranged. If so, there was an analytical method to his madness. In the House, Randolph charged that what drove the War Hawks was "a scuffle and scramble for plunder," and that a large chunk of the land they sought would come through the conquest of Canada. To the discomfiture of the war party, Randolph shrilled, "Ever since the report of the Committee on Foreign Affairs came into the House, we have heard but one word — like the whip-poor-will, but one monotonous tone — Canada! Canada! Canada!"

He warned, with remarkable prescience, that territorial expansion would be perilous to the American Union, that it would bolster the anti-slavery forces and would ultimately compel the South to secede. Randolph opposed the conquest of Canada for that reason.[17]

In a head-to-head debate with Calhoun, Randolph cautioned that war with Britain could result in American slaves, inspired by the

French Revolution, rising up against their masters. To this, Calhoun replied that while Randolph "may alarm himself with the disorganizing effects of French principles, I cannot think our ignorant blacks have felt much of their baneful influence. I dare say more than one-half of them have never heard of the French Revolution."[18]

The House of Representatives elected in 1810, ever after to be known as the War Congress, included 59 freshmen members, among them Henry Clay and John Calhoun, out of a total of 142. The Republicans — who had begun to label themselves Democratic-Republicans — had 108 members to 36 Federalists. In the Senate, they outnumbered the Federalists 30 to 6.[19]

The presence of the War Hawks in Congress tilted the national debate toward war with Britain. And those in charge of British military and political strategy were acutely aware of the rising tensions with the United States.

Chapter 4

Isaac Brock and the Defence of the Canadas

THE FATE OF THE GLOBAL ENTERPRISE that became the second British Empire — the first British Empire having been destroyed by the American Revolution — hung in the balance at the turn of the century. The struggle between Britain and France would determine which power would dominate the world in the nineteenth century. If the French succeeded in landing an army on British soil, Britain would lose the war and would be reduced to an offshore island in France's imperial sphere. Political and military leaders in London were keenly aware that all means at their disposal must be mobilized for the struggle.

Britain had two services in its arsenal: the great shield provided by the Royal Navy, and the sword in the hand of the British army. Take away its naval supremacy and Britain would have been doomed. The leaders of the British government and the admirals of the Royal Navy were prepared to do whatever was needed to sustain British command of the seas around the world. In the years prior to the War of 1812, the dominance of the Royal Navy over the fleets of other states is captured in the fact that it deployed 152 ships of the line, compared with 46 by the French, 13 by the Netherlands, 28 by Spain, and 33 by Russia, with some of the Russian ships interned under British command. The Royal Navy had 183 cruisers, France 31, the Netherlands 7, Spain 17, and Russia 10.[1]

During the wars between Britain and France from 1793 to 1815, 103,660 men died while serving in the Royal Navy. Illness and personal accidents carried off 84,440 (81.5 percent) of these men. A further 12,680 (12.2 percent) of the deaths resulted from non-combat calamities, mostly shipwrecks, the foundering of vessels, and fires. Enemy action took the lives of 6,540 (6.3 percent) of the naval force.[2]

Over the course of the Napoleonic War, the Royal Navy was globally pre-eminent, not only as a weapon of war but also as an industrial enterprise. Together, the dockyards of the navy were the world's leading industrial operations. In 1803, 100,000 seamen and marines served in the Royal Navy. The navy sustained this complement and then increased it to 145,000 men in 1810 and kept it at that level through 1812, after which the number of seamen and marines declined to 117,000 in 1814 and 90,000 the following year. Maintaining this huge fighting force severely strained the British treasury. In 1803, the Royal Navy received a grant of just over ten million pounds, and that sum increased year by year to a peak of just over twenty million pounds in 1813.[3]

The immense effort to sustain and expand the Royal Navy, in addition to the risks faced by men in the service, pressured those in charge of the Admiralty — the strategy was crafted by a small group of senior officers and civilians in the Admiralty Board Room in London[4] — to take decisions that were bound to generate intense conflict, and possibly war, with the United States.

In theory, service in the Royal Navy and in the army was voluntary. In practice, the masters of the Royal Navy had to resort to desperate measures to keep up the complement of men on the ships. Impressment was the solution. The British state took unto itself the right to bodily carry off men for service — and not just the deserters they found on American ships. Lieutenants in British port towns organized gangs of ruffians to seize able-bodied men to serve on ships. Exempt were gentlemen (those of sufficient means), those under eighteen or over fifty-five, seamen already in the Royal Navy, fishermen, tradesmen, apprentices, and a few others. Royal Navy ships also stopped merchant ships returning to home ports and impressed their most promising sailors. Once impressed, men were often offered the opportunity to "volunteer," which made them eligible to receive a bonus that varied over the period of the wars with France from one pound ten shillings to ten pounds. Genuine volunteers may have accounted for as few as one-quarter of those serving on the ships of the Royal Navy.[5]

Early-nineteenth-century warships combined the most advanced industrial technology of the day with the technology of a much earlier period. Wooden vessels, propelled by wind and deploying as much sail as possible to ensure maximum speed and manoeuvrability, coexisted with the rising firepower of guns — cannon, we would call them — and mortars. The ships of the line were packed with enormous firepower. They were the most concentrated engines of destruction in existence at the time. Although most of those who died while serving on ships were not killed in action, casualties were extremely high when naval battles erupted. When warships fought each other broadside, unleashing their firepower at close range, ships and masts were torn asunder and men were blown to bits.

The most crucial battle of the age was Vice Admiral Horatio Nelson's decisive victory at Trafalgar in 1805, fought off the southwestern corner of the Iberian Peninsula. Against the combined fleets of France and Spain, Nelson managed a triumph that was the very opposite of the normally inconclusive battles at sea. Nelson used his uncanny understanding of the dictates and tactics of naval war to achieve Britain's most strategically important victory on the seas.[6] And he died in the fight, becoming as a result Britain's pre-eminent naval hero.

At Trafalgar the British did not overturn Napoleon's empire, but they gained for themselves much needed protection against a French invasion of the British Isles. In the end, it would be a soldier, not an admiral, who would finish off Napoleon — the Duke of Wellington, at the Battle of Waterloo in 1815.

Similarly, in North America, the Royal Navy would be indispensable to Britain's defence of its holdings in North America. But it was soldiers who would have to mount a defence along an all-too-lengthy border when the Americans launched their war. While soldiers in the United States were most often farm boys, in Britain they were as likely to be recruited from the urban poor, from coal-mining or cloth-manufacturing towns.

The men who served in the army's rank and file were drawn from among the poorest segments of society in the British Isles. English, Irish, and Scots, they manned the regiments that served at home and in the colonies. Common soldiers were paid a pittance — seven shillings a week — from which were subtracted sums to cover rations, personal equipment, and materials for washing and cleaning. The soldier was fortunate to receive one and a half shillings after these deductions. British soldiers were poorly housed and clothed and inadequately fed. They spent long periods of time stationed away from wives and children. A small number of wives — ranging from six to twelve, depending on where the unit was stationed — were allowed to accompany about one hundred men. These women were charged with doing the washing and often cared for the wounded and the sick.[7]

Officers, who regularly purchased their posts, came from higher rungs on the social ladder, from prosperous merchant families and families of the gentry. For them, as for enlisted men, the army was a calling for life. It was a tough, wearisome existence, especially for those posted in distant colonies. The generous consumption of alcohol made the drabness more endurable. Wars and battles punctuated army life with excitement, danger, and fear.

Reliability was the quality most prized in the British army. Regiments were trained to perform on battlefields the way the new machines in British industry performed. Soldiers were disciplined to follow orders while under fire, and officers learned how to give those orders and maintain cohesion when it counted.

Many of the top officers were better suited to politics or administration. But among them were men with genuine military talent, and, more rarely, warriors with the skills to inspire men and the

foolhardiness and daring to throw caution to the wind on the battlefield. One of these was Isaac Brock.

Isaac Brock was a career soldier from a very early age. The British
army was much more than his vocation. It was his entree to the
world; it was his taskmaster, his school, his life.

Brock was born in a setting that could hardly have been more different from that of Tecumseh, his future comrade-in-arms. The two
did share one crucially important commonality: both were born on
the front line, Tecumseh in the Ohio country and Brock on the Channel
Island of Guernsey, off the coast of Normandy, in a centuries-old
conflict zone between England and France. Although Brock fash-
ioned himself a British general in appearance and manners, and even
in his exquisitely crafted letters and superb penmanship, he was at
heart a Guernseyman.

The eighth son among fourteen children, Brock was born in St.
Peter Port, the chief town and capital of Guernsey, on October 6,
1769. Brock's father, John, had married Elizabeth de Lisle, the daughter of the bailiff of Guernsey. With deep roots in island society, the
Brock family was linked to other leading families through marriage.
Although John Brock died at the age of forty-eight while taking the
waters at Dinan in Brittany for his health, he managed to endow his
wife and their large brood with the means for a comfortable middle-
class life.

The Brock family traced its history in Guernsey to the sixteenth
century, a turbulent time in the Channel Islands during an often violent transition from Catholicism to Protestantism. With Jersey only
fourteen kilometres from the Norman coast at its closest point, and
Guernsey farther west, the major Channel Islands were caught amid
sociopolitical forces from England and France. The government of
Elizabeth I wanted to impose Anglicanism on the islands, but the
population was heavily influenced by French Calvinism as well as by
the Protestantism of the Huguenots, some of whom fled to Guernsey

and Jersey and the smaller Channel Islands to escape Catholic perse-
cution in France. Pockets of Catholicism survived in the islands;
among Anglicans, the Calvinist hue remained.

The societies of Guernsey and Jersey hummed with commercial
energy. The leading families of Guernsey developed trading links
with many parts of the world. They shared little in common with the
English aristocracy — making money and dirtying their hands in
commerce, much abhorred by the great English aristocrats, was the
lifeblood of the Guernsey merchants. This put them on the leading
edge of the rising international capitalism, much in the manner of
Holland. Many of the leading Guernsey families, including the
Brocks, set up as privateers, licensed pirates who obtained letters of
marque from the English Crown. They attacked Spanish and French
ships carrying bullion on the high seas, handing most of it over to
the Crown but keeping an important share for themselves. It is not
unlikely that some ambitious Guernsey privateers acquired letters of
marque from France as well as England, which allowed them to
attack English ships in addition to those of France and Spain. Energy,
vitality, and the ability to adapt to changing conditions were the hall-
marks of the leading families of Guernsey, and Isaac Brock was
unmistakably in their mould.

In his youth, Brock excelled at swimming and boxing. One of his
favourite activities was to swim to Castle Cornet, a military strongpoint six hundred metres offshore. He attended school in Southampton
when he was ten and spent a year in Rotterdam, where he was taught in
French by a Protestant clergyman. After school, he devoted a great deal
of time to devouring books on military tactics and science, as well as
on ancient history. He grew to a height of six foot two, unusually tall in
his day. At the time of his death, measurements taken from his uniform revealed an ample waist size of forty-seven inches. A few inches
can be subtracted from this girth, since his uniform had to be loose fitting so he could move in it on a battlefield.

At the time, it was a common practice for men of means to purchase a rank and then sell it when they purchased a higher rank. In

1785, when Brock was fifteen, his family purchased for him the rank of ensign in the 8th (King's) Regiment of Foot, in which his eldest brother, John, also served. In 1790, Brock purchased the rank of lieutenant. That same year, he raised his own company of soldiers, for which he was promoted to captain. Soon after, he was transferred to the 49th (Hertfordshire) Regiment of Foot, joining the unit in Barbados in 1791 and serving subsequently in Jamaica. In 1793, he contracted a fever and nearly died, only recovering fully during sick leave after his return to England in 1793.[8]

Captain Brock was assigned the task of recruiting men into the army, initially in England and later in Jersey. Discontent and threats of mutiny were all too common in the British forces. In 1797, by which time Brock had purchased the rank of lieutenant colonel, major mutinies broke out among Royal Navy sailors at Spithead, near Portsmouth, and Nore, in the Thames estuary. The mutinous sailors wanted their living conditions improved and they demanded a pay raise to make up for the high inflation of recent decades. At a time when Britain was at war with revolutionary France, there were fears within the upper classes and the higher ranks of the Royal Navy that the mutinies could spark a revolution in Britain.

As the mutinies gained strength, the objectives of the leaders of the movement spread beyond the typical trade-union-style demands of better working conditions and a raise in pay; they included pardons for mutineers, the election of a new parliament, and peace with France. In the end, the movement was divided and the radical elements among the mutineers lost the support of many of the sailors. The authorities prevailed and the mutinies collapsed.

Richard Parker, the leader of the Nore mutiny, was convicted of treason and piracy and was hanged from the yardarm of the HMS *Sandwich*, the vessel on which the uprising had begun. In all, twenty-nine leaders of the mutinies were hanged; others were flogged, and still others were sent to Australia.

In the summer of 1797, when the naval mutinies were reaching their peak, Brock's regiment was stationed on the banks of the

Thames. Many of the men in the regiment felt sympathy for the mutineers and identified with their goals. Brock acted to deal with grievances and to restore discipline. When the regiment was stationed in Jersey in 1800, Brock went on leave for several months, during which time the men were commanded by a much disliked junior lieutenant colonel. The regiment was standing at ease in front of the barracks at St. Helier when the men recognized Brock striding into view. They gave him three loud cheers. He immediately rebuked them for unmilitary conduct and sent them to their barracks, where they were confined for a week.[9] Brock was popular, but he was a staunch disciplinarian.

By this time, British military strategy was devoted to the conflict with France's rising military star, soon to be the country's ruler, Napoleon Bonaparte. Missions across the Channel along the coast of French-dominated Europe had become a principal task of the British army.

In September 1799, in command of the 49th, Brock was sent with his regiment and other units on an expedition against the Batavian Republic (the Netherlands), where they were joined by a Russian army.* Brock and his unit did not see heavy fighting when they first came ashore. But a few weeks later, on October 2, the unit was involved in a fierce battle at Egmont-op-Zee. Brock led his men — his younger brother Savery was among them — across the sand dunes. He later wrote that the ground they covered could only be compared "to the sea in a storm." When his men were threatened on their flank by the enemy, Brock led six companies of his regiment — the other four being led by Colonel Roger Sheaffe, who would join Brock in the defence of the Canadas — on a charge against the foe. Camouflaged French

---

* The Batavian Republic was proclaimed in 1795, as a consequence of a popular revolution in the Netherlands, with the armed support of revolutionary France. It later became a vassal state of the French Republic, as it was at the time of the British assault in which Brock was involved. Later still, the French Empire of Napoleon Bonaparte dominated the Batavian Republic. In June 1806, the Kingdom of Holland succeeded the republic when Napoleon coerced the Dutch into accepting his brother Louis as their monarch.

sharpshooters poured a volley of fire on the members of the 49th. During the long battle, Brock's regiment lost thirty men. A spent bullet struck Brock in the throat. It is likely that what saved him was a thick cotton handkerchief, which he wore over a black silk cravat.[10]

In a letter written from London about seven weeks later to his brother John — also a lieutenant colonel, he was serving with the 81st regiment at the Cape of Good Hope — Brock reported, "I had every reason to be satisfied with the conduct of both officers and men, and no commanding officer could be more handsomely supported than I was on that day, ever glorious to the 49th." He informed John that when he was hit by the spent bullet he "got knocked down . . . but never quitted the field, and returned to my duty in less than half an hour." He also wrote that his brother Savery "had a horse shot under him."[11] Brock's charge had been decisive. His adversaries panicked and withdrew from their position.

The victory at Egmont-op-Zee was reversed four days later, when enemy cavalry attacked the British and the Russians, driving them back and ultimately forcing them to evacuate their position in Holland.[12] Nonetheless, Brock had discovered during his baptism of fire that he had nerve and that he could use it to rally his men and lead them to success.

By the early years of the new century, Brock had learned his trade. He was a first-rate soldier and leader of men, a professional. In 1802 he was transferred to Canada, a corner of the empire in which he would spend the rest of career.

When the Treaty of Paris was signed in 1783, the British possessed key posts that were now legally on American soil. British military units clung to Oswego, Niagara, Detroit, and Michilimackinac, strategic points from which they could supply arms and provisions to their erstwhile native allies. During the tense first decade of the nineteenth century, the British played a double game with the native peoples who had been their allies during the American Revolutionary War. Well aware of the fury of the natives against the westward march of American settlers, the British sought to maintain their ties with the native peoples whose lands lay inside the boundaries of the new republic, in order to sustain the viability of the fur trade south of the Great Lakes. But their support for the natives on the land question stopped short of backing them if they should take up arms in support of their cause; they did not want a new war with the United States.

The British kept their posts on American soil until the mid-1790s. In 1794, a new treaty was negotiated in London by an American special envoy, John Jay, the first chief justice of the United States. Even with Jay's Treaty in effect, it took two more years for the British to abandon their posts.[13]

Ambitious British officers like Isaac Brock did not welcome the idea of being transferred to British North America. On the British military agenda, the interminable struggle against France topped the list of priorities. North America was of secondary importance. Despite that, the British government and military were all too aware that the expansionary ambitions of U.S. politicians could easily generate renewed conflict with native peoples, and that such conflict could spill over into Canada. They also knew that a renewal of war against France would impel Britain to adopt measures on the seas that would be deeply resented in the United States. Like it or not, one price of empire was the need to station units of the regular British army along the lengthy frontier shared with the U.S.

The British North America Brock experienced was more a collection of odds and ends left over from the vast empire that had existed before the American Revolution than the promising kernel of a new country. The Atlantic colonies — Newfoundland, Nova Scotia, New Brunswick, and Prince Edward Island — had little to do with the sprawling colonies of Lower and Upper Canada. Indeed, Newfoundland had few commercial connections to the Maritimes. More than half the population of British North America lived in Lower Canada and was overwhelmingly francophone. Upper Canada had fewer than one hundred thousand residents of European descent.

While many of them were Loyalists, a large number had come from the United States after the Revolutionary War in search of land. These newcomers often had no particular attachment to the British Crown.

The St. Lawrence River and the Great Lakes imposed a powerful logic on the Canadas, despite the deep linguistic and cultural differences between the populations of Lower Canada and its younger, less populous western neighbour. The waterways of the North had long drawn the French and the English into the interior of the continent in their quest for beaver pelts. Spread across a vast territory, with their commercial centre in Montreal, the Canadas were subordinate to the political, military, and economic power of Great Britain.

In the event of an American military assault, the long frontier provided numerous possible invasion routes from the south. The farther west one journeyed in the Canadas, the sparser was the population. In Lower Canada most people lived on farms next to the St. Lawrence River between Quebec and Montreal, with the two big towns anchoring the settlements along what amounted to Lower Canada's main street. Upper Canada was lightly populated, with a thin line of settlement on the north shore of the St. Lawrence and Lakes Ontario and Erie. Here and there, the few small towns in the colony — among them, Kingston, York, Fort Niagara, Fort Erie, Newark (today's Niagara-on-the-Lake), Amherstburg, and Sandwich — were the nerve cells for commerce, the military, and government. In Upper Canada, most of the population lived dangerously close to the American border.

In 1802, when Brock and the 49th were first posted to Canada, they were initially quartered in Montreal. What preoccupied Brock was the prospect of a U.S. invasion. He did not know when it would come, but with the rise and fall of tensions between Britain and the United States, it was an event for which he had to prepare.

Bedevilling British regiments in Canada during those years was the ever-present temptation for men to desert and disappear across the border into the United States to begin a new life there. A posting in Canada was potentially depressing not only for British officers but for enlisted men as well.

In the summer of 1803, Brock had to deal with two serious episodes of disobedience in the ranks, the first the desertion of six men from York and the second a mutiny at Fort George, on the Niagara Frontier. In the latter case, conspirators plotted to confine officers in cells and then to cross over to New York State. The rebellious contagion spread to Chippawa and Fort Erie, also along the Niagara Frontier.

The deserters were pursued and caught in the United States and brought back to Canada in a cross-border operation that U.S. officials would have loudly protested had they known about it. Brock and his second-in-command, Colonel Roger Sheaffe — they had served together earlier in Europe — acted quickly to quell the planned mutiny. The ringleaders were arrested at Fort George. Those charged were sent to Quebec to face courts martial. Seven men — three of the deserters and four of the mutineers — were sentenced to death. On March 2, 1804, on a cold, windy morning at Quebec, with the entire garrison present, the prisoners were led to their coffins. For close to an hour they kneeled on the coffins in prayer. Then the shooting began. At first the rounds were fired from a distance of fifty yards. Some of the condemned were only wounded and had to be repeatedly shot. Finally the executioners were ordered to fire their muskets into the breasts of the sufferers.[14]

Upon receiving news that the men had met their deaths, Brock spoke to the soldiers at Fort George and told them of the "grief" he felt. That he won the adherence of his troops is evidenced in an 1807 inspection report praising the state of his regiment, which at that time was stationed in Lower Canada.[15] Brock had that unfathomable quality that won the respect and admiration of those he led, even when he disciplined the men harshly. It was a quality that Sheaffe did not possess. Each time Brock went away and left Sheaffe in charge, discontent bubbled up in the regiment.

⁓

Following a period of leave in England in 1805–6, Brock returned to
Canada, by then a colonel. For a time, he commanded all of the
British soldiers in the colony. Continuing to rise through the
ranks — he became a brigadier general in 1807 — he was charged
with improving the defences of Canada at a time when U.S. hostility
toward Britain was rising to a crisis point. Brock's efforts included
strengthening the fortifications at Quebec City, reorganizing the
defences and shipping capacity of rivers and lakes, and recruiting
and training Canadian militia volunteers. While militia service was
long established in British North America, with fit males aged sixteen to sixty required to participate, it usually amounted to little
more than showing up for meagre training once a year.[16] In Brock's
mind this was far from adequate. He wanted the members of the
militia to undergo serious training in preparation for war, not for an
annual parade. Weighing on his mind was the enormous extent of
the territory that would have to be defended in the event of an
American invasion, and the paucity of British regulars on hand to
defend it.

Brock's energetic attention to duty and his efforts to improve the
defences of the Canadas did not mean that he was happy to be stuck
in such a backwater. In November 1808, he wrote from Quebec to
two of his brothers, saying, "My object is to get home as soon as I can
obtain permission; but unless our affairs with America be amicably
adjusted, of which I see no probability, I scarcely can expect to be
permitted to move." He feared that he would "remain buried in this
inactive, remote corner, without the least mention being made of
me," and hoped that "should Sir James Saumarez [an admiral and
fellow Guernseyman] return from the Baltic crowned with success,
he could, I should think, say a good word for me to some purpose."[17]
In a later letter, Brock expressed pure envy to his brother Irving
about the life he was leading "in the bustle of London" compared to
"the uninteresting and insipid life I am doomed to lead . . ."[18]

The desire for respectable female companionship emerges in
some of his letters. Brock was far too well-mannered to put this

directly. Instead, he wrote wistfully of the arrival of officers' wives, who bestowed a dash of glamour, beauty, and refinement to the dull Canadian social setting. He was buoyed by the excitement such women brought to army and government soirees.

In a note to his sister-in-law Mrs. William Brock, written from Quebec in June 1810, he lamented, "It was my decided intention to ask for leave to go to England this fall, but I have now relinquished the thought." This time the problem was the "spirit of insubordination lately manifested by the French Canadian population of this colony," which "called for precautionary measures." He reported to his sister-in-law that Sir James Craig, the governor of Lower Canada and top British official in the Canadas, had concluded that he needed "to retain in this country those on whom he can best confide." While flattered to be included among this group, he could not help remarking that "fate decrees that the best portion of my life is to be wasted in inaction in the Canadas."[19]

This was not the first time Brock expressed concern about the loyalty of the French Canadians. In an earlier letter to his brother William, in December 1809, Brock opined that "Bonaparte, it is known, has expressed a strong desire to be in possession of the colonies formerly belonging to France. A small French force, 4 or 5000 men, with plenty of muskets, would most assuredly conquer this province."

"The Canadians," he remarked, "would join them almost to a man — at least, the exceptions would be so few as to be of little avail. It may be surprising that men, petted as they have been and indulged in every thing they could desire, should wish for a change. But so it is — and I am apt to think that were Englishmen placed in the same situation, they would shew even more impatience to escape from French rule."[20] Professional realism underscored Brock's view of the Canadas, which he regarded as imperial possessions that supplied essential primary goods to the mother country.

Brock was similarly anxious about the political outlook of recent American immigrants to Upper Canada; he regarded them much more warily than he did the original Loyalists who had arrived immediately following the conclusion of the American Revolutionary War.

Everywhere Brock looked, he saw the need for improvements to prepare for the possibility of a U.S. invasion. Harbours and forts had to be brought up to standard. Transportation had to be made efficient to ensure supplies where and when they were needed. Lakes Ontario and Erie required robust British fleets to prevent these crucial waterways from falling into American hands. Brock wanted the standards set by the British army's Medical Department to be met in Canada. He was well aware that his units were appallingly short of medical supplies and surgeons.

In September 1810, Brock was dispatched to take over the command of British forces in Upper Canada. Sir James Craig, who had served as governor since 1807, departed for England on sick leave in June 1811. Before departing, he bestowed a very special gift on Brock. Colonel Edward Baynes, writing from Quebec on behalf of the ailing Craig, informed Brock that he was to receive the governor's favourite horse, Alfred. Baynes wrote, "The whole continent of America could not furnish you so safe and excellent a horse. Alfred is ten years old, but being a high bred horse, and latterly but very little worked, he may be considered as still perfectly fresh."[*21]

In Upper Canada and during a brief stint back in Lower Canada from June to September 1811, Brock had to deal in an official capacity with civilian officials. And while he was a born leader of men on a battlefield, he found it exasperating to work with members of an elected legislature. Democracy was not his strong suit.

Back in Upper Canada for the last months of 1811, Brock took up the final posts of his life: commander of British forces in the province and head of the provincial government. As he began this ultimate

---

[*] Brock was to work out how to transport Alfred from Quebec to Fort George. Historians disagree about whether Brock ever had Alfred shipped to him. Some believe that the horse did arrive at Fort George, and that on the day Brock was killed he rode Alfred, who also died that day. In any case, there is a small monument to Alfred at Queenston, near the spot where Brock died.

chapter in his career, Brock brooded long and hard about the military strategy to be pursued in the likely event of war with the United States. His strategic conception differed from that of the other British military commanders in the Canadas, because he understood that an effective alliance with native peoples would hold the key to the defence of Upper Canada's western reaches. That idea would be central to his triumphs in the last months of his life.

Chapter 5

Showdown

WHILE BROCK PREPARED the Canadas for hostilities against the Americans, U.S. state representatives, very much in tune with the expansionist War Hawks in the capital, were busy making land-transfer deals with a host of native tribes. The most important of these representatives was future president William Henry Harrison. Born in 1773 into a prominent political family in Virginia, Harrison arrived in the Indiana Territory at the age of twenty-seven, having been appointed its first governor. In January 1801, he took up residence in Vincennes, the capital of the newly established territory. Harrison was a military man — he had fought at the Battle of Fallen Timbers — but also an ambitious politician who forged close relations with land speculators.

Between 1802 and 1805, encouraged by President Jefferson,[1] Harrison used bribery, intimidation, subterfuge, and whiskey to extract seven treaties from a number of tribes, including the Delawares, Miamis, Weas, Piankeshaws, Eel Rivers, Potawatomis, Kickapoos, Shawnees, Kaskaskias, Sacs, and Foxes. These treaties purported to give the United States legal title to vast tracts of land in present-day Indiana, sections of Missouri, Wisconsin, and most of Illinois. The U.S. government paid two cents an acre for these dubiously acquired lands. In addition, Harrison strove to attract enough settlers that the Indiana Territory could qualify for statehood.[2] By 1809, he had overseen the development and execution of a total of thirteen treaties, through which the United States acquired 240,000 square kilometres of land from native peoples.

Harrison's efforts in the Indiana Territory complemented those of the War Hawks in Congress. As a consequence, the United States found itself on the brink of two wars that would soon become one: a war against the native peoples led by Tecumseh and a war with Great Britain.

In August 1810, Tecumseh met face to face with William Henry Harrison at a council convened in Vincennes, located in present-day Knox County, Indiana. The Shawnee chief—who had become the leader of a growing native confederacy, travelling far and wide to unite members of disparate tribes—was in Vincennes to express his fury at the land-transfer deals.

Accompanied by an escort of forty warriors, Tecumseh objected to Harrison's plan to hold the meeting under the portico of his house, where seats had been set up in preparation. Through an interpreter, he told the Indiana governor that he preferred to meet in a nearby grove of trees. When Harrison said that he had no problem with the alternative site but no seats were in place there, the Shawnee chief replied that that posed no difficulty, since native people preferred to repose upon the bosom of their mother. After benches and chairs were set up for the U.S. representatives, the meeting began with Tecumseh and his warriors seated on the ground.[3]

Tecumseh rose dramatically to his feet and opened the talks with a lengthy objection to the treaties Harrison had negotiated with native peoples in recent years. But the treaty that infuriated him the most, the one that had driven him to confront Harrison, was the Treaty of Fort Wayne, through which Harrison had acquired twelve thousand square kilometres of land from representatives of the Delaware, Eel River, and Potawatomi tribes, later joined by the Kickapoos and the Weas. As a consequence, the United States secured its hold on southern Indiana. The native leaders who signed the treaty received annuities and the paltry sum of 5,250 dollars' worth of goods.[4]

Tecumseh regarded the Treaty of Fort Wayne as theft, pure and simple, the extortion of land from weak chiefs overwhelmed by the growing poverty of their peoples as game grew scarce. The treaty was the last straw for the Shawnee leader.

In his speech, Tecumseh spelled out the principle to which he and his warriors and their allies adhered — that the native peoples formed one nation and that he would resist any cession of land unless the transfer was agreed to by all the tribes. He stated that he was determined not to allow the village chiefs to make deals such as the Treaty of Fort Wayne and that, in the future, power would be invested in the war chiefs, who would act for all of the native peoples.

The Shawnee chief recounted the history of the relationship between the Americans and the native peoples. He said the Americans had driven the natives from the seacoast and now threatened to push them from the lakes. He declared that he was unalterably resolved to take a stand, warning that he would resolutely oppose any further intrusion of settlers on native lands. He reviewed the numerous aggressions perpetrated by Americans against native peoples from the beginning of the American Revolutionary War to the present day.[5]

According to one report, the Shawnee chief declared, "You have taken our land from us, and I do not see how we can remain at peace if you continue to do so. You endeavour to make distinctions. You wish to prevent the Indians doing as we wish them — to unite, and let them consider their lands as the common property of the whole . . . in future we are prepared to punish those chiefs who may come forward to propose to sell the land . . . If the land is not restored to us you will see, when we return to our homes, how it will be settled. We shall have a great council, at which all the tribes will be present . . . We will see what will be done to those chiefs that did sell the land to you . . . I am not alone in this determination . . . I tell you because I am authorized by all the tribes to do so. I am the head of them all.

"Brother, do not believe that I came here to get presents from you. If you offer us any, we will not take. By taking goods from you, you will hereafter say that with them you purchased another piece of land from us . . . Should you not return the land, it will occasion us to call a great council that will meet at the Huron village, where the council-fire [preparatory to a meeting] has already been lighted, at which those who sold the lands shall be called, and shall suffer for their conduct.

"As we intend to hold our council at the Huron village, that is near the British, we may probably make them a visit. Should they offer us any presents of goods, we will not take them but should they offer us powder and the tomahawk, we will take the powder and refuse the tomahawk."[6]

Following Tecumseh's blunt challenge to the Treaty of Fort Wayne and the treaties that had come before, Harrison stood up and issued a forthright reply. He denied the Shawnee chief's contention that the native tribes constituted one nation, having a common property in the lands. If the Great Spirit had intended the native peoples to make up one nation, he would not have given them different tongues. He said that Tecumseh had no business challenging the United States and the treaties.

Partway through the translation of the governor's speech, Tecumseh leapt up and began to speak in menacing tones. Harrison did not understand what was being said, but one of his officers who understood Shawnee warned, "Those fellows intend mischief; you had better bring up the guard." Tecumseh's followers sprang to their feet, brandishing their tomahawks. Harrison drew a short sword that he kept at his side. For a few moments, the tense standoff continued. An army captain drew a dagger, and a native chief friendly to the Indiana governor cocked his pistol. When guards ran up and seemed about to fire, Harrison ordered them to stand down. He demanded that the translator convey to him the meaning of Tecumseh's remarks. When he learned that the Shawnee chief had charged that everything the governor had said was false and that he and the Seventeen Fires — in 1803 Ohio had become the seventeenth state — had cheated the native peoples, Harrison told Tecumseh that he would not continue the meeting. Since Tecumseh had come to Vincennes under the protection of a council fire, he could depart in safety, but Harrison made it clear that Tecumseh and those accompanying him must leave the village at once.[7]

That evening, back at his camp, Tecumseh decided that he had gone too far. The following morning he sent a message to the governor, requesting an opportunity to explain his conduct at the council, and declared that he had no intention of attacking Harrison. On the understanding that the two sides would have the same number of armed companions present, the governor agreed to another session.

Restrained in tone when the council resumed, Tecumseh stuck to his position and firmly reiterated that he and his followers were determined to insist on the boundaries that had been in place before the signing of the treaties. Adding to the force of his position was the presence of chiefs from the Wyandots, Kickapoos, Potawatomis, Ottawas, and Winnebagoes. They spoke in succession, making it clear that they had entered the confederacy and supported the principles set out by Tecumseh.

Harrison concluded the conference by saying that he would inform President James Madison of the claims being made by Tecumseh and his supporters on the land issue. But he warned that the U.S. government would never back away from the principles on which it had negotiated the Treaty of Fort Wayne. The United States would sustain its ownership of the lands it had acquired, if necessary by resort to the sword, he warned.[8]

The next day, Harrison made a further effort to sound out Tecumseh. Accompanied only by his interpreter, he visited the Shawnee chief's camp and was cordially received. During his lengthy conversation with the governor, Tecumseh explained the purpose of his native confederacy, an informal alliance of leaders and tribes, and set out the terms for a peaceful resolution with the United States. He compared the U.S. land purchases to a mighty water that was ready to overflow his people; the confederacy he was establishing would stop any individual tribe from selling land without the consent of the others, he explained, and it was the dam that would resist this mighty water.

Testing the possibilities of a deal with the Americans, Tecumseh said he would be drawn into war with the United States only reluctantly. If the governor could convince the president to give up the lands that had been purchased in the recent treaties, and would agree never to negotiate another treaty without the consent of all the tribes, Tecumseh would become the faithful ally of the Americans. He would, he pledged, assist the U.S. in the war he knew was soon coming with Great Britain. He said he would rather be the ally of the Seventeen Fires, but warned that if the Americans did not go along with his request he would have no choice but to side with the British. The hostility between the British and the Americans was no secret, and Tecumseh was adept at playing on the tensions between the two powers to seek a deal that would be beneficial to the confederacy.

When Harrison responded that he would present the confederacy's case to the president but that there was little probability of his conditions being met, Tecumseh replied with more sorrow than anger. "As the great chief is to determine the matter," he said, "I hope the Great Spirit will put sense enough into his head to induce him to give up this land: it is true, he is so far off he will not be injured by the war; he may sit still in his town and drink his wine, whilst you and I will have to fight it out."9

Following his meeting with Tecumseh, even Harrison could not help being impressed by the mettle of his foe. In a letter to the War Department in which he referred to Tecumseh as "one of those uncommon geniuses," he went on to say, "If it were not for the vicinity of the United States, he would, perhaps, be the founder of an empire that would rival in glory Mexico or Peru. No difficulties deter him. His activity and industry supply the want of letters. For four years he has been in constant motion. You see him today on the Wabash and in a short time hear of him on the shores of Lake Erie or

Michigan, or on the banks of the Mississippi and wherever he goes he makes an impression favourable to his purposes."[10] And in an earlier letter to U.S. Secretary of War William Eustis, Harrison compared Tecumseh with other native leaders who had pursued the goal of a union of native peoples: "Tecumseh has taken for his model the celebrated Pontiac, and I am persuaded he will bear a favorable comparison, in every respect, with that far famed warrior."[11]

Harrison understood that Tecumseh followed in the footsteps of others in undertaking the task of uniting the diverse peoples of the continent to make common cause against the westward tide of white settlement. The project that engaged all of Tecumseh's energies was the construction of a native confederacy to stand up to the Americans along a vast front — one that arced across the continent from the upper Great Lakes through the Indiana Territory, the Ohio Valley, and upstate New York, down the Mississippi, and along the boundary of white settlement in the South, all the way to Florida.

He faced the challenge of fashioning a defensive military alliance capable of putting men in the field along a perimeter thousands of kilometres long. Divisions of language and culture, traditions of self-reliance and jealously guarded independence, and inter-tribal antagonisms stood in his path. He showed at Vincennes that he knew the tricks of the enemy. The Americans were masters of bribery, assimilation, and sowing seeds of division among the native peoples. When necessary they used force, at times on a genocidal scale, as they were to do again in the years to come. They also sent in missionaries to convert natives to Christianity. As a result, the native peoples had been swept off almost all their land. Reduced to poor farmers, toiling on a fraction of the territory they had once held, they were shorn of their former freedom and way of life.

At Vincennes, Tecumseh made it clear that if the United States did not change its policies on the issue of native land, there would be war. And in the event of war, he warned, he would accept gunpowder from the British.

Tecumseh had not really expected a deal with Harrison, and he did not get one. The prospect of peace with the United States was closed at Vincennes.

In October 1810, Tecumseh turned to the British at Fort Malden, in the southwestern corner of Upper Canada. Constructed between 1797 and 1799, Fort Malden was the most important British military post on Lake Erie. Prior to the implementation of Jay's Treaty between Britain and the United States in 1796, which required the British to evacuate all forts located on American soil, the main British post had been at Detroit. Fort Malden was located at the site of the present-day town of Amherstburg, Ontario, a few kilometres south of Windsor. From the fort, the Indian Department maintained contact with native tribes that were friendly to the British. These tribes were vitally important to the defence of Upper Canada against a potential American assault. Fort Malden was also key to the protection of the crucial Amherstburg Naval Yard, where the British built and equipped ships to expand their fleet on Lake Erie.[12]

Arriving at the fort in mid-November 1810, accompanied by 134 men, 28 women, and 8 children of Shawnee, Potawatomi, Ottawa, Winnebago, and Sac descent, Tecumseh announced in a speech to British officers and officials that he wanted to rekindle their former alliance. At Fort Malden two years prior, Tecumseh had been unwilling to commit himself to backing the British side in an armed struggle with the United States. This time, he told the British that he expected war and his goal was to have the British on side. "We sit at or near the borders where the contest will begin," he said. At the very least, he wanted supplies from the British. He had brought an old wampum belt, which signified the former native alliance with the British. During the meeting, he asked all those in attendance to touch the belt.

Then he said, "Father, intend proceeding toward the Mid Day [the south], and expect before next autumn and before I visit you again that the business will be done. I request, Father, that you will be charitable to our king's [old men], women and children. The young men can more easily provide for themselves than they."[13]

The British wanted to keep Tecumseh on side in case hostilities with the United States erupted into armed conflict, but they did not want to be blamed by the Americans for a war between the native confederacy and the U.S. On November 25, 1810, Sir James Craig, who had not been present at Fort Malden, sent a message to the British chargé d'affaires in Washington telling him to alert the American government that the native confederacy was planning for war. On February 2, 1811, Craig again expressed his anxiety about a native attack on the Americans in a letter to Francis Gore, Upper Canada's lieutenant-governor, stressing that British policy was to urge the native peoples against war with the U.S. The message should be, he told Gore, that although the British would remain friends to the native confederacy, Tecumseh should not expect aid if his people went to war against the Americans.[14] The British, as Tecumseh already believed, were not to be trusted as allies in a war against the United States, unless it was their war as well.

For the two years prior to the outbreak of the War of 1812, Tecumseh continued to travel throughout the regions on the western rim of American settlement. He was tireless in his campaign to win native peoples over to his cause. Some of his journeys are well documented, while others are less certain, handed down to future generations in the form of oral history. That he spent time with militant Muscogees (Creeks) is well established. Much less certain is the claim that he visited Cherokee leaders in the mountainous terrain of North Carolina. We hear of him in Chickasaw territory en route to the Mississippi. Other stories tell of him among the Cherokees in Tennessee, not far from the region where he and Cheeseekau had once spent time. There is evidence that he visited the Osages west of the Mississippi, counting on their anger at the Americans to offset a dispute with the

Missouri Shawnees. On the northwestern leg of his journeys, Tecumseh traversed the Illinois country and the upper Mississippi. In this vast terrain, he was courting Potawatomis, Winnebagoes, Sacs, Foxes, Dakotas, Kickapoos, Ojibwas, and Ottawas.[15]

During these travels, which were monitored with concern by the Americans, Tecumseh was building an informal political organization, a grouping of peoples who shared a common vision. The Shawnee chief met with both successes and failures: he won some to his banner; others chose to sit on the sidelines; still others aligned themselves with the Americans (some of the latter group had grown dependent on annuities from the U.S. government).

On September 20, 1811, Tecumseh rode into Tuckhabatchee, the capital of the Muscogee people, in present-day Alabama. Twenty warriors — members of the Shawnee, Kickapoo, and Winnebago nations — rode with him. The last months of a tense peace between the United States and the native peoples were quickly passing. And with the War Hawks stoking the fires in Washington, the U.S. and Britain were well down the path to war.

Thousands of people watched the dramatic arrival of Tecumseh and his followers. Tuckhabatchee was overflowing with visitors, in town for the meeting of the Muscogee national council. Big Warrior, Hopoithle Miko, and other important chiefs were in attendance. Longtime North Carolina politician Benjamin Hawkins, the government-appointed representative to the Muscogee nation, came to Tuckhabatchee to serve as the eyes and ears of the United States and to speak up for U.S. interests. A number of white traders were also on hand, as well as representatives from the Choctaw, Chickasaw, and Cherokee tribes, and even some from the Seminole nation in Spanish-ruled Florida.[16]

The Muscogee lived in settlements in the area now known as the Old Southwest (present-day Alabama and Mississippi) and western portions of Georgia, building their towns along the rivers and creeks of that lush territory, which is why settlers called them the "Creeks." Tuckhabatchee was strategically located at the junction of the Tallapoosa and Coosa Rivers.

As was the case with the native peoples of the North, the arrival of white settlers in their territory had led to a growing crisis within Muscogee society. In the new territories, settlers could purchase land cheaply, at between $1.25 and $2.00 an acre, but many preferred simply to squat on the land in the hope that they wouldn't be bothered by the U.S. government or by the native peoples. Outfitted with slaves — some settlers bought their own and others purchased slaves from the Spaniards farther south — they aspired to become wealthy members of the planter class. During the first decade of the nineteenth century, the slave-owning settlers introduced the cotton gin in the Mississippi Territory (present-day Alabama and Mississippi). By 1810, slaves made up almost 40 percent of the population of the settlements along the Tombigbee River, one of the two major rivers (along with the Alabama) flowing from Mississippi south through Alabama.[17]

Slave ownership was also widespread among the Muscogees in the late eighteenth and early nineteenth centuries. During the American Revolution, Muscogees allied to the British captured black slaves from southern whites. In the 1790s, the use of the cotton gin, which did so much to reinvigorate slavery in the South, promoted the institution of black slavery among the upper crust of Muscogee society. In some cases, Muscogee women were removed from work in the fields to be replaced by black slaves of both genders.[18] The Muscogee chief Big Warrior was among those who grew wealthy and owned slaves.[19]

In 1805, the Muscogee ceded close to three million acres of land between the Oconee and Ocmulgee Rivers in Georgia. Within a short space of time, the settlers pushed across this area and moved into the lands west of the Ocmulgee River that remained, in theory at least, in the hands of the Muscogee. Big Warrior declared, "The Muscogee land is become very small . . . What we have left we cannot spare, and you will find that we are distressed."[20] The chief protested directly to President Thomas Jefferson that white settlers were violating the agreement and were seizing native land. In 1809, federal soldiers drove about seventeen hundred squatters off the land of the Muscogee and the territory of the Chickasaws, farther to the northwest.

But such occasional attempts by Washington to stem the advance of
the settlers proved utterly ineffectual. The federal government lacked
both the means and the political will to stop that westward tide.

In the same years that the Muscogees endured the full brunt of
the settler migration, they also were cursed with a sharp decline in
the number of deer on their traditional lands. The herds had been
overhunted. The Muscogees wrestled with two broad approaches.
Some wanted to adapt to the ways of the white man; others passion-
ately believed their survival as a people depended upon resisting the
Americans and, if possible, driving them back, or at least holding the
line against further cessions of land.

A small but powerful group of mixed-blood planters, some of
them slave owners, emerged as a new upper class in the native society, rupturing the long-held communal land ownership traditions of
the Muscogees. This group, whose members embraced American
concepts of land tenure and the acquisition of wealth, was reinforced
in 1796, when Hawkins was appointed as the federal government's
agent to the Muscogees. He was an avid advocate of winning the
Muscogees over to the techniques of white agriculture. Instead of
continuing as hunters, he proselytized, they should become farmers,
raising livestock and growing cotton, using slave labour, and adopting the plantation system.[21] At the meeting of the Muscogee National
Council in 1811, Tecumseh regarded Hawkins as his foe.

Hawkins believed that by promoting class divisions among the
Muscogees and encouraging intensive methods of agricultural land
use, he could quickly assimilate this people and draw them into
American life. But Muscogees who were strongly attached to traditional ways and who saw no economic advantage in the American
approach fiercely opposed those who counselled a deal with the
United States.

In 1811, the U.S. government insisted on opening a federal road
through Muscogee territory, which inevitably meant more settlers.
With its starting point in Augusta, Georgia, the road crossed
Muscogee country all the way to Fort Stoddert, just forty-eight

kilometres north of Mobile, still under Spanish rule. In the first six months of its use, thirty-seven hundred people travelled the road in search of land. In 1806, the Cherokees ceded land that opened the Tennessee River Valley, in what is now northern Alabama, to settlers from Tennessee.[22] Big Warrior, while not openly backing the construction of the road, profited from the monopolies along its route, taking his share in the earnings from toll bridges, ferries, and taverns.[23]

When the pliant political leadership in the Muscogee National Council failed to stop the road and deal effectively with the issue of white settlement, a militant opposition formed. In growing numbers, Muscogees turned to the spiritual leadership provided at the village level by shamans, who had previously been of little consequence politically but had considerable local influence. Just as peoples in the North had been drawn to the teachings of the Prophet and Tecumseh's native confederacy, a spiritual movement to rid the Muscogee people of the ways of the white man became a force to be reckoned with in the South.[24] Hawkins found that the socio-economic program he favoured was being rejected, and along with it the viability of the national council.

This spiritual revolt, which took its most militant form among the Red Sticks, cut right across Muscogee society. Even some of the well-to-do with mixed-blood ancestry joined the movement. It was not a simple matter of conservative elements fighting to retain traditional ways; it was fierce resistance to assimilation. At stake was Muscogee sovereignty.

So there was great anticipation in Tuckhabatchee about what Tecumseh, the famous Shawnee chief, would say in his address. He had reason to believe that his message would be well received by many, but not all, in Tuckhabatchee. Although he came from the distant Ohio country with its markedly different terrain, Tecumseh had personal ties to the Muscogees; this visit was partly a homecoming, not just a diplomatic venture to win over peoples who were not his own.

On the day he arrived, the Shawnee chief marched with his accompanying warriors to the square. They were naked except for their breechcloths and ornaments. Their faces were painted black and their heads were decorated with eagle feathers. Suspended from their waists and arms were buffalo tails, which dragged behind them. Though some in attendance regarded their appearance as hideous, Tecumseh and his party drew the fascinated attention of all who were present.[25]

Tecumseh stayed at the council for a number of days but refrained from speaking as long as Hawkins remained in town. He had no intention of sharing his message to the Muscogee council with a representative of the United States government. Each day, Tecumseh remarked laconically, "The sun has gone too far today. I will make my talk tomorrow."[26] More than a week passed before Hawkins departed. That same evening, with a multitude gathered, Tecumseh entered the council house and offered a wampum bag and a peace pipe to Big Warrior. Big Warrior smoked the peace pipe before passing it to the other chiefs. Tecumseh stood before the assemblage for a few minutes, looking out at the crowd.

Accompanying Tecumseh that memorable evening, as he had throughout the long tour, was Sikaboo, his interpreter. A proficient linguist, Sikaboo spoke Muskogean, Choctaw, and English in addition to Shawnee.[27] When Tecumseh spoke to a crowd or negotiated with American or British political or military leaders, he did so in Shawnee. His knowledge of English was very limited, and he rarely attempted to speak to whites in their language.[28]

A masterful performer who punctuated his remarks with theatrical gestures, Tecumseh used rhetoric to drive home his arguments and leave an indelible impression on his listeners. There is no record of Tecumseh's speech in Tuckhabatchee,[29] but he had been delivering essentially the same set of remarks on a number of occasions during his tour. We do have a record of his words spoken a few months later, and that gives us a good idea of what he had to say to the Muscogee national council.[30]

"Brothers — We all belong to the same family; we are all children of the Great Spirit; we walk in the same path; slake our thirst at the same spring; and now affairs of the greatest concern lead us to smoke the pipe around the same council fire.

"Brothers — We are friends; we must assist each other to bear our burdens. The blood of many of our fathers and brothers has run like water on the ground, to satisfy the avarice of the white men. We, ourselves, are threatened with a great evil; nothing will pacify them but the destruction of all the red men.

"Brothers — When the white men first set foot on our grounds, they were hungry; they had no place on which to spread their blankets, or to kindle their fires. They were feeble; they could do nothing for themselves. Our fathers commiserated their distress, and shared freely with them whatever the Great Spirit had given his red children. They gave them food when hungry, medicine when sick, spread skins for them to sleep on, and gave them grounds, that they might hunt and raise corn.

"Brothers — The white men are like poisonous serpents: when chilled, they are feeble and harmless; but invigorate them with warmth, and they sting their benefactors to death. The white people came to us feeble; and now we have made them strong, they wish to kill us, or drive us back, as they would wolves and panthers.

"Brothers — The white men are not friends to the Indians: at first they only asked for land sufficient for a wigwam; now, nothing will satisfy them but the whole of our hunting grounds, from the rising to the setting sun.

"Brothers — The white men want more than our hunting grounds; they wish to kill our warriors; they would even kill our old men, women, and little ones.

"Brothers — We must be united; we must smoke the same pipe; we must fight each other's battles; and more than all, we must love the Great Spirit; he is for us; he will destroy our enemies and make his red children happy."[31]

In his stirring address at Tuckhabatchee, Tecumseh drew on his close ties to the Muscogee people. "Oh, Muscogees!" he shouted. "Brethren of my mother! Brush from your eyelids the sleep of slavery, and strike for vengeance and your country!"[32]

The effect was overwhelming. A thousand warriors raised their tomahawks in the air. But throughout Tecumseh's address, Big Warrior sat with a disapproving frown on his face.[33] At the end of his talk, Tecumseh searched out those who had appeared unmoved during his speech, and then fixed his gaze on Big Warrior. Pointing his finger toward the Muscogee leader's face, he told him, "Your blood is white: you have taken my talk, and the sticks and the wampum, and the hatchet, but you do not mean to fight: I know the reason: you do not believe the Great Spirit has sent me: you shall know: I leave Tuckhabatchee directly, and shall go straight to Detroit: when I arrive there, I will stamp the ground with my foot, and shake down every house in Tuckhabatchee."[34]

Big Warrior's attitude toward Tecumseh was almost certainly influenced by his personal circumstances. Along with other upper-crust Muscogees, he had grown wealthy through the use of slave labour and the cotton gin to profit from the sale of cotton, much in the manner of the southern slave owners.[35]

Big Warrior did not respond to Tecumseh's accusation. Instead, the first to reply to Tecumseh following his speech was William Weatherford, a mixed-blood Muscogee also known as Lamochattee ("Red Eagle"), who would play a vital role over the next few years. He was far from convinced by what he had heard. If Tecumseh was so set on war with the whites, Weatherford demanded to know why he had not already led the northern tribes into battle against them. Tecumseh replied that all of the native peoples needed to come together in the struggle at hand. Weatherford shot back that the Shawnee chief's suggested path would lead to war with the United States and that the native peoples could no more count on the British than on the Americans. Relying on the British for military assistance would be sheer folly.

There were others who rejected Tecumseh's suggestion of a native alliance against the United States. During a conversation later that evening between Tecumseh and Cherokee leaders, one chief vowed to kill Tecumseh if he carried his message to Cherokee country.[36]

Tecumseh did win adherents to his cause, however. His words stirred many of the warriors present. The Muscogees faced their own struggle to halt the seizure of their lands by the Americans, and they would remember Tecumseh's speech during the perilous events to come.

The Shawnee chief then departed for the North, but the prophecy he had hurled at Big Warrior was not forgotten. Some of the Muscogees counted the days, calculating how long it would take Tecumseh to reach Detroit. In the early hours of December 16, the day when the Muscogees had reckoned Tecumseh would complete his journey, the earth trembled as the first waves of a powerful series of earthquakes struck the eastern United States. Every house in Tuckhabatchee was shaken to the ground. "Tecumseh has got to Detroit!" was uttered by many Muscogees on that day.[37]

That the earthquake struck is an indisputable fact. And it is no less a fact that many Muscogees connected the trembling of the earth with Tecumseh's prophecy and drew the conclusion that the Shawnee chief's call to arms must be heeded.

By the time Tecumseh reached Detroit, the conflict between the United States and the native confederacy had already exploded in armed struggle. While the Shawnee chief was presenting his case to the Muscogees at Tuckhabatchee, William Henry Harrison was preparing a pre-emptive military strike against Tecumseh's brother, the Prophet.

Chapter 6

The Prophet

IN THE AUTUMN OF 1811, William Henry Harrison set out to attack a town established by Tecumseh and his younger brother, Lalawethika, who had renamed himself Tenskwatawa and was known to his followers as "the Prophet." Located next to cultivated fields by the Wabash River, Prophetstown was a thriving settlement with sixty lodges, a guesthouse, a large council house, and a medicine lodge. Two hundred bark-sided houses overlooked the river. Over the previous three years,[1] a thousand warriors from a number of tribes had been attracted to the town by the teachings of its spiritual leader.

While Tecumseh became the renowned warrior and political leader around whom a native confederacy coalesced, it was his brother who fed it the spiritual and ideological sustenance that bound the movement together. Lalawethika soared in influence among the Shawnees and other tribes in the Ohio country by preaching the message that native peoples must return to their traditional ways, reject American ideas and material goods, and fight for their land.

During the winter of 1774–75, Tecumseh's mother, Methoataaskee, had given birth to triplets, all boys. One of the triplets died at birth. The two who survived were Kumskaukau (meaning "A Cat that Flies in the Air" or "A Star that Shoots in a Straight Line over Great Waters") and Laloeshiga ("A Panther with a Handsome Tail"). The latter grew up under the name Lalawethika ("He Makes a Loud Noise" or "The Noise Maker"), but he later took the name Tenskwatawa ("The Open Door").[2]

Lalawethika's early years were difficult and seemed to foreshadow a sad and failed life. He spent his youth aimlessly, often drunk and dissolute. An accident cost him an eye, and he used a handkerchief to cover the socket.

One day in the autumn of 1805, smoking in his wigwam, he dropped his pipe and fell into a coma or trance so deep that those around him believed he was dead. When he regained consciousness, he told his fellow tribesmen that he had been transported up to the clouds, where he spoke with the Great Spirit. Calling himself Tenskwatawa, he started preaching a religious doctrine to wean his people from the ways of the white man and back to the course they had been created to follow. Those who became his followers called him the Prophet. The mantle of "prophet" was a respectable calling among the Shawnees; Tenskwatawa assumed it shortly after the death of an elderly prophet named Penagashega.[3]

He told others of his life-altering experience, in which he had embarked on the spectral journey taken by the souls of the departed. At a critical point, Tenskwatawa reached a crossroads. There he saw a few natives taking the fork to the right, which led to heaven; far more of them, though, took the fork to the left. Three houses appeared at the side of this fateful road. Beside the first two houses, paths led the journeyers back to the road to salvation. These houses were "last chance" way stations offering the souls of the dead a final opportunity to redeem themselves and come back to the light. Most, however, continued past them on the road to perdition, the road to the last house, named Eternity, from which there was no return.

Having seen the point of no return, Tenskwatawa came back to consciousness. From then on, he was on a mission. He believed that the Great Spirit had chosen him to convey the message to the people that they must change. Tenskwatawa amazed others, including his brother Tecumseh, with his sudden transformation. Because revelations transmitted through a dream were an accepted part of Shawnee culture, and since these were fearful times, people listened. Not only people from his own village but other Shawnees, Ottawas, Senecas, and Wyandots beat a path to his door to hear what he had to say.[4] Propelled by the necessity to pay heed to his dream, and undoubtedly reinforced and energized by the positive responses of so many others, Tenskwatawa's message grew into an agenda.

Tenskwatawa taught his tribe that they were the original creations of the Masters of Life and that this imposed a great responsibility on them. They had to return to the traditional customs of the tribe and to eschew the ways they had borrowed from the white man. Henceforth, native women must not marry white men. Tenskwatawa preached against all innovations in clothing and declared that the Shawnees must continue to wear the original dress of their people. He issued a powerful warning against drunkenness, claiming that when he was lifted into the clouds, the first place he reached was the dwelling of the Devil, where those who had died drunkards were confined. Flames shot out of the mouths of the unfortunate wretches; this terrible scene had put an end to his own excessive drinking. He insisted that native peoples should practise a code of community property, and proclaimed that the young must cherish and respect the aged and infirm.[5]

Above all, the Prophet took a very hard line where the Americans were concerned. He declared that they "grew from the scum of the great water, when it was troubled by the Evil Spirit. They are numerous, but I hate them. They are unjust. They have taken away your lands, which were not made for them." As for commercial dealings with the Americans and British, the Prophet had pithy advice: "Pay the white traders only half of what you owe, because they have cheated you."

The Prophet's gospel affected many people, including his brother Tecumseh. It drove home a powerful ideological message: the Great Spirit intended a separation between natives and whites, a fundamental division that must not be breached. Becoming dependent on the ways of the whites was the path to demoralization. Instead, native people needed to return to their old ways. Not only should men dress the way their ancestors had, they should shave their heads, leaving only a scalp lock. The crowns of their heads should be adorned with eagle feathers, and they should paint their faces.

He did not want natives to be reduced to settler-style farmers. Instead, he advocated a lifestyle that combined growing food with hunting over a wide area of land. When doubters complained that there was no longer enough game to sustain the native people, he responded that the animals were being laid waste to meet the appetites of the whites and those natives who had taken up the whites' customs. He directed his people to give up animals introduced by the Europeans, with the exception of the horse, which had been fully integrated into traditional native hunting practices and had become indispensible to the hunters.

As one of his followers transcribed it, the Prophet preached that the message of the Great Spirit was clear: "My children, you complain that the animals of the forest are few and scattered. How shall it be otherwise? You destroy them yourselves, for their skins only, and leave their bodies to rot or give the best pieces to the whites. I am displeased when I see this, and take them back to the earth that they may not come to you again. You must kill no more animals than are necessary to feed and clothe you."[6]

Where previously Lalawethika had been the object of derision, he now was taken very seriously by a growing number of people in his own tribe and eventually other tribes as well.

Tenskwatawa's emergence as the Prophet occurred at a time of deep unease among the Shawnees. The winter of 1804–5 was unusually cold, and floods accompanied the spring that followed, resulting in severe damage to the cornfields. Disease struck many native villages, including Tecumseh's. Fever struck suddenly, carrying people off within days. Native doctors did their best to combat the severity and spread of the malady, but to no avail. Called "bilious fever" at the time, the disease was likely influenza or smallpox.

For the native peoples of North America, virulent and deadly outbreaks of illness were already an old story by the beginning of the nineteenth century. From the first days of their conquest of the Americas, Europeans brought diseases against which the native peoples had no immunity, and these were far more destructive than the weapons of the white man. In the first decades, whole villages were felled. Even in Tecumseh's time, sudden epidemics in native villages wiped out large swaths of the population.

When disease struck, it brought in its wake not only suffering and death but also anxiety and fear. Many natives believed that such misery could only mean that the Great Spirit was deeply displeased. Another explanation was that witches were at work in the villages and that they had caused the epidemic. Those suspected of being witches could be either male or female. The accused were usually elderly people who were believed to use medicine to the detriment of those around them.[7]

Witch hunts could tear communities apart. People were terrified of being accused next. For example, George Blue Jacket, the son of the famous warrior chief who had been educated by whites, pronounced, "This witchcraft is a very wicked thing. They [witches] can go a thousand miles in less than an hour and back again, and poison anybody they hate and make them lame, and torment them in many wicked and cruel ways." He believed that witches could "go into houses with their poison even if the doors are locked ever so tight, and the people cannot get awake till they are gone. This witchcraft has prevailed greatly and been very common among our people, and some of the white people have learned it and practice it, and it's a very wicked thing."[8]

While the Prophet was developing the *Weltanschauung* on which the native confederacy of Tecumseh would be based, he was also drawn into the dark task of outing the witches and punishing them. In March

1806, a great council of the Delawares was convened at Woapicamikunk, and people from the surrounding area were pressured to attend. Especially anxious were the elderly and those unfortunate enough to be regarded as anti-social or strange. Such people feared that if they attended the council they could be singled out as witches. If they failed to participate in the ceremonies at the council, on the other hand, this could heighten suspicions against them.

By the time the Prophet arrived at Woapicamikunk, the council was already underway and the principal suspects had already been identified. Two Delaware chiefs, Tetepachsit and Hackinkpomska, who had been centrally involved in ceding land to white settlers, had been placed under guard and were being forced to confess that they were witches. Young men bound the elderly Tetepachsit and tortured him with flaming torches. To assuage his tormenters, the old chief at last admitted to having practised sorcery. He claimed, though, that he had left his medicine bag in the house of a Christian-born native named Joshua, who spoke a number of native languages and served as an interpreter.[9]

A search party set out for the nearby Moravian mission to fetch Joshua and bring him back to act as a witness. Tetepachsit swore, when Joshua was paraded before him, that his testimony while he was being tortured had been false and that the poisonous medicine was hidden elsewhere. That was enough to keep Joshua from harm for the moment, but it did nothing to end the ordeal for the old chief.

As soon as the Prophet arrived, men and women were walked past him in a circle so that he could search for signs that some among them were practitioners of witchcraft. He confirmed that Tetepachsit and Hackinkpomska were witches. Although Joshua was deemed to possess no evil medicine, he too was condemned because he was said to have influence with an evil spirit.

The first person to be put to death, though, was an old woman. While enduring torture — she was slowly roasted over a fire for four days — the old woman confessed to having given her medicine to her grandson, who was away hunting at the time of the trials. Fortunately for the young man, he was spared when he admitted that his grand-mother's story was true and that he had used the evil medicine to fly from Kentucky to the Mississippi and back in a single day.[10]

Then Tetepachsit met his death. He claimed to have hidden his medicine in several places, which were duly searched. Nothing was found. The old man, aware that he could not escape death, dressed in his finest apparel and assisted in the building of the pyre on which he would be burned. His dignity and age moved one of the executioners to tomahawk him. The old chief's body was placed in the blazing fire. The executioners then proceeded to put Joshua to death.[11] Further executions ensued, but soon the hysteria declined as fewer Delawares succumbed to the epidemic.

In the spring of 1806, when William Henry Harrison learned of the executions, he dispatched a messenger to deliver a speech to the Delawares that denounced the Prophet as a fraud and counselled an end to the executions of those accused of witchcraft. "Who is this pretended prophet who dares to speak in the name of the Great Creator," challenged Harrison. "Examine him. Is he more wise or virtuous than you are yourselves, that he should be selected to convey to you the orders of your God? . . . Clear your eyes, I beseech you . . . No longer be imposed upon by the arts of an imposter."

"Let your poor old men and women sleep in quietness, and banish from their minds the dreadful idea of being burnt alive by their own friends and countrymen," read Harrison's message. "I charge you to stop your bloody career . . . if you value the friendship of your great father, the President — if you wish to preserve the good opinion of the Seventeen Fires . . ."[12]

Tecumseh's brother had launched a new career. His harsh message grew out of the profound insecurities facing the tribes of the region. His was an ideology that brooked no compromise with the United States and its advancing line of settlements. It was, in that sense, an ideology of resistance.

Undoubtedly, such personalities are present in all societies. But they gain an audience and become significant societal actors only in times of great crisis. They are products of their communities as much as they are unique individual actors. What repels us about the Prophet are the witch hunts. The Prophet did not initiate the witch hunts, but he lent himself to them with no reservations. He was immersed in kindred cultures that sought personalized explanations for great calamities. Finding evildoers and determining responsibility for plagues, famines, and natural disasters has been commonplace in the civilizations of the world.

The rise of the Prophet had a visible effect on Tecumseh, influencing him to stop wearing European-style shirts and trousers, instead clothing himself in soft deerskin suits and moccasins embroidered with dyed porcupine quills.[13]

The change gave him the appearance of a warrior from an earlier time, which added to his distinctiveness as he rose to fame and helped him to promote his cause of native unity. Significantly, Tecumseh borrowed some ideas from his brother's revelations, but he kept his own counsel in important ways. From a very early age, he strongly opposed cruelty toward others. When he was in a position to do so, he forbade the torture of prisoners and would not countenance physical abuse of women and children.

While the Prophet was a fundamentalist in his manner and in his unbending certitudes, Tecumseh was much more flexible. He was prepared to work with native groups quite different culturally from his own. And while he had no illusions about the possibility of a complete understanding with the Americans or the British, he was ready to work with or against either of them in pursuit of his goals. In that sense, he was a political leader. It was exactly his clarity of purpose that made him so formidable and adept at commanding respect from his opponents.

The brothers were on a parallel course, though sharp disagreements did flare between them at times. The Prophet was set on establishing a theocracy with himself at the head. Tecumseh was determined to establish a confederacy that could launch a native state with the full rights and recognition of the other states on the continent. Differences aside, the brothers were both leaders, building a bold resistance movement among the native peoples.

Alarmed by the growing number of warriors who had congregated at Prophetstown, and by the rising strength of the native confederacy, William Henry Harrison decided that the United States must take action against the native threat. Even prior to his meeting with Tecumseh at Vincennes, Harrison had sent a dispatch to U.S. Secretary of War William Eustis, seeking permission to attack Prophetstown. Two months later, on July 17, 1811, Eustis replied, "If the Prophet should commence, or seriously threaten, hostilities, he ought to be attacked; provided the force under your command is sufficient to ensure success."[14] In a further missive, on October 20, the Secretary of War was less bellicose. Stating that he had "been particularly instructed by the President, to communicate to Your Excellency his earnest desire that peace may, if possible, be preserved with the Indians . . . Circumstances conspire, at this particular juncture, to render it peculiarly desirable that hostilities of any kind, or to any degree, not indispensably required, should be avoided."[15]

In those days of slow communications, field commanders were much freer to follow their own inclinations. Aware that Tecumseh was away on a journey to win the southern tribes to his confederacy, Harrison believed the moment for action was at hand. "There can be no doubt," he wrote to Eustis, "but his [Tecumseh's] object is to excite the Southern Indians against us . . . I do not think there is any danger of any hostility until he returns. And his absence affords a most favourable opportunity for breaking up his Confederacy . . . I hope . . . before his return that that part of the fabrick [sic], which he considered complete will be demolished and even its foundations rooted up."[16]

Harrison sent couriers with secret messages to key military and political figures so that troops would be readied for the assault on

Prophetstown. He alerted Kentucky to have troops in readiness to march by September 20. He rallied Governors Ninian Edwards of Illinois and Benjamin Howard of Upper Louisiana to prepare their militias to join the battle if necessary.

While Harrison was preparing for conflict, which was clearly his preferred option, he was assuring the Madison administration that he was doing everything possible to achieve a peaceful outcome. On August 13, Harrison wrote to Eustis to assure him that while he had alerted the other governors of the growing hostilities, he still hoped for a peaceful outcome: "The President may rest assured that our united councils and exertions will be directed to preserve peace with the Indians . . . recourse to actual hostilities shall be had only when every other means shall have been tried in vain to effect the disbanding of the Prophet's force."[17]

As he prepared to march, Harrison resorted to the time-honoured tactic of seeking to divide his potential foes. He dispatched a warning to the residents of Prophetstown urging them to save themselves by abandoning the Prophet. He also sent a message to the nearby Miami, Eel River, and Wea tribes, cautioning them to stay neutral. "My children," he wrote, "be wise and listen to my voice. I fear that you have got on a road that will lead you to destruction. It is not too late to turn back. Have pity on your women and children. It is time that my friends should be known. I shall draw a line. Those that keep by me by the hand must keep on one side of it and those that adhere to the Prophet on the other."

The governor's warning did not intimidate Laprusieur, the Wea chief, who replied that he considered himself to be a friend of both the Prophet and the Americans, but went on to let Harrison know in no uncertain terms where he stood. "Father," he said in his message, "Your speech . . . has not scared us, we are not afraid of what you say . . . We have our eyes on our lands on the Wabash with a strong determination to defend our rights, let them be invaded from what quarter they may; that when our best interest is invaded, we will defend them to a man."[18]

In late September 1811, Harrison marched north at the head of his force of more than a thousand men. One-third were U.S. Army regulars and over four hundred were Indiana militiamen. Eighty Indiana riflemen and 120 mounted Kentucky volunteers filled out the ranks. In less than two weeks, the force marched two-thirds of the way to Prophetstown. They halted at a location close to the present-day city of Terre Haute, and Harrison's men spent the next half-month building Fort Harrison.

When the fort was nearing completion, a small band of Shawnee warriors from Prophetstown shot a sentry, wounding his legs. The incident gave Harrison the opening he sought to attack Tenskwatawa in his lair. "I had always supposed that the Prophet was a rash and presumptuous man," he wrote to Eustis. "He has not contented himself with throwing the gauntlet but has absolutely commenced the war."[19]

In a final bid to achieve a peaceful outcome, Harrison dispatched a party of Delawares to negotiate with Tenskwatawa. The three conditions he advanced, via his messengers, amounted to an ultimatum Harrison knew would be refused. The conditions were to expel all the Potawatomis, Kickapoos, and Winnebagoes from Prophetstown; to surrender all the warriors who had committed offences against the United States and its citizens; and to return horses that had been stolen from settlers.[20] Not surprisingly, on their return, the messengers reported to the governor that the offer had been received with hostility and contempt.

Having been reinforced with the arrival of more troops, on November 6 Harrison set out for Prophetstown, advancing to within 1.6 kilometres of the settlement. With the American force on his doorstep, Tenskwatawa had to decide whether to stay on the defensive or to launch an attack. Tecumseh had solemnly warned his brother not to engage in combat while he was away — he was sure they would eventually come to blows with the Americans, but he believed the best time to strike would be when the confederacy was fully mobilized.

Under pressure from the militants among his followers, Tenskwatawa organized a pre-emptive strike. He sent a negotiating party to meet with Harrison to request a parley the following day. Harrison acquiesced and both sides agreed to a truce until their conference had been held the following day.

That night, Tenskwatawa dispatched a party of one hundred warriors on a pre-dawn mission to attack the Americans. They were to use the advantage of darkness to elude the sentries, enter the camp, find Harrison's tent, and kill him. Drawing on his spiritual powers, Tenskwatawa promised his warriors that the darkness would dim only the eyesight of the Americans and that the Native warriors would be able to see clearly. He further undertook to send rain to dampen the soldiers' gunpowder and render his warriors invulnerable. The one hundred warriors who were to infiltrate the camp were to be followed by a second wave of five or six hundred others who would attack when the battle had been joined.

Things did not go according to plan, however. At about 4:30 a.m., a U.S. sentry spotted a warrior and fired his rifle to alert the camp. All of the sentries rushed back to camp, and the soldiers, who had been sleeping on their weapons as instructed by Harrison, dove out of their tents and formed ranks. Confused fighting erupted. From the perimeter of the camp, warriors with blackened faces unleashed a deadly volley of fire, aided by the visibility the fires in the camp afforded. The soldiers returned fire blindly into the darkness.

Some of Harrison's troops were on the verge of panicking, but Harrison rallied them. The fight continued for two hours, until Tenskwatawa's warriors retreated to Prophetstown at the approach of daylight.[21]

Tenskwatawa's bold plan had been thwarted by one sentry and a dwindling supply of ammunition. Daylight would inform the Americans that they outnumbered the warriors two to one. As the tide turned in favour of the Americans, the Prophet stood on a nearby hill, where he prayed, danced, and shouted incantations, calling on the warriors to hold their ground and promising them that the Great Spirit would soon bestow victory upon them.[22] When the fighting ended, the Prophet returned to his settlement, where disgusted warriors, convinced that he was a fraud, threatened him with death. Tenskwatawa tried to rally them to continue the fight, but the tribesmen deserted Prophetstown.

Expecting a renewed attack, Harrison ordered his men to build fortifications and care for the wounded. Late on November 8, when it seemed certain that the warriors were not returning, the U.S. force marched to Prophetstown and found the settlement deserted. They seized the cooking utensils and then set fire to the lodges and more than five thousand bushels of corn and beans. Harrison proclaimed the Battle of Tippecanoe a major military triumph. "The Indians have never sustained so severe a defeat since their acquaintance with the white people," he boasted in a message to Eustis. "I think upon the whole that there will be no further hostilities."[23]

Harrison continued to reap the glory and political benefits of Tippecanoe for the rest of his life. In a successful campaign for the U.S. presidency in 1840, Harrison and his running mate, John Tyler, campaigned on the slogan "Tippecanoe and Tyler too." Inaugurated as president on a cold March day, Harrison didn't enjoy his triumph for long. A few weeks after he delivered the longest inaugural address in history, he came down with a cold. The malady worsened, turning into pneumonia and pleurisy, and he died after only thirty-one days in office.

But at Tippecanoe, Harrison launched the United States into war against Tecumseh's confederacy, a war that would fold into the larger conflict with Great Britain just seven months later.

Chapter 7

Brock on the Eve of War

IN LATE 1811, THE UNITED STATES was already at war with Tecumseh's native confederacy, and the signals flashing from American political actors, including the War Hawks, indicated that war with Great Britain was a very real possibility.

Brock was posted to Upper Canada to serve as the senior commander of the armed forces and shore up the defences of the Canadas against a U.S. invasion. But he had also taken on the role of president of the province's governing council. This required him to work with the other council members, the executive branch of the government, and the elected members of the legislative assembly. Brock operated under the orders of the newly appointed senior commander in the Canadas, General George Prevost.

Born in New Jersey in 1767, Prevost was the eldest son of Major General Augustine Prevost, a Swiss-born officer who had fought in the British army and served under Major General James Wolfe in the capture of Quebec in 1759, during the Seven Years' War. In 1779, at the tender age of twelve, George joined the 60th Foot, his father's regiment. He had attained the rank of major by 1790, the result of rapid promotions, likely purchased. After a series of posts in the Caribbean and Nova Scotia, Prevost was dispatched to Canada to stiffen the defence, but he was no lion. Prevost was named governor of the

Canadas and commander-in-chief of the British forces. His bilingualism equipped him for dealing with the francophone majority in Lower Canada and its elected assembly. Sir George — he was knighted in 1805 — had the difficult task of combining the two roles of head of government and commander of British forces in both Upper and Lower Canada. In Upper Canada, a lieutenant-governor headed the government except when the governor, normally based in Lower Canada, was present. Although the system established by the Constitutional Act of 1791 provided for a popularly elected assembly in each of the two provinces, most of the power rested in the hands of the governors and their appointed executives and legislative councils.

Brock and Prevost could not have been more different. Brock was a warrior; Prevost was a cautious, bureaucratic general and administrator. He did not want to make waves — with the French Canadians, with his home government, or with the Americans.

Brock's natural inclination to take the offensive was reinforced by his reasoned calculation that only victories on the field of battle could cement such a disparate mix of men — British regulars, Canadian militia, and native allies — and interests. He also knew that regiments that didn't see combat for long periods of time were in danger of lapsing into somnolence.

"The 41st is an uncommonly fine regiment," he wrote, "but wretchedly officered . . . The 49th has been ten years in this country, drinking rum without bounds; but it is still respectable and apparently ardent for an opportunity to acquire distinction."[1]

British regulars formed the backbone of the land defence of both Upper and Lower Canada. On both the British and American sides of the coming conflict, the regulars were superior to the militias, although some militias were certainly better than others. On the eve of the war, there were 4,450 British imperial regulars in Canada. This quite small force was made up of four line battalions of the 8th, the 41st, the 49th, and the 100th regiments. The British imperial forces in Canada included no cavalry, a paucity of artillery, not many engineers, and little in the way of transport and medical services.

The British army of the period was divided into regiments for organizational purposes. In the infantry, regiments ("of Foot," as they were
known) were made up of one or more battalions. A fully manned battalion had ten companies of about one hundred men each. The
battalion was the principal tactical unit on the battlefield. A brigade
was made up of three or sometimes just two battalions, normally
drawn from different regiments. The army's largest unit, the division,
was composed of two or more brigades. A division with a full complement could have as many as ten thousand men, but an under-strength
division could have as few as three or four thousand men.

The companies that made up a battalion were designed to play particular roles. Two of the ten companies were called "flank" companies.
The "grenadier" company—the most fearsome of the flank companies—normally was positioned on the right-hand side of the battalion
during a battle. The men in this unit were typically battle-hardened
and physically imposing. The other flank company, usually deployed
on the battalion's left, was a "light" company. Its members were skilled
soldiers, and the unit could be used to provide a screen in front of the
main body of the battalion. These men could fire at enemy formations
to weaken them and disrupt their ranks before the main body of the
battalion came to grips with them. The members of the light company
could also protect their battalion from enemy skirmishers. Between
these flank companies were the eight "line" companies.[2]

In the British army, a colonel commanded a regiment, but this
was an administrative post that did not necessitate his presence on
the field of battle. In the field, a lieutenant colonel commanded the
actual fighting unit, the battalion.

The Americans used different terminology to describe their fighting units. What the British called a battalion, the Americans called
a regiment. American regiments deployed eight companies rather
than ten. A few months before the outbreak of the War of 1812, the
American army set up some regiments consisting of two battalions,
on the British pattern. Most of these units were rapidly reorganized
on the old pattern, with regiments consisting of a single battalion,

but during the first year of the war some kept the new organizational form. The Americans also, on occasion, called a grouping of at least two companies from different regiments a battalion. An officer who held at least the rank of major commanded a unit of this kind. The Americans also ordered soldiers to "form a battalion," which meant to form a line.[3]

Generally speaking, battles were fought across a deadly killing space at close range between opposing infantry drawn up in companies and battalions. The standard weapon of the day was the smooth-bore musket. In order to load and fire this weapon, the soldier had to bite off the tip of a greased paper cartridge containing gunpowder and a lead ball. He then poured a small quantity of powder into the pan of the firing mechanism. The mechanism was snapped shut and the hammer was pulled back to the half-cock position. The soldier then poured the remaining contents of the cartridge down the barrel, followed by the cartridge itself. Using a rod that was stored below the barrel of the musket, he forced the contents down to the base of the barrel. The musket was then fully cocked and ready to fire. The soldier held the weapon against his shoulder and waited for the command to fire. Most muskets did not possess sights. Pulling the trigger released the lock, which snapped forward and struck the flint, setting off a spark that ignited the powder. The initial explosion was forced through the touch hole, where it set off the main charge. The musket was effective over a range of up to two hundred yards. The mass firing of muskets released clouds of white smoke into the air, and this quickly reduced visibility on the battlefield.

The cumbersome procedure for loading, firing, and reloading a musket, especially when facing volleys from the opposing side, required a great deal of training. Most soldiers could only get off two or three shots per minute, although British veterans who had fought the French in Spain were known to be capable of firing five rounds per minute. Smooth-bore muskets, unlike rifled bores that imparted a spin to a bullet in flight, were notoriously inaccurate. Muskets also misfired often. Musket fire was effective when it was unleashed in volleys, when the men in a company, platoons within a company, or an entire battalion fired simultaneously. Well-timed volleys took a toll on the opposing line, and they could cause an inexperienced unit to panic, break ranks, and flee. In a well-trained battalion, each platoon could be ordered to fire one by one along the line, creating a terrifying rolling effect.

Reloading and firing muskets was not always effective against an infantry charge by opposing units. When hand-to-hand fighting could not be avoided, soldiers were ordered to deploy the socket bayonet, which was fifteen to seventeen inches long and fitted around the muzzle of the musket. The sight of a tight row of bayonets was often sufficient to halt charging infantry. Bayonets were essential against cavalry. Large cavalry units were not a factor in the War of 1812, because supplying feed for horses on a large scale was more trouble than it was worth on the battlefields of North America.

The Napoleonic Wars and the War of 1812 were fought during the golden age of drilling soldiers. British officers were constantly drilling their units to a pitch of perfection.[4] A highly trained British battalion — the British army reckoned it took three years to turn a recruit into a dependable fighter on the field of battle — could change direction and follow complex orders while under fire. British infantry stood in a line two deep to maximize their firepower on the battlefield.[5] During the War of 1812, the Americans usually fought in a line that was three deep.

As the leading British officers, including Brock, were well aware, the Royal Navy would play a crucial role in the defence of British North America in the event of war with the United States. The navy had the power to blockade the U.S. coast and to carry out raids and major incursions into U.S. ports and cities.

The Royal Navy classified warships into three types and six "rates," according to the number of guns they deployed. Ships of the line were ship-rigged and were outfitted with at least two covered gun decks; frigates were similarly rigged but had only one covered gun deck and were intended for scouting and other tasks outside of the major battle fleet; all other craft, mostly schooners, sloops, and brigs, filled out the third type. These latter craft were assigned convoy duties and carried dispatches. The "rates" enumerated the firepower of vessels as follows: "first-rate," at least one hundred guns; "second-rate," ninety to one hundred; "third-rate," sixty to ninety; and "fourth-rate," fifty to sixty (there were few such vessels by this date; they were not regarded as powerful enough to fight in the line). Frigates that deployed thirty to forty-four guns were classed as "fifth-rate," and even smaller vessels, commanded by a "post-captain," were sixth-rate.[6] By 1812, the rating system was somewhat out of date. The short-barrelled carronade, a new weapon introduced in the 1780s, allowed more guns to be deployed on vessels.

"Ship-rigged," as opposed to other vessels, carried three masts — fore, main, and mizzen. The masts supported square sails hung on horizontal yards. In addition, ship-rigged vessels could carry sails between the masts and along the bow. Brigs carried two masts, each deploying square sails, and, in addition, a spanker sail. The foremast of a brigantine sported square sails. Farther back, on the main mast, sails were rigged both fore and aft. Two-masted schooners — schooners often had more masts in later decades — deployed fore and aft sails, and some were outfitted with square sails as well. A sloop carried a single mast, on which was mounted a fore and aft sail and sometimes a square sail above the others.[7]

In the Royal Navy, the traditional term for a cannon was "gun." By the early nineteenth century, the British had adopted the French word "cannon," and the words "cannon" and "gun" were used interchangeably. The British fired their ship-borne cannon with a flintlock apparatus, using the same principle as a musket. In naval engagements, the British preferred cannonballs of solid iron. The gun was designated according to the weight of the shot — for example, the Royal Navy's cannon were called 18-pounders. In combat, the Royal Navy and its adversaries manoeuvred as close to each other as possible so that their guns could be used to maximum effect. Guns that could be fired over a range of two thousand yards on land had less range at sea. Firing from the decks of shifting vessels made cannon much less accurate than artillery pieces fired on land.

The more recently adopted carronades, with their shorter and wider barrels, could fire a heavier shot. They were deadly at ranges of three hundred yards or less. The Royal Navy used grapeshot and chain shot to assault the personnel and tear up the rigging on an enemy ship. Grapeshot consisted of stacks of round shot wrapped in canvas and stuffed into the barrel of a gun. Three or more packs could be fired at a time. When fired, they split open, scattering the small balls over a wide area. At close range, grapeshot was used against the enemy quarterdeck to kill or maim the officers. Chain shot consisted of two iron balls joined by a length of chain that whirred through the air in a vicious circular pattern. Aimed effectively, chain shot devastated sails and rigging.

The technology of the time dictated that major battles for "command of the seas" were fought quite close to land, because fleets found it exceedingly difficult to find the ships of their enemies in the vastness of mid-ocean.[8] Once fleets found their opponents, battle tactics were dictated by the strengths and limitations of wooden ships, the power and range of cannon, and the need for attackers and defenders to use the power of wind to propel themselves. Attacking fleets sailed downwind to close in on the enemy. Defending fleets had the option of sailing downwind to escape from the foe, which they often did. Great battles at sea in the age of wooden sailing ships usually ended inconclusively.

While Brock understood the indispensable role of the Royal Navy, deep in the heart of North America where he was stationed, the blessings the navy could bestow were rather a cold comfort. Over the long haul, the navy could play a huge role in convincing the Americans that the war was not worth fighting. In the immediate future, though, the fate of Brock's turf would be decided by the sharpness of his regulars, the morale of the local militia, the inclinations of Tecumseh's confederacy, and even the postures adopted by Upper Canadian politicians.

~

During the final months of what turned out to be the last year of peace with the Americans, Brock undertook a strategic military review, bringing to it his characteristic energy and his preference for an offensive approach to war. From December 1811 until early 1812, in a series of letters to General George Prevost and to his adjutant general, Colonel Edward Baynes, Brock summarized his thoughts about the defence of the Canadas.

The conventional British perspective was to hold on to Quebec and as much of Lower Canada as possible. With a citadel and seaport to which British warships could readily sail, the old capital at Quebec equalled Halifax as the most vital strategic point in British North America. As long as the British held Quebec, the theory went, they could later regain any regions of the country they lost over the course of a war. General Prevost adhered to this conventional wisdom, which viewed the defence of Quebec and Lower Canada as much more important than the defence of Upper Canada.

While Brock naturally agreed that holding Quebec was crucial, he had different views about the defence of the upper province. He reckoned that because Upper Canada now had a substantial population the defence of the province had become a top priority. In 1759, when the British had invaded against the French, or 1775, when the Americans invaded against the British, retaining the old capital on the St. Lawrence may well have been the key to defending the territory. But conditions had changed. Brock saw real advantages in emphasizing the defence of the upper province, which everyone recognized was a great challenge becuase of its lengthy frontier with the United States. He believed that British regular soldiers were better than their American counterparts. He calculated that the potential for bringing large numbers of native warriors into the field against the U.S. was an advantage that had to be seized. And he knew that to win the adherence of the native tribes, the fight had to be made in Upper Canada, indeed, in its vital southwest corner along the shore of Lake Erie opposite Detroit.

With his preference for going on the offensive, and well aware that the Americans were deeply split on whether to declare war,

Brock believed that swift moves to seize Detroit and Michilimackinac (located on the strait connecting Lake Huron and Lake Michigan) in alliance with native forces would throw the enemy back on its heels.[9] In his letters, he returned more than once to the issue of the southwestern frontier of Upper Canada. "Unless Detroit and Michilimackinac be both in our possession at the commencement of hostilities," he calculated, "not only the district of Amherstburg [near present-day Windsor, Ontario], but most probably the whole country as far as Kingston, must be evacuated." He reminded Prevost through Baynes that former governor Sir James Craig had contemplated a similar strategy three years earlier.[10]

Unlike the other senior British commanders, who could see only the vulnerability of Upper Canada, Brock perceived the region as a geographical arrow that pointed straight into the heart of American territory, from which offensive action could be launched. So it was that, with respect to the western reaches of Upper Canada, Brock's strategic thinking focused most attentively on the crucial importance of the native alliance. In the southwestern corner of Upper Canada around Amherstburg, where Fort Malden was situated, Brock calculated that strong preparations would deter the Americans from attempting to occupy the territory west of Niagara. He wanted additional British regulars moved from York and from Fort George, on the Niagara Frontier, to Fort Malden. Such a deployment would raise the morale of militiamen in that corner of the province, and reassure native allies that a serious fight could be made there to counter a U.S. invasion.

"I have always considered that the reduction of Detroit would be a signal for a cordial co-operation on the part of the Indians," he wrote, and went on to warn that "if we be not in sufficient force, to effect this object, no reliance ought to be placed on them."[11] Within a year, these views opened the door to his close working relationship with Tecumseh.

In addition, Brock wanted increased naval forces to be developed on both Lake Erie and Lake Huron. Lake Erie was key to the viability

of Fort Malden, and a force on Lake Huron could serve as a springboard for an attack on Michilimackinac. He wanted older commanders
to be replaced with younger officers, and recommended building
sailing vessels and gunboats.[12]

Along the Niagara Frontier, soon to become the epicentre of the
war, Brock reckoned that a strong contingent of regulars could serve
as the backbone for a force that would also include close to three
thousand militiamen and five hundred native warriors. There was,
along this vital frontier, a volunteer corps of farmers who used their
horses to move cannon. To shore up the volunteers, he requested the
dispatch of more gunners, drivers, and horses. He also wanted a
stock of weapons that could be used to outfit a volunteer cavalry
contingent.[13]

Not surprisingly, Brock placed his greatest faith in the security of
the old fortress town of Kingston, with its vital location at the junction of the eastern end of Lake Ontario and the St. Lawrence River.
He reckoned that the militiamen in the Kingston district were Upper
Canada's most dependable. Kingston was a vital supply point for
men and weapons for operations farther west in the province, and
attacks could be launched from there against Sackets Harbor, the
principal American base on the lake.[14]

Brock was also keenly aware that high morale among the settlers in
the province was essential if an active militia was to be raised and
maintained in the field. In December 1811, from York, Brock wrote
Prevost that during his recent visit to Niagara "I received the most satisfactory professions of a determination on the part of the principal
inhabitants to exert every means in their power in the defence of their
property and support of the government . . . unless the inhabitants give
an active and efficient aid, it will be utterly impossible for the very limited number of the military who are likely to be employed, to preserve
the Province."[15] In Upper Canada, responses to the threat of war ranged
from loyalism to neutrality to outright support for the Americans.
Even though the colonies did not yet have responsible government—a
parliamentary system in which cabinet ministers had to enjoy the

support of the majority of the members in the elected assembly — they did elect legislatures that played a role in financing their own militias. Brock displayed considerable acumen in weighing the opinions of the settler population in Upper Canada on the question of war. Many of them were migrants from south of the border. A large percentage were genuine Loyalists with a strong attachment to the British Crown, and some of them had suffered personally at the hands of the Patriots. Many of the "Late Loyalists," on the other hand, had lukewarm political loyalties; they could be swayed either way in a conflict between the British and the Americans.

Toward the end of 1811, Brock detected a shift in the mood of settlers along the Niagara Frontier. While the residents there had formerly thought that the military situation was so bad that no real resistance to a U.S. invasion was intended, the steps taken to shore up defences had changed many minds.[16] Despite his conviction that civilian morale had improved on the Niagara Frontier, Brock harboured concerns about governing a province in which loyalty was a slippery commodity. In a letter to Prevost, he said frankly that he was "perfectly aware of the number of improper characters" with whom he had to deal, men whose "principles diffuse a spirit of insubordination very adverse to all military institutions." He reckoned, though, that despite the presence of "improper characters," "the best policy to be pursued . . . will be to act with the utmost liberality, and as if no mistrust existed."[17]

On February 4, 1812, General Isaac Brock opened the final session of the fifth Parliament of Upper Canada with an address to the members of the appointed Legislative Council and the elected Legislative Assembly. Under the shadow of impending war with the United States and the more distant shadow of the war against Napoleon, Brock declared, "I should derive the utmost satisfaction, the first time of my addressing you, were it permitted to me to direct your attention solely to such objects as tended to promote the peace and prosperity of this Province." This was not such a time, however. He warned the members of the assembly about the disposition of the

American government. "Insulting threats are offered," he stated, "and hostile preparations actually commenced." While he expressed the hope that "cool reflection and the dictates of justice may yet avert the calamities of war," he said it was time to prepare for the worst.

Brock wanted the assembly to pass an amendment to the Militia Act of 1808, which stipulated that fit males in Upper Canada attend an annual muster to receive more serious training. "Principally composed of the sons of loyal and brave bands of veterans, the militia, I am confident, stand in need of nothing but the necessary legislative provisions to direct their ardour in the acquirement of military instruction, to form a most efficient force."

Warning against the clear risk of a U.S. invasion of Canada, Brock asserted that "the growing prosperity of these provinces, it is manifest, begins to awaken a spirit of envy . . . Heaven will look favourably on the manly exertions which the loyal and virtuous inhabitants of this happy land are prepared to make."[18]

John Graves Simcoe, who served as the first lieutenant-governor of Upper Canada from 1791 to 1796, had set up the province's militia system, whereby all males in the province from sixteen to sixty years of age were required to become active militia members when called up by the government. What concerned Brock was the poor attendance of Upper Canadian males at the militia and the abysmal level of training.

Brock was correct in his suspicions that the members of the legislative assembly of Upper Canada were not particularly interested in military affairs and that they were inclined to question and often oppose the initiatives of the appointed council and its head. It was entirely natural for an elected assembly that enjoyed relatively little power to chafe at the limitations imposed on it, much the way the assemblies in the pre-revolutionary Thirteen Colonies had pushed for greater powers.

The members of the assembly did not belong to clearly defined political factions. To use a term common later in nineteenth-century Canada, they were often "loose fish." Among those who typically opposed the council, the strongest figure was Joseph Willcocks, a sometime newspaper publisher and sheriff. Born in Palmerstown, Ireland, in 1773, Willcocks had emigrated to York when he was twenty-seven years old. He led the fight in the assembly to reject the proposed amendments to the Militia Act.

In the ensuing debates, Willcocks and the members who followed his lead managed to block the passage of Brock's proposed legislative measures. By small majorities, the assembly rejected the government's bill that would have required the subjects of the province to swear an oath of loyalty declaring that they owed no allegiance to foreign powers, and another bill that would have suspended habeas corpus in a time of threatened invasion. The assembly was willing to approve Brock's proposed changes to the Militia Act, but only until the end of the ensuing session of Parliament.

After Brock closed the session of the legislature, much disappointed by the results, he reported to Sir George Prevost, "I had every reason to expect the almost unanimous support of the two houses of the legislature to every measure the government thought it necessary to recommend; but after a short trial, I found myself egregiously mistaken in my calculations . . . The great influence which the numerous setters from the United States possess over the decisions of the lower house is truly alarming, and ought immediately, by every practical means, to be diminished."[19] Writing from Quebec, General Prevost agreed with Brock that the limits placed on "the operation of the Militia Act for Upper Canada" were deplorable.[20]

In the months immediately prior to the American declaration of war against Great Britain and during the first months of the conflict itself, the differences in temperament and inclination between Brock and Prevost were clearly displayed in their correspondence. Brock understood the need to avoid provoking the Americans and thus making a peaceful settlement between the two countries more difficult, but he could see the advantage in a test of arms as a way to settle outstanding issues. Prevost's inclinations were exactly the opposite. He behaved like the head of government and a "political general," whose job was to encourage a peaceful resolution of the issues at stake between Washington and London, even after the guns began firing. While praising Brock for the steps he was taking to prepare Upper Canada to meet an American attack, he persistently sought to restrain the major general and hold in check his inclination to strike at the enemy.

On April 30, 1812, Prevost wrote Brock a letter marked "confidential," informing him that the U.S. secretary of war had sent orders to Governor Daniel D. Tompkins of New York to send units of five hundred men each to border points adjacent to Canada, on the Niagara Frontier, at Kingston, and south of Montreal at Lake Champlain. He conveyed the concern of the British government that dispatching troops to the border could be designed to "produce a quarrel with the British Troops, which may lead to retaliation on both sides, and occasion hostilities to commence." He warned, "This way alone, it seems . . . an unjust War can be forced on the American people." Cautioning Brock, he said that the British must strive "to prevent any collision from taking place between our forces and the Americans."[21]

On May 27, General Prevost wrote again to Brock, this time to express his support for the precautions that Brock had taken "to prevent any act occurring within your control that should afford the Government of the United States a legitimate pretext to add to the clamour artfully raised by it against England."[22]

Brock had done invaluable service preparing the available forces to defend the Canadas. With only a few months left for him to live, the greatest days of Brock's career still lay in the future.

Chapter 8

The United States Declares
War on Great Britain

O N JUNE 1, 1812, PRESIDENT James Madison crossed his personal and political Rubicon and sent his war message to both houses of Congress. In sharp contrast to more recent U.S. declarations of war, memorably Franklin Roosevelt's against Japan in December 1941, a clerk read the document, with no emotion.

In his three-page message, the president made the case that for a number of years the British government had been guilty of "a series of acts hostile to the United States as an independent and neutral nation . . . British cruisers have been in the continued practice of violating the American flag on the great highway of nations, and of seizing and carrying off persons sailing under it; not in the exercise of a belligerent right founded on the law of nations against an enemy, but of a municipal prerogative over British subjects," Madison charged. "We behold our vessels, freighted with the products of our soil and industry, or returning with the honest proceeds of them, wrested from their lawful destinations, confiscated by prize-courts, no longer the organs of public law, but the instrument of arbitrary edicts," the president continued, widening his case from impressment to the effects of the British blockade on American shippers.

Although most of Madison's message dealt with Britain's alleged wrongdoings on the sea, one paragraph charged that the British were instigating native hostility toward the United States on America's inland frontier: "Our attention is necessarily drawn to the warfare just renewed by the savages on one of our extensive frontiers: a warfare which is known to spare neither sex nor age, and to be distinguished by features peculiarly shocking to humanity. It is difficult to account for the activity and combinations which have for some time been developing themselves among tribes in the constant intercourse with British traders and garrisons, without connecting their hostility with that influence . . . We behold, in fine, on the side of Great Britain, a state of war against the United States; on the side of the United States, a state of peace towards Great Britain," concluded Madison.

Having made his case for war, the president passed the matter to Congress to decide whether the U.S. would "continue passive under these progressive usurpations, and these accumulating wrongs; or, opposing force to force in defence of their natural rights, shall commit a just cause into the hands of the Almighty Disposer of events . . ."[1]

Significantly, Madison closed his message to Congress with a warning to France. "I proceed to remark," noted the president, "that the communications last made to Congress on the subject of our relations with France, will have shown, that since the revocation of her decrees as they violated the neutral rights of the United States, her government has authorized illegal captures, by its privateers and public ships, and that other outrages have been practiced on our vessels and our citizens. . . . I abstain at this time from recommending to the consideration of Congress definitive measures with respect to that nation, in the expectation, that the result of unclosed discussions between our minister plenipotentiary at Paris and the French government, will speedily enable Congress to decide, with greater advantage, on the course due to the rights, the interests and the honour of our country."[2] Madison delivered his war message to an "executive session" of Congress that was closed to the public and, therefore, to the feedback of public opinion.

The response to the message in the House of Representatives exposed deep divisions between Madison's Republicans (the ancestors of today's Democrats) and the Federalists (the ancestors of today's Republicans via the Whigs). The more liberal Republicans, in the Jeffersonian tradition, were broadly inclined to identify with the Enlightenment, the French Revolution, and even Napoleon, the heir of the Revolution, rather than monarchical Britain. The more conservative Federalists were more sympathetic to Britain than to revolutionary France. At least as important as these ideological inclinations were the major sectional rifts that divided the United States. Federalists who opposed war with Britain tried three times without success to open the session to the public, in the hope that negative popular sentiment would halt the passage of the declaration of war.

On June 4, 1812, the House passed the motion by a vote of 79 to 49. West of the Appalachian Mountains, where the issue was the desire to settle on native land and the conflict was with Tecumseh's confederacy, Congressmen voted solidly for war. The rest of the country was split. The majority of the delegations from Virginia and Pennsylvania assented to the declaration. The large majority of New York's congressmen voted against the motion, as did all of Delaware's members. In New England, where opposition to the war was so strong that it threatened the unity of the nation, the votes in the House were split. Delegations from Connecticut and Rhode Island unanimously voted in opposition to war. Majorities from Vermont and New Hampshire voted yes, as did six Massachusetts congressmen.

The Senate was so deadlocked that it appeared for a time that the declaration would fail. Following a week of deliberations, Senator Alexander Gregg of Pennsylvania moved that the war bill be sent back to a select committee to be amended so that in place of a full declaration of war, the United States would issue letters of marque and reprisal, licensing privateers to attack and seize British vessels.[3] The Senate passed Gregg's motion by a vote of 17 to 13. But three days later, when the limited-conflict proposal emerged out of committee to go before the full Senate, the upper chamber cast a tied vote on the measure, 16 to 16, and thus it went down to defeat.

With the compromise off the table, Madison's motion again went before the Senate. On June 17, 1812, senators voted 19 to 13 in support of the declaration. It was by far the narrowest vote for war in the history of the United States. The following day, Madison signed the declaration.

On June 27, Brock received the news at Fort George that the United States had declared war against Britain nine days earlier. He immediately dispatched missives to his key subordinates along the Niagara Frontier. By June 30, the news had reached Colonel Thomas Bligh St. George, an experienced British officer who had served in Europe before being transferred to Canada as commander of Fort Malden. And by July 8, Captain Charles Roberts, in command at Fort St. Joseph, had been alerted, which gave him a clear edge against the Americans at Fort Michilimackinac.

Although Brock was urged by Prevost to remain cautious and defensive-minded, he did send two letters to Roberts on June 26 and 27, ordering him to assault Fort Michilimackinac if he felt he could take it. Roberts commanded an outpost on the St. Mary's River just off the northern shore of Lake Huron, manned by a small contingent of Royal Artillerymen and a single company of the 10th Royal Veteran Battalion. His fort was located eighty kilometres northeast of Michilimackinac, a strategically important island that dominated the strait connecting Lakes Huron and Michigan and sat astride a major fur trade route. The very day that Roberts received his missives from Brock, he also received a letter from Prevost with orders to act with caution, offer aid to the North West Company, and ready himself to retreat "in case of necessity." Even Brock was not entirely committed to the offensive in the Northwest. On July 15, Roberts received another letter from his commanding officer with orders "to adopt the most prudent methods of offence or defence which circumstances might point out." But this was not an order to prepare to retreat.[4]

With these ambiguous instructions from two distant commanders, Roberts was left to decide on his own what course to follow. On July 17, with a force of about 700 native warriors (including Sioux, Winnebagoes, Tallesawains, Chippewas, and Ottawas), 260 Canadian militia, and just under 50 British regulars, Roberts swooped down on Michilimackinac and seized the island from the surprised American garrison. U.S. Lieutenant Porter Hanks, in charge there, only learned on the day he surrendered his post that war had been declared — Roberts informed him. The swift capture of the post, which was held by the British until the end of the conflict, helped open the way for Brock's attack on Detroit and had long-term consequences for the course of the war in the Northwest.[5] Michilimackinac was also strategically crucial to the Canadian fur trade and to winning over native peoples of the region to the British side.

In his roles as the head of the government of Upper Canada and the commander of armed forces in the province, Brock issued a proclamation to steady the nerves of the populace: "Whereas on the seventeenth day of June last the congress of the United States of America declared that war then existed between those States and their territories, and the United Kingdom of Great Britain and Ireland and the dependencies thereof: And whereas, in pursuance of such declaration the subjects of the United States have actually committed hostilities against the possessions of his Majesty and the persons and property of his subjects in this province: now therefore by and with the advice of his Majesty's executive Council for the affairs of the Province, I do hereby strictly enjoin and require all his Majesty's liege Subjects to be obedient to the lawful authorities, to forbear all Communication with the Enemy or persons residing within the Territory of the United States, and to manifest their Loyalty by a zealous Co-operation with his Majesty's land Force in Defence of the Province & repulse of the Enemy. And I do further require and command all officers civil and military to be vigilant in the discharge of their Duty, especially to prevent all Communication with the Enemy; and to cause all Persons suspected of traitorous Intercourse to be apprehended & and treated according to Law."⁶

On July 3, Brock wrote to Prevost that he had "been anxiously expecting for some days, to receive the honor of Your Excellency's Commands" to deal with "the present emergency." He told the commander-in-chief that while he believed the declaration of war against Britain by the Americans "would have justified in my opinion, offensive operations," he calculated that attacks could later be mounted against a number of American positions, including Fort Niagara, which was across the river from Fort George. Therefore, he "relinquished" any such immediate intentions and "attended only" to defensive measures such as "calling out the flank companies" of the local militia. He informed General Prevost that he believed the Americans had about twelve hundred regulars and militia at Fort Niagara, and added, "I consider myself at this moment perfectly safe against any attempt they can make."⁷

A few days later, Prevost replied to Brock in characteristic fashion, telling him, "I am convinced you have acted wisely in abstaining from offensive operations . . ." Still in a cautionary frame of mind, he wrote, "It is highly proper you should secure the services of the Indians but restrain and control them as much as you can."⁸ On July 10, again counselling restraint, Prevost advised Brock, "I consider it prudent and politic to avoid any measure which can in its effect have a tendency to unite the People in the American States."⁹

While Brock and Prevost attempted to calculate the correct balance between offence and defence, the Americans were acting on a plan of attack that they had conceived months earlier. The Madison administration had one big idea about how to prosecute the war. The idea was to conquer Canada.

Shortly after war was declared, Governor Daniel D. Tompkins of New York was confident that "one half of the Militia of both provinces [Upper and Lower Canada] would join our standard."¹⁰ And in Washington, Henry Clay told the House of Representatives in the summer of 1812, "We have the Canadas as much under our command as she (Great Britain) has the ocean; and the way to conquer her on the ocean is to drive her from the land. I am not for stopping at Quebec, or anywhere else; but I would take the whole continent from them, and ask no favors. Her fleets cannot then rendezvous at Halifax as now; and, having no place of resort in the north, cannot infest our coast as they have lately done. It is as easy to conquer them on the land, as their whole navy would conquer ours on the ocean. We must take the continent from them. I wish never to see a peace till we do."[11]

A week after the U.S. declared war, Secretary of State James Monroe gave himself over to the rising belligerence where Canada was concerned when he said that public opinion could make it "difficult to relinquish Territory which had been conquered."[12]

Also at the beginning of the war, former president Thomas Jefferson wrote in a letter that the conquest of Canada must be a goal of the United States. He referred to his hope for "the successful course of our war, and the addition of Canada to our confederacy. The infamous intrigues of Great Britain to destroy our government . . . and with the Indians to tomahawk our women and children, prove that the cession of Canada, their fulcrum for these Machiavellian levers, must be a *sine qua non* at a treaty of peace."[13] In a further letter he wrote in late 1812, Jefferson said that he believed that "the acquisition of Canada this year, as far as the neighbourhood of Quebec, will be a mere matter of marching, and will give us the experience for the attack on Halifax, the next and final expulsion of England from the American continent."

For the Americans, a successful invasion of Canada would achieve three goals simultaneously: by denying British war aid to the native enemies of the United States, it would ensure U.S. control of the lands the Americans were contesting with Tecumseh's confederacy; it would lead to the annexation of Canada, which was much desired by the land-hungry War Hawks; and it was the one way the United States could get at the British. Potentially, Canadian soil could be held as a bargaining chip to force the British to end the practice of impressment and interference with U.S. commerce across the seas.

In April 1812, the Americans conceived a strategy that had the endorsement of both President James Madison and U.S. Secretary of War William Eustis. The plan was to attack Canada with simultaneous assaults against Montreal and Kingston and across the Niagara River between Lakes Erie and Ontario. Some of President Madison's advisors concluded that because Canada's defences depended on the Great Lakes, the St. Lawrence, and other major rivers, the U.S. needed to seize control of the waterways by constructing a fleet of ships as soon as possible. That was a far-sighted idea, but the Americans failed to follow through amid fierce debates about how much the war would cost and who would pay for it.

If American planning was desultory, their selection of senior commanders could hardly have been worse. Henry Dearborn, a sixty-one-year-old veteran of the American Revolutionary War, was put in charge of the first plan to conquer Canada. Dearborn had long since devoted himself to politics, not military affairs. Nonetheless, Madison appointed Dearborn, who was known to his troops as "Granny," to command the Northern Department with a rank of major general.[14] At the same time, the administration picked sixty-three-year-old Thomas Pinckney, another veteran of the American Revolution, to run the Southern Command.

A third key commander whose military experience during the American Revolution had long since passed, was fifty-nine-year-old William Hull. Short and pudgy, more epicurean than Spartan, Hull was the genial governor of the Michigan Territory, the first holder of that office, with an appointment that had begun in 1805. As governor, Hull was the nominal commander of the Michigan militia. Originally from Massachusetts, he displayed few of the martial qualities of a man fit to lead soldiers into battle. Whatever his military prowess decades earlier, Hull was now fearful. Above all, he quavered at the prospect of native warriors gaining the upper hand against his troops and his family, a fear that would have important consequences in coming weeks.[15]

Shortly after his arrival at Fort Detroit on July 5, General Hull received a packet from William Eustis that contained the text of the American declaration of war and gave Hull written authorization "to commence offensive operations." While Eustis cautioned Hull to protect his own posts, he urged him to "take possession of Malden and extend your conquests as circumstances may justify."[16]

Hull replied with a written message of his own that combined bluster against the British with anxiety about the native population. "Every effort has been and is still making, by the British to collect the Indians under their standard," he wrote. "The British have established a post, directly opposite this place — I have confidence in dislodging him, and being in possession of the opposite bank . . . I have little time to write: every thing will be done that is possible to do. The British command the water and the savages . . . you therefore must not be too sanguine."[17]

On July 12, after collecting boats on the Detroit River for three days, Hull led his troops across the river. Greeted by friendly residents in the settlement of Sandwich, Hull issued a proclamation to Canadians, inviting them to regard the American forces as liberators. "Inhabitants of Canada!" Hull's proclamation read. "After 30 years of peace and prosperity, the United States have been driven to arms. The injuries and aggressions, the insults and indignities of Great Britain, have once more left them no alternative but manly resistance or unconditional submission. The army under my command has invaded your country, and the standard of union now waves over the territory of Canada. To the peaceable, unoffending inhabitant, it brings neither danger nor difficulty."

Asserting that Canadians had no interest in Britain's wars and had "felt her tyranny," he pressed, "I tender you the invaluable blessing of civil, political and religious liberty . . . That liberty which has raised us to an elevated rank among the nations of the world, and which afforded us a greater measure of peace and security, of wealth and improvement, than ever fell to the lot of any country."

The general's honeyed words were followed by a stern warning: "If, contrary to your own interest and the just expectation of my country, you should take part in the approaching contest, you will be considered and treated as enemies, and the horrors and calamities of war will stalk you. If the barbarous and savage policies of Great Britain be pursued, and the savages be let loose to murder our citizens, and butcher our women and children, this will be a war of extermination. The first stroke of the tomahawk, the first attempt with the scalping knife, will be the signal of one discriminate scene of desolation. No white man found fighting by the side of an Indian will be taken prisoner; instant destruction will be his lot." And then he added a final admonition: "The United States offer you peace, liberty and security — your choice lies between these and war, slavery and destruction."[18]

From the American point of view, the immediate response to Hull's invasion of Canada and to his proclamation was favourable. Several hundred Canadian residents quickly accepted the entreaty to identify themselves with the American cause, and dozens of militiamen deserted Fort Malden to join Hull's army. Hull had been expecting this support. He later wrote that "a large portion of the population of that province had emigrated from the United States. They had been educated with the principles of freedom and independence; and some of them, and many of their fathers, had fought and bled in our revolutionary contest. They were situated more than three thousand miles from the country to which they were subjected, and had no participation or interest in the measures it adopted."[19] The positive reception the Americans received from a sizeable number of residents showed that Brock's concerns about the loyalty of segments of the population were well-founded.

Confident that he was on the way to a major and easily won victory, Hull set himself up in the best-appointed house in Sandwich, the residence of a British colonel who was then away in York, the capital of Upper Canada. The American general sent out parties of troops to commandeer provisions for his men from the local farmers,[20] a practice that over the course of the war convinced most Upper Canadians that the Americans were thieves, not liberators. The demands of the invaders devastated some of the farmers. One farmer had 408 bushels of grain confiscated, and another lost 620 skins and all of his livestock.

On July 16, the first shots in the War of 1812 rang out not far from Fort Malden. Advance units of General Hull's army, based at Detroit, had crossed the Detroit River onto Canadian soil four days earlier. Under the command of Colonel Lewis Cass, the invading force consisted of one company of the U.S. 4th Regiment, one company of Ohio volunteers, four companies of Ohio riflemen, and some dragoons — in total about three hundred men.[21] Leaving a small force to hold a bridge across the Canard River, Cass marched up the river to a ford and crossed. There he surprised a small force of British regulars, Canadian militia, and native warriors, under the command of Lieutenant John Clemow. The outnumbered British fell back to their main position at Amherstburg. During the confused retreat, two British privates, James Hancock and John Dean, were left behind. They defended their position until both were wounded and taken prisoner. Hancock died the same evening, the first soldier to be killed in the defence of Canada.[22]

Ten days after Hull's proclamation to the residents of Upper Canada, Brock issued his own counter-proclamation from Fort George. In the words of the head of the military and civil government of the province, Hull had insulted Upper Canadians "with a call to seek voluntarily the protection of his government." Brock warned that an American conquest of Canada would quickly be followed by the country's re-annexation by France, which would result in the inhabitants of Canada becoming "willing subjects, or rather slaves, to the despot who rules the nations of continental Europe with a rod of iron."

Then Brock took aim at Hull's warning about the dire consequences that would follow if any white soldier stood side by side with a native warrior. "Be not dismayed at the unjustifiable threat of the commander of the enemy's forces to refuse quarter, should an Indian appear in the ranks," he declared. "The brave bands of aborigines which inhabit this colony were, like his majesty's other subjects, punished for their zeal and fidelity, by the loss of their possessions in the late colonies, and rewarded by his majesty with lands of superior value in this province . . . The Indians feel that the soil they inherit is to them and their posterity . . . They are men, and have equal rights with all other men to defend themselves and their property when invaded."[23]

After affirming the rights of the native peoples to their lands, Brock declared that the war was not just about whether Britain or the United States would rule Upper Canada — the war was a struggle for the rights of all of the subjects of the king. With this statement, Brock made common cause with the native enemies of the U.S.

On July 27, Brock met the newly elected legislative assembly at York, under circumstances dramatically different from those of his first meeting with the assembly a few months earlier. Again he pressed for amendments to the Militia Act and sought the suspension of habeas corpus. The members of the assembly did agree to amend the Militia Act to strengthen the government's ability to insist that orders be obeyed. They also passed a measure to raise ten thousand pounds to fund the militia. But the assembly refused to revoke habeas corpus. Even under these dire circumstances, the elected members were not prepared to give the government carte blanche. It was a unique situation faced by the democratic branch of the Upper Canadian regime, and in the end the members of the assembly insisted that the government not completely abridge the rights of the subjects of the Crown in the province. Brock accused them of wasting time during an emergency.

On August 3, Brock turned to the appointed Executive Council, whose members could be expected to be more compliant, and spelled out for them the threat of the American invasion of the western corner of Upper Canada. The following day, in a letter to Prevost, he reported that the council had adjourned for deliberation. He was confident that the members would recommend the prorogation of the assembly and a proclamation declaring martial law.[24]

A few weeks earlier, uncertain about how to proceed on the question of martial law, Brock had sought the advice of Prevost on how far his authority extended. On July 31, the governor wrote back advising, "I believe you are authorized by the Commission under which you administer the Government of Upper Canada to declare Martial Law in the event of Invasion or Insurrection. It is therefore, for you to consider whether you can obtain anything equivalent from your Legislature." And then he let Brock know that he had been having his own problems with his legislature: "I have not succeeded in obtaining a modification of it in Lower Canada, and must therefore upon the occurrence of either of those Calamities [invasion or insurrection], declare the Law Martial unqualified . . ."[25]

Despite the unease he felt dealing with politicians and acting as head of government, there was one place where Brock did feel at home — on a battlefield, where he would soon find himself.

In the first days of the war, with a foothold secured in Upper Canada, Hull had the opportunity to achieve a decisive victory for the United States. With bold moves, he could have won over much of the Upper Canadian population with the proposition that the Americans were going to win and it made sense to side with the victors. Decisiveness could also have convinced many of the native peoples who were hostile to the U.S. that they should sit on the sidelines rather than rally to a losing British cause.

This was the moment for an audacious general to take advantage of the fact that the Americans had twice as many men as the British in the immediate zone of conflict. Hull needed to strike from his base on Upper Canadian soil and seize Fort Malden, the principal British strongpoint, in a dramatic coup. Hull, however, was anything but audacious. He was the classic ditherer, so fearful of threats to his position that he threw away his opportunities.

On August 4, Porter Hanks wrote to Hull with the devastating
news that he had surrendered Michilimackinac. He explained that
he had been compelled to give up the post to a superior force without
a shot being fired in its defence. He concluded his letter with a personal plea: "In consequence of this unfortunate affair, I beg leave, sir,
to demand that a court of inquiry may be ordered to investigate all
the facts connected with it; and I do further request, that the court
may be specially directed to express their opinion on the merits of
the case."[26] Hand-wringing combined with self-justification was to
be characteristic of missives written by American commanders following their defeats in the coming months.

Shocked by the bad news from the north, Hull also grew anxious
about the security of his lengthy supply lines south to Ohio. An
intrepid commander would have understood that war, especially in
its early phases, is highly fluid; he would have brushed aside the bad
news and put off concerns about his supply lines for the moment.
Capturing Fort Malden would have more than offset the problems
that were beginning to immobilize Hull.

Hull's opponents were fortunate to have a leader on their side who
was anything but a ditherer. At this critical moment, Tecumseh
brought his towering skills to the aid of the British, who themselves
were poorly prepared to meet the American assault. At the end of June,
when the Shawnee chief reached Fort Malden, news had just arrived
that war had broken out. Tecumseh was immediately prepared to
throw himself into the fight, although he had few warriors with him.
In the days that followed, he managed to convince other native leaders
and their followers not to back the Americans, and he pulled some
neutral tribes off the fence to side with the British. The British quickly
realized that Tecumseh was the decisive figure in determining how
much military support they could receive from the native peoples. In a
series of small-scale clashes with the Americans north of Fort Malden,
Tecumseh showed his offensive spirit while fighting alongside the red-
coats. While the battles were indecisive, the initial sense that an
American victory was inevitable was quickly fading.

~

During the critical early weeks of the conflict, General Brock behaved as though he had nothing on his mind but the upcoming battle against the Americans. In truth, Brock and Prevost had been thinking about whether a deal might be negotiated to bring an early end to the war. They were acutely aware that one of the U.S. government's major quarrels with Britain was the British Orders in Council directing the Royal Navy to blockade all continental ports and halt the entry of foreign ships, including U.S. vessels, unless they first landed at a British port and paid customs duties.

Having rather reluctantly led the United States into war with Great Britain, the Madison administration was also not averse to seeking ways to end the conflict. A few weeks after the declaration of war, Secretary of State James Monroe instructed the administration's chargé d'affaires in London, Jonathan Russell, to attempt to work out a deal to end the conflict. Monroe required two concessions from the British. The first was the repeal by the British of the Orders in Council; the second was an end to the practice of impressment.

In fact, on the eve of the outbreak of the War of 1812, the British had decided to offer the Americans an olive branch by repealing the Orders in Council. Two days before the United States declared war, the Parliament at Westminster took steps to repeal the Orders, and three days after the declaration of war, they were repealed. The Americans, of course, were not aware that the British had made this conciliatory gesture.

Meanwhile, Monroe's other demand — that impressment be stopped — had not been met. Toward the end of August 1812, when Russell outlined the American case to Britain's foreign minister, Lord Castlereagh, he added as a further inducement that the U.S. Congress would swiftly pass legislation prohibiting the use of British seamen on American vessels, a policy that the Americans believed would end the practice of impressment.

Castlereagh responded that he believed that the repeal of the Orders in Council gave sufficient incentive to stop the American rush to war. He rejected the impressment demand with derision. "I cannot refrain on one single point from expressing my surprise," declared Castlereagh, "that as a condition preliminary even to a suspension of hostilities, the Government of the United States should have thought fit to demand that the British Government should desist from its ancient and accustomed practice of impressing British seamen from the merchant ships of a foreign state, simply on the assurance that a law shall hereafter be passed to prohibit the employment of British seamen in the public or commercial service of that state." Castlereagh closed the matter by saying that his government could not "consent to suspend the exercise of a right upon which the naval strength of the empire mainly depends."[27] As far as direct negotiations between the two belligerent powers were concerned, that was that, for the time being.

Several weeks earlier, on July 31, 1812, still hopeful that a deal might be reached to bring about an early end to the war, General Prevost, writing from Quebec, alerted General Brock at Fort George that "should the intelligence which arrived yesterday by the way of Newfoundland, prove correct, a remarkable coincidence will exist in the revocation of Our Orders in Council as regards America, and the declaration of war by Congress against England, both having taken place on the same day in London and at Washington, the 17th June."[28]

In a further letter, sent two days later, on August 2, and marked "private and confidential," Prevost acquainted Brock with a communication he had received "referring to a declaration of Ministers in Parliament, relative to a proposed repeal of the Orders in Council, provided the United States Government would return to relations of amity with us." Prevost held out the prospect to Brock that a deal might be worked out that would "induce the American Government to agree to a suspension of Hostilities as a preliminary to negotiations for Peace."[29]

Hoping for an early end to the war, Prevost at once sent Colonel Edward Baynes, the adjutant general for British forces in Canada, under a flag of truce to meet with General Dearborn in Albany to propose an armistice. Dearborn was favourable to the idea, but he lacked the authority to negotiate an armistice. He was willing, none-theless, to order his officers to limit themselves to defensive measures until he received word from the U.S. government about its wishes. As it turned out, President Madison was completely hostile to Dearborn's proposal of an armistice. As far as the president and the members of his administration were concerned, only one of their two demands had been addressed with the repeal of the Orders in Council. And to halt the war only a few weeks after it had been declared would leave the United States looking weak and foolish.

While U.S. political leaders were preoccupied with matters of high policy, General Hull became ever more obsessed with his supply lines. He dispatched two hundred U.S. Army regulars under the command of Major Thomas Van Horne to proceed to the River Raisin south of Detroit and meet an expected supply convoy under the command of Captain Henry Brush. Van Horne's men planned to escort Brush's convoy back to the American base at Sandwich. A native scout discov-ered Van Horne's marching route and reported it to Tecumseh. With seventy warriors, the Shawnee chief lay in wait in a wooded position beside the road and launched a surprise attack on the Americans. Having failed to send scouts ahead of his main force, Van Horne was thrown into panic by Tecumseh's well-planned ambush. Before the Americans could disengage and escape, one hundred troops were killed.

Tecumseh's attack took advantage of the strengths of native war-riors against a European-style foe. Native forces were more mobile than those of the Americans and the British and they were less dependent on water transport. Both sides deployed native forces, the Americans much less effectively than the British. While the native warriors relied on the British or the Americans for ammunition and sometimes for food, they were far more capable of living off the land. They were also most effective fighting in the open and ambushing enemy units. Because they lacked artillery, they were less successful in sieges of forts.

Among the items Tecumseh retrieved from the shattered American force was a mailbag containing a letter from Hull to U.S. Secretary of War William Eustis, in which the general admitted that he feared being besieged by thousands of native warriors. The letter could only raise the morale of Tecumseh and his men, as well as that of the British. By the time of the assault on Van Horne's men, Hull's officers were growing restive under his command. Some of his Ohio officers circulated a petition "requesting the arrest and displacement of the General."[30]

Hull took the news of the ambush hard. Panic was in the air. Hull decided that he had to go on the defensive at Detroit. On August 7, he ordered the evacuation of Sandwich, and his troops crossed the Detroit River. His invasion of Canada had lasted just twenty-seven days. Still preoccupied with his supply lines to the south, Hull chose Lieutenant Colonel James Miller to lead a force of six hundred men to complete the job that had eluded Van Horne.

Meanwhile, Tecumseh's scouts kept him apprised of Miller's slow progress, which was dangerously retarded by the unwise decision to take along heavy pieces of artillery. Cannon were immensely difficult to tow on poor roads and tracks and across open countryside. Teams of horses dragged a gun and its ammunition on a limber. This slow process stalled infantry, leaving it more vulnerable to enemy attack.

Usually, cannon were deployed on the flanks of a force of artillery. Fired at a rate of about one round per minute, their preferred use was against foot soldiers rather than against opposing cannon. There was always the risk of gunners' being exposed to an enemy flanking attack or assaults from sharpshooters or skirmishers. When attacked from the flank, the first choice of gunners was to hitch up the horses and tow the guns and ammunition out of danger. As a last resort, if their position was likely to be taken by the enemy, they spiked their guns, disabling them by driving a nail into the touch hole.

In his pursuit of the Americans, Tecumseh was joined by ten British regulars and by militiamen under the command of Major Adam Muir. Tecumseh and his warriors lay flat on the ground, hiding themselves in tall grass to await the Americans, while Muir's men positioned themselves on a nearby rise. The U.S. troops, advancing slowly across the plain, walked straight into the trap. When they were within range, the warriors leapt to their feet and opened fire.

In a desperate battle that lasted for two and half hours, the Americans fixed bayonets and repulsed an enemy charge. The horses used to haul the U.S. artillery pieces bolted. Muir's men, brightly clad in red, made easy targets for the Americans, and fell back. Tecumseh and his warriors held their ground and prevented Miller from going after the retreating British. The Shawnee chief, though nicked by a bullet in the neck, fought alongside his warriors.

Eighteen Americans died in the fight, and sixty-four were wounded. Five of Muir's men died, fourteen were wounded, and two went missing. According to the best estimate — neither the British nor the Americans made exact counts of native casualties — eleven of Tecumseh's warriors died and six or seven were wounded. A brief episode of friendly fire increased the casualties. When the British mistook some of the warriors for Americans and fired on them, the natives returned their fire. Despite this mishap, Miller was forced to halt his march and to return to Detroit.[31]

The momentum of the war was shifting. What looked at the outset like a triumphal American occupation of western Upper Canada now took on the appearance of an American fortress under siege. Hull and Tecumseh had been the key actors in the first weeks of the war. Another major player was about to arrive on the scene.

Chapter 9

Two Warriors

IN EARLY AUGUST, General Isaac Brock left York with a small force. He travelled to Burlington Bay, at the western edge of Lake Ontario, and then by land to Long Point, on Lake Erie, where 40 British regulars, 260 Canadian volunteers, and about 60 Mohawk warriors joined him. Brock's men commandeered all the boats they could find in the area, and in this rather ramshackle convoy they set out on the five-day passage up the lake, rowing in heavy rain to Fort Malden.[1]

When Brock arrived at Fort Malden to take command of a larger force and work out a plan with native allies, his presence would stiffen the spines of the men he had to rally. The general was far from vainglorious, but he was well aware of his ineffable ability to transmit spirit and energy to a body of men. He would not have described himself as charismatic, but he was exactly that. He insisted that his fitness to lead his men was a function of his rank. But he understood that there was much more to it. He knew that his unusual height made him physically imposing and that the sight of him in his scarlet uniform made soldiers confident of what they could do. For thousands of years, warriors have followed such leaders into battle, gaining strength from the sight of them. Brock drew much of his power from the ancient code of the warrior, while his scarlet uniform announced that British power was alive and well in the heart of North America.

Late on the evening of August 13, Brock's flotilla reached Amherstburg, near Fort Malden. Native warriors fired muskets into the night air to welcome the general and the recruits he had brought with him. Brock immediately sent Matthew Elliott, who had served for decades as the British Indian agent in the region, to find Tecumseh. Elliott had two messages for the Shawnee chief. The first was to ask Tecumseh to tell his warriors to stop shooting and save their ammunition for the Americans. The second was that Brock wanted to meet Tecumseh immediately. Brock knew that Tecumseh commanded native forces that he himself could not control, forces that could well prove decisive on the battlefield over the next few days.

Tecumseh, too, was anxious to meet Brock. His opinion of British commanders was not high — he remembered the numerous occasions when the British had played a double game with the natives and the Americans — but he was ready to make up his own mind about the major general. As a show of respect, Tecumseh dressed more ornately than was his custom for the occasion. He wore a large silver medallion of George III, the long-serving British monarch who had sat on the throne since 1760, attached to a coloured wampum string around his neck. Suspended from the cartilage of his nose were three small silver crowns. He was attired in a tanned deerskin jacket and trousers of the same material, and he wore his leather moccasins decorated with dyed porcupine quills.[2]

Tecumseh set out with Elliott for the meeting. By the time they arrived, the major general had already received the good news that Hull had pulled his remaining troops at Sandwich back across the river to Fort Detroit, ending the American invasion of Upper Canada. Brock had been sitting at a candlelit table, reading the packets of mail captured from the Americans, which told of Hull's low morale and the lack of confidence of the men under his command, when the door opened and Tecumseh entered.[3]

The general, taller and stouter than Tecumseh, rose to his feet and stepped forward to shake the hand of his visitor. The two men were physically imposing, the Shawnee chief with his muscular grace and the British general with his unusual size. Both had the indefinable ability to attract notice and command respect, even awe.

Observers have described Tecumseh at this stage of his life as a striking man, handsome, with large, dark, penetrating eyes and heavily arched brows that reinforced his grave and severe expression. He moved easily, despite the slight limp that was the consequence of his old leg injury. He was nearly six feet tall, with a compact build that displayed his capacity for physical endurance. He had even features, high cheekbones, an aquiline nose, a well-formed mouth, and regular teeth.[4] Though not as classically handsome as Tecumseh, Brock had boyish good looks. Portraits show an open, attractive face with a smallish nose and an unruly shock of hair.

Each man was at the height of his powers. Tecumseh was forty-four years old; Brock was nearly forty-three. The tall general in his scarlet uniform with gold-fringed epaulettes and the lithe, athletic Shawnee chief sized each other up and concluded that they could work together. They had come to their fateful meeting in very different ways, but it was apparent that they had much to offer each other.

Aware that morale in the American camp was low and that the ageing General Hull was terrified of the native warriors, Brock was quickly developing a strategy. With a swift assault on Fort Detroit, and with Tecumseh's warriors highly visible in the attack, Hull could be psychologically undermined. The fort, Brock reasoned, could be taken in a *coup de main* that would flow from a *coup de théâtre*. And if that didn't work, the Americans could be provoked to come out of their fort, where they could be beaten in a classic European-style battle. In his canny judgement of his opponent, an essential skill for a general, Brock was confident that a coup might work.

According to an account written by British Captain John Bachevoyle Glegg, who was present at the meeting, Brock commended Tecumseh for his leadership and courage in the native warriors' recent

engagements against the Americans. "I have fought against the enemies of our father, the king beyond the great lake, and they have
never seen my back," he continued. "I am come here to fight his enemies on this side of the great lake, and now desire with my soldiers to
take lessons from you and your warriors, that I may learn how to
make war in these great forests."

Glegg recorded that Brock outlined his plan for a swift attack on
Fort Detroit, while the British officers shook their heads and strongly
dissented. Tecumseh responded positively to the proposed offensive,
and when Brock asked him about the lay of the land en route to
Detroit, the Shawnee chief spread out a long strip of elm bark on the
table. He secured the corners with stones, unsheathed his knife, and
proceeded to create a map with its tip. Brock was impressed as
Tecumseh drew in the roads, waterways, and valleys and hills of the
neighbouring terrain.[5]

With this, the meeting concluded, and Brock arranged to meet
with Tecumseh and his warriors the next day to plan the campaign.

The following morning, a thousand warriors drawn from different
tribes — the fruit of Tecumseh's mobilization effort — assembled at
Fort Malden. Once ceremonial greetings were completed, Brock
addressed the multitude and declared that together they would drive
the Americans from Fort Detroit. The general's words drew loud
cheers. Tecumseh replied to Brock, saying that he was pleased that
"their father beyond the great salt lake had at last consented to let his
warriors come to the assistance of his red children, who had never
ceased to remain steadfast in their friendship and were now all ready
to shed their last drop of blood in their great father's service."[6]

According to one account, Tecumseh remarked in English that
while the previous British commander at Fort Malden had said,
"Tecumseh, go fight Yankee," General Brock said instead, "Tecumseh,
come fight Yankee."[7] Another often repeated version of events has it
that Tecumseh said of Brock to his fellow warriors: "This is a man."[8]

Over the next three days, Brock and Tecumseh led their men — British regulars, Canadian militia, and native warriors — onto American soil to capture Detroit. Outnumbered by the Americans, the British general and the Shawnee chief were breaking cardinal rules of warfare, aiming to seize an American fortress and dash American assumptions about an easy conquest of Canada.

More than mere chance brought Tecumseh and Brock together. Tecumseh's career as a warrior, and lately as the leader of the native confederacy in alliance with the British, pointed him inexorably to the battlefield in the southwestern corner of Upper Canada next to the Ohio country, where the struggle to hold on to native land had reached fever pitch. Nor was it an accident that Brock, the most offensive-minded senior British officer in the Canadas, should rush to meet Hull's invasion. Brock was betting heavily on Tecumseh. Unlike the other British commanders in Canada, he regarded the alliance with native forces as absolutely crucial to the success of the campaign in the western theatre of war. Without Tecumseh, he calculated that the British cause could only go down to defeat in the west. With Tecumseh and with a daring assault, they just might win. Brock was that rare commander who was prepared to wager it all on a single calculation. The stakes were nothing less than the fate of a continent.

Tecumseh and Brock sealed their commitment to fight side by side with a handshake and a few brief meetings. Lengthy protocols and precise terms of alliance did not have to be negotiated and signed. The two men simply sized each other up and resolved to entrust their respective fates to one another.

Chapter 10

The Capture of Fort Detroit

O N AUGUST 15, BROCK'S MEN and Tecumseh's warriors marched to Sandwich, establishing British headquarters in the house Hull had recently vacated. Brock had about seven hundred British regulars at his disposal, and Tecumseh's native force was about the same size.

The fort across the river was a formidable defensive stronghold. Built in the shape of a parallelogram, Fort Detroit was well constructed and heavily buttressed. Its rampart was twenty-two feet in height and had openings for cannon. A twelve-foot-wide and eight-foot-deep moat surrounded the fort. Hardwood stakes, ten feet in length and sharpened at the tips, encircled the area, placed at a forty-five-degree angle.[1]

Brock dispatched two officers under a flag of truce to deliver a message to General Hull, demanding that he surrender. "The force at my disposal authorizes me to require of you the immediate surrender of Fort Detroit," Brock wrote. Brock's letter played on Hull's fears of native warriors: "It is far from my inclination to join in a war of extermination [the word Hull had earlier used in his message to Canadians], but you must be aware, that the numerous body of Indians who have attached themselves to my troops, will be beyond my control the moment the contest commences."[2]

Despite his anxieties, which were heightened by the presence of his own family and numerous civilians inside the walls of the fort, Hull showed no sign of timidity in his staunch answer: "I have no other reply to make, than to inform you that I am prepared to meet any force, which may be at your disposal, and any consequences which may result from any exertion of it you may think proper to make."[3]

While Brock and Tecumseh readied their men for the crossing to the American side of the river and the assault on the fort, the major general ordered his gunners to open fire with their cannon from Sandwich. Hull's gunners returned fire with salvos from his fort's 24-pounder guns. On the first day, the exchange of cannon fire inflicted little damage on either side. But the next morning a cannonball fired from Sandwich struck the fort's mess hall and killed two men. One of the dead was a doctor from the Ohio volunteers. The other was Lieutenant Porter Hanks, the U.S. officer who had recently surrendered Fort Michilimackinac.

During the War of 1812 the rules of engagement dictated that both sides exchange captured soldiers to avoid having to feed and guard them. Those released swore an oath that they would not resume fighting until an enemy soldier of equivalent rank had also been released. Once the exchange was made, the soldiers could again take up arms. The unfortunate Hanks had been released by the British under such an arrangement and had been sent to Fort Detroit.[4]

On the morning of the bombardment, a young mother in Detroit wrote down her reaction to the roar of the guns: "Hour after hour how I passed thus alone, listening to the booming cannon and the startling and shrieking as a ball whizzed by the house, sometimes feeling almost sure that it was a mark for the enemy and thinking perhaps the next shot should terminate my existence."[5]

While early-nineteenth-century artillery pieces were unwieldy in the field, larger guns could be used to both defend fortifications and to assault them. In the War of 1812, these included large-bore guns mounted on carriages of the kind used at sea.

Another artillery piece deployed in the war was the howitzer. Invented in Sweden in the late seventeenth century, the howitzer had a short barrel that allowed it to fire at a sharp angle. By the middle of the eighteenth century, light and mobile howitzers were often deployed in the field by European armies; in the War of 1812, they were mounted on wooden field carriages in the manner of guns (cannon). With this weapon, adroit gunners honed the art of lobbing a metal shell, filled with powder and equipped with a wooden fuse, into an enemy fort. Ideally, it would explode above the heads of the defenders, showering them with deadly splinters. A howitzer could also be armed with an incendiary shell to set enemy fortifications alight or, better yet, strike enemy powder magazines and set off a giant explosion. Howitzers of the time could not be aimed with any precision, but they could cause real damage. When the defenders of a fort were running low on supplies, their morale was wavering, and their commanders were shaky, a howitzer was an effective psychological weapon.

A third type of artillery deployed during the conflict was the mortar. Normally held in place on a wooden bed at a forty-five-degree angle, the mortar was outfitted with a double chamber. The projectile was loaded into the larger chamber, and the smaller chamber, housed at the rear, was filled with gunpowder. Mortars fired what were called "bombs." On the outside, a bomb looked like a solid cannonball, but its hollow interior was filled with gunpowder. Just before firing the weapon, a gunner would place a wooden fuse in a hole in the bomb. The fuse would be cut to the desired length to time the distance it would fly before it exploded. When the fuse was lit, it burnt down to the bomb, setting it off. Well timed, the bomb would fly over the wall of a fort, exploding to strike personnel or powder magazines. Because of the fixed emplacement of the mortar, which could not easily be adjusted, the amount of gunpowder used in the charge was varied to achieve the desired range.

Henry Shrapnel, a British army officer and inventor, added to the arsenal available to the British during the War of 1812. He invented the "spherical case," a hollow cannonball that was filled with shot and burst in midair. Adopted by the British army in 1803 as an anti-personnel device, the weapon came at once to be called the "shrapnel shell," after its inventor.

In addition, there was the rocket, which was invented by Sir William Congreve in 1804. The rocket was housed in an iron case containing the black powder that was used to propel it. Attached to this was a warhead. Launched from an upright wooden guide pole, the rocket had a maximum range of about 3.2 kilometres; the distance was adjusted by setting the angle of the launching frame. The rockets were notoriously inaccurate, but they were an effective psychological tool that the British deployed both at sea and on land.

The night before the British guns took the lives of two men at Fort Detroit, Tecumseh and about six hundred warriors paddled quietly across the Detroit River and landed undetected three kilometres south of the fort. The following morning, a sunny and pleasant August 16,[6] Brock's force, made up of three hundred British regulars and four hundred Canadian militia, was divided into three groups for the crossing. With the guns at Sandwich providing cover, the British and the Canadians crossed the river. The general stood at the prow of the lead boat. As soon as the landing was complete, Brock positioned himself at the head of the column. As was his practice, he led from the front, attired in his scarlet uniform. A British quartermaster who had crossed the river with Brock urged him to make himself less of a target for the Americans. "If we lose you, we lose all," he said to the general, pleading with Brock to let the troops be led by their own officers.

"Many here follow me from a feeling of personal regard," replied Brock. He thanked the quartermaster for his concern but said, "I will never ask them [his soldiers] to go where I do not lead them."[7]

Shortly after the landing, a scout brought the alarming news to Brock that several hundred American soldiers were behind him, only a few miles distant. These were the men from Ohio whom Hull had dispatched to the River Raisin in a quest for supplies but then called back to help defend Fort Detroit. Brock was between the fort and the Ohio men. Caught in such a vise, a less intrepid commander would have withdrawn his force back to the Canadian side of the river.

Brock did no such thing. He pressed ahead, calculating that he had little time to lose. In two columns, the British and the Canadians marched to within a mile of the fort. Playing on the American general's anxiety, Brock had had his Canadian militia men decked out in the discarded uniforms of British regulars. In addition, Tecumseh's men crossed in front of the fort several times, sneaking back under cover each time, to convince Hull that he faced a much greater presence of native warriors than was actually the case.

Brock halted his troops and Tecumseh joined him. The two men climbed a small hill to scout their position. What they saw was certainly unexpected. The gates of the American fort suddenly swung open and a rider galloped in their direction. From the stick he carried, there fluttered a white handkerchief. What Brock and Tecumseh did not know was that the man waving the symbol of surrender was Hull's own son, Abraham. The general had reached the conclusion that he was not able to sustain an effective defence of the fort. On his mind, in addition to his fear of the native warriors, was the protection of the civilian population of the nearby town of Detroit. General Hull had ordered his son to instruct a major to display the white flag outside the fort. But the major refused, saying that he would be damned if he would disgrace his country. So Abraham Hull hoisted the symbol of capitulation and rode out with it himself.

General Brock, who had been girding for a difficult siege, sent an officer ahead to inquire about the meaning of the white flag. The officer returned to give Brock the stunning news that General Hull was surrendering the fort forthwith. Along with his offer to surrender, the general sought two things from Brock. First, he wanted three days to ready the fort and his men for evacuation; Brock replied that he could have three hours. Hull's second request, that the Canadians who had abandoned the British forces to join the American side should be treated leniently, was refused outright.

When Brock rode through the open gates of Fort Detroit, he encountered U.S. officers and soldiers in tears, so bitter was their feeling of humiliation. General Hull was in a shabby state. For hours he sat transfixed, as though in a daze, with spittle and tobacco juice dribbling down his chin.

In a lengthy letter to U.S. Secretary of War William Eustis, written while in captivity at Fort George a few days after the surrender, General Hull set out the reasons for his decision to hoist the white flag. His case rested heavily on his claim that after the surrender of Michilimackinac "almost every tribe and nation of Indians, excepting a part of the Miamies and Delawares, north from beyond Lake Superior, west from beyond the Mississippi, south from the Ohio and Wabash, and east from every part of Upper Canada, and from all the intermediate country, joined in open hostility, under the British standard, against the army I commanded, contrary to the most solemn assurances of a large portion of them to remain neutral."

At the head of the list of chiefs who led the warriors against the Americans was Tecumseh. Hull informed the secretary of war that native warriors were able to totally "obstruct the only communication I had with my country." He related the sorry fate of the forces he had sent out to reopen communications, and then argued that he did not have enough men at his disposal both to "fight the enemy in the field" and to leave "any adequate force in the fort." Outnumbered by the British troops and warriors opposing him, he chose capitulation. "A large portion of the brave and gallant officers and men I commanded," he wrote, "would cheerfully have contested until the last cartridge had been expended . . . I could not consent to the useless sacrifice of such brave men, when I knew it was impossible for me to sustain my situation."[8]

Within an hour of the surrender, the Ohio troops who had been dispatched to the River Raisin arrived outside the fort. They were shocked to discover the victorious British occupying the American installation. Most of the troops surrendered peacefully, laying down their weapons. A few, however, broke their swords, disabled their muskets, and uttered epithets concerning General Hull. The disgusted commander of the Ohio troops said that if Hull had fought, his men could have fallen on the British from the rear.

The U.S. soldiers marched out of the fort as the American flag was lowered. A British sailor pulled a Union Jack out from under his coat, and it was raised to loud cheers.

General Brock sent the news of his brilliant success to General Prevost, dating his report "Detroit, August 16, 1812."

"I hasten to apprize Your Excellency of the capture of this very important post: 2,500 troops have this day surrendered prisoners of war, and about 25 pieces of ordnance have been taken without the sacrifice of a drop of British blood," Brock wrote. "I had not more than 700 troops, including militia, and about 600 Indians to accomplish this service. When I detail my good fortune, your excellency will be astonished."[9]

Americans saw the capitulation at Detroit as an act of ignominy. Other American soldiers who had been involved in the engagement furiously and vociferously countered Hull's case for the need to surrender the fort. Lewis Cass, colonel of the third regiment of Ohio volunteers, wrote a lengthy letter to Eustis setting out the way Hull had acted to produce "so foul a stain upon the national character." He argued that the United States had available at Fort Detroit sufficient forces, weapons, and ammunition to make a successful stand, and that Hull had vastly exaggerated the size of the enemy he faced. "I was informed by General Hull the morning after the capitulation, that the British forces consisted of 1,800 regulars, and that he surrendered to prevent the effusion of human blood. That he magnified their regular force nearly five fold, there can be no doubt ... Confident I am, that had the courage and conduct of the general been equal to

the spirit and zeal of the troops, the event would have been as brilliant and successful as it now is disastrous and dishonourable."[10]

The day after the Union Jack was raised, the British celebrated
their triumph by firing a salute in front of Fort Detroit. The gun they
used to mark their victory was a brass 6-pounder with a brass plaque
on it. The plaque read "16 October 1777." The gun had been captured
from British General John Burgoyne's defeated army following the
Battle of Saratoga during the American War of Independence. Firing
a return salute from the lake were the guns of the British ship *Queen
Charlotte*.

Brock and Tecumseh feted their common victory with gestures of
praise toward one another. The Shawnee chief told Brock that the
Americans had been denying the valour of British generals, but what
he had seen at this battle had removed any doubts on that score. Brock
made a gift of a pair of pistols to Tecumseh and took the silk sash from
his own uniform and placed it across Tecumseh's shoulders. Tecumseh
presented a decorative scarf to the general. The exchange was sponta-
neous. The two men had known each other so briefly and had achieved
so much together in that short time.[11] Tecumseh's warriors, following
the American surrender, considered the lives of the prisoners to be
theirs to protect. No massacres or scalpings ensued.

Hull's officers were in a bitter mood during the traditional surrender ceremony. The 47th U.S. Regiment and the Ohio volunteers
turned over 1,900 muskets, and 1,150 weapons were surrendered by
members of the Michigan militia and other units. Among the cache
of weapons the British acquired were thirty-nine brass and iron cannon of various kinds, four hundred rounds of 24-pound shot, and
one hundred thousand cartridges.[12] The 1,606 members of the Ohio
militia who laid down their weapons were paroled and allowed to
return to their homes. Their names were duly placed on the roll of
prisoners, meaning that they could not serve in the military again
until they had been formally exchanged for British prisoners. British
soldiers escorted them on the first leg of their journey home.[13] General
Brock also paroled the members of the Michigan militia.[14]

Back in York at the end of August 1812, Brock reflected on his encounter with Tecumseh and on the cause for which the Shawnee chief was fighting. In a letter to the Earl of Liverpool written on August 29, 1812, he noted, "Among the Indians whom I found at Amherstburg . . . I found some extraordinary characters . . . He who attracted most my attention was a Shawnee Chief, Tecumseh, brother to the Prophet, who for the last two years has carried on (contrary to our remonstrances) an active warfare against the United States. A more sagacious or a more gallant warrior does not, I believe, exist. He was the admiration of everyone who conversed with him. From a life of dissipation he is not only become in every respect abstemious but has likewise prevailed on all his Nation, and many other Tribes, to follow his example."

On the war aims of Tecumseh and his warriors, Brock wrote, "They appear determined to continue the contest until they obtain the Ohio for a boundary. The United States Government is accused, and I believe justly, of having corrupted a few dissolute characters, whom they pretend to consider as Chiefs, and with whom they contracted engagements, and concluded Treaties, which they have been attempting to impose on the whole Indian Race. Their determined opposition to such fictitious and ruinous pretentions which if admitted would soon oblige the Indians to remove beyond the Mississippi is the true ground of their enmity against the Americans."[15]

Brock's reference to Tecumseh's earlier "life of dissipation" is a theme picked up by others who have written about the Shawnee chief. Significantly, it was a view not shared by Stephen Ruddell. In his account of Tecumseh's younger years, Ruddell wrote, "He rarely ever drank ardent spirits to excess — when inebriated he was widely different from other Indians — perfectly good humoured and free from those savage ideas which distinguished his companions."[16]

During the months prior to the assault on Fort Detroit and during the brief time he spent with Tecumseh, Brock came to comprehend the politics and goals of the native confederacy. He understood they had war aims that were quite distinct from those of the British

government, and he geared his military strategy to complement the
goals of Britain's native allies, calculating that it was the only way to
prevail in the southwestern corner of the province.

While the victors at Detroit savoured their hour of glory, the losers
suffered a different fate. General Hull and the 582 U.S. regulars who
had been taken prisoner began their journey by boat to Fort Erie and
then to Kingston, and from there to Montreal on foot. The arrival of
the American captives in Montreal generated a carnival-like atmo-
sphere in the city. A Montreal journalist who dubbed the spectacle
"an exhibition equally novel and interesting" went on to note that "it
unfortunately proved rather late in the evening for the vast con-
course of spectators assembled to that gratification they so anxiously
looked for. This inconvenience was, however, in great measure rem-
edied by the illuminations of the streets through which the lines of
march passed."

The Americans were the centrepiece of the parade, which was
held to cheer the inhabitants. A military band and British soldiers led
the procession. Next came General Hull, who rode in a carriage
alongside a British captain. Four carriages carrying wounded
American officers followed. On foot came American officers and
then non-commissioned officers and finally private soldiers. The
Montreal journalist told readers, "The general appears to be about
sixty years of age, and is a good looking man . . . He is communica-
tive, and seems to bear his misfortunes with a degree of philosophical
resignation that but few men in similar circumstances are gifted
with."[17] General Hull was taken to the residence of General Prevost,
the officers were housed in a hotel, and the soldiers had to make do
with a British barracks.

News of the catastrophe at Detroit did not reach President James
Madison for a couple of weeks. By then the president, who hated
Washington's intolerable summer weather, had left town with his
wife, Dolley, to spend some time at his estate in Montpelier, Virginia,

in the cooler clime of the foothills of the Blue Ridge Mountains. They had arrived at Dumfries Tavern, where a messenger raced to deliver the terrible news. Madison read the missive from Eustis, which told him that Hull had surrendered Fort Detroit and its 2,500 men without firing a shot.

The following morning, he returned to the capital, where he called the second full cabinet meeting of his presidency. The fall of Detroit stiffened the spines of the members of the administration. The president posed two questions to the cabinet: First, should the United States undertake a swift recapture of Detroit? And a second, longer-term, strategic question: did the U.S. need to establish a viable naval force on the Great Lakes? The cabinet answered both questions in the affirmative.

Despite Madison's injunction to the members of his administration that he did not want General Hull to be publicly pilloried until all the facts were known, the nation's rush to judgement was already well underway. The president directed Richard Rush, his comptroller, to write a piece about the debacle at Detroit for the *National Intelligencer*. However, Rush failed to adhere to Madison's instructions to be even-handed, saying of Hull, "The nation had been deceived by a gasconading booby."

Even Dolley Madison had trouble sticking to the president's line. "Do you not tremble with resentment at the treacherous act?" she wrote of Hull's surrender to a friend. She did, however, add, "We must not judge the man until we are in possession of his reasons."[18]

The surrender of Detroit would haunt the disgraced General Hull for the rest of his life. On January 17, 1814, in Albany, New York, he had his day in court. At the military tribunal, where he faced a court martial, Hull pleaded not guilty to the charge of treason. Hull's officers testified that the general had spoken in a trembling voice during the brief British siege of Fort Detroit. They told the court of Hull's dishevelled demeanour as tobacco-stained spittle dripped from his mouth.

While the twelve-member court did not find Hull's behaviour treasonous, its members did find him guilty of neglect of duty and conduct unbecoming an officer. Two-thirds of the judges concluded that he should be executed by firing squad. Three months later, President Madison reviewed the sentence and wrote that in view of Hull's contribution to the United States during the American Revolution, "the sentence of the court is approved, and the execution of it remitted." Hull was allowed to return home to Massachusetts.[19]

Hull spent his latter years in an effort to recover his lost reputation. He wrote two books, *Detroit: Defence of Brigadier General William Hull* and *Memoirs of the Campaign of the North Western Army of the United States, A.D. 1812*. The publication of the latter in 1824 convinced at least a part of the public to view him more favourably. In the spring of 1825, a dinner was held in his honour in Boston. In June of that year, the Marquis de Lafayette visited him and declared, "We both have suffered contumely and reproach; but our characters are vindicated; let us forgive our enemies and die in Christian love and peace with all mankind." A kindly word from this hero of the American Revolution could only help the general's standing with his fellow countrymen. On November 29, 1825, Hull died at his home in Newton, Massachusetts.

The triumph of Tecumseh and Brock at Detroit threw the American invasion of Canada off stride. Conquering Canada would not be "a mere matter of marching," as Thomas Jefferson had forecast. The twin victories at Detroit and at Queenston Heights a few months later were as important to the future independence of Canada as was the victory of the Americans against General Burgoyne at Saratoga in 1777 during the American Revolutionary War.* At Detroit and later at Queenston Heights, the Americans discovered that wresting Canada from the grip of the British Empire would be no easy matter. It would take two more years of bitter fighting for that lesson to sink

---

* An 1822 painting by John Trumbull titled *The Surrender of General Burgoyne* hangs in the rotunda of the United States Capitol.

in. And indeed, many later episodes in the relationship of Canadians with their more powerful southern neighbour would show that the lesson was a hard one to learn. The path of American expansion, it turned out, would be to the west and the southwest, and not to the north, at least militarily. In later decades, the Americans would tear off a large portion of the territory of Mexico, not British North America.

What made Tecumseh and Brock such natural allies, not merely from a personal point of view, was their approach to combat. Both were inclined to fight offensive battles, to strike quickly, and to cede as little ground as possible to the enemy. Realizing that when the Americans mobilized to their full capacity they would outnumber the native warriors, British regulars, and Canadian militia, they counted on a war of movement, in which swift attacks would disrupt the enemy, endanger his lines of supply and communication, and prevent him from assembling his superior numbers on a field of battle where he could achieve a strategic victory. Brock's regular army, outfitted with cannon, was an ideal match for Tecumseh's warriors, who were much more akin to a guerilla force, relying on an unexcelled knowledge of the terrain and a capacity to strike swiftly at points of their choosing.

During the battle for Detroit, Tecumseh and Brock reinforced each other's strengths, marrying the speed and flexibility of the native force to the firepower and solidity of the British regulars. That potent combination proved lethal for the cumbersome Americans and their shaky commanders. The consequence was a victory that should not have been won.

It was on the evening of August 13 that Brock arrived at Fort Malden and met Tecumseh; three days later, the Union Jack flew over Fort Detroit. This was a moment when the fate of the continent hung in the balance. But now the brief triumph shared by Tecumseh and Brock was over. Each continued to fight the Americans, but never again together.

Chapter 11

Death of the General

WARRIORS WHO FALL in battle appear in retrospect to have been journeying all their days to their appointed places of death. The Spartans led by King Leonidas who fell fighting the Persians are inexorably journeying to Thermopylae. No matter what part of Nelson's career we explore, he is always en route to Trafalgar on the deck of the HMS *Victory*. So it is with Brock and Queenston Heights. It can scarcely be doubted that Brock was likely to die on a battlefield. He could have died at Egmont-op-Zee in 1799, when a spent bullet struck the handkerchief he wore over his cravat. If Hull hadn't been so anxious to surrender at Detroit, it is not hard to imagine Brock leading a charge and being picked off there.

The story of Queenston Heights does not begin heroically with Brock, however. It begins in the weeks before the fall of Detroit, this time at the Niagara Frontier. Over the previous two decades, both the Americans and the British had regarded this frontier, along the gorge through which the Niagara River roared, as a crucial flashpoint in the event of a future war. In 1791, the British decided that this location at the foot of the Heights was a propitious place to locate a post. The village that consequently developed drew its name, Queenston, from the detachment of Queen's Rangers located there. On the

Heights, the British embedded an 18-pounder and a mortar in an earthwork that faced in two directions at right angles.

In 1791, the capital of Upper Canada was located at Newark, at the northern end of the river where it emptied into Lake Ontario. (In 1796, the capital was moved to the more militarily defensible position of York.) Farther upstream from Newark was Fort George, the main British military base in the region. Directly across the river from Newark was Fort Niagara, the principal base of the United States.

The Americans were determined to avenge the disaster at Fort Detroit. From Monticello, his retirement home in Virginia, Thomas Jefferson, the nation's most esteemed elder statesman, wrote a letter to President Madison warning that the Americans must move quickly to put things right. "I fear that Hull's surrender has been more than the mere loss of a year to us," he wrote. "Besides bringing on us the whole mass of savage nations, who fear and not affection, had kept in quiet, there is a danger that in giving time to an enemy who can send reinforcements of regulars faster than we can raise them, they may strengthen Canada and Halifax beyond the assailment of our lax and divided powers."[1]

To lead the assault at Niagara, the U.S. Department of War had endorsed the selection of Stephen Van Rensselaer by New York Governor Daniel Tompkins prior to the disaster at Detroit. Although he held the rank of major general of volunteers, Van Rensselaer had no military experience. His was a political appointment, pure and simple. The New York governor reasoned that by appointing a distinguished Federalist and a member of the party that was out of power in the nation's capital, he could help heal the country's political divisions and encourage other Federalists to back the war effort. It was hoped that the major general would receive advice from his cousin, Colonel Solomon Van Rensselaer, New York's adjutant general. The colonel had seen action in 1794 at the Battle of Fallen Timbers, where Tecumseh had fought in a losing cause.

The major general travelled to Ogdensburg, a post on the St. Lawrence River. Arriving on July 16, he found the position threatened by the presence across the river of two British warships, the *Duke of Gloucester* and the *Earl of Moira*. Van Rensselaer's first thought was to take offensive action, but of the four hundred militiamen assembled for the task, only sixty-three were fit for duty. The major general thought better of attacking the British, and on July 29 he and his men left Ogdensburg for the two-week journey to the Niagara River.

He set up his headquarters in Lewiston, located on the narrow, swift-flowing Niagara downstream from Niagara Falls. His task was to guard the crucial fifty-two-kilometre line from Fort Niagara in the north, on the shore of Lake Ontario, to Black Rock in the south, on the shore of Lake Erie.[2] British regulars, Canadian militia, and their native allies were posted opposite him on the Canadian bank of the Niagara River.

On his arrival, Major General Van Rensselaer found a rather a wretched force of troops — only 691 were fit for duty, out of a force of about 1,600 men — badly equipped and clamouring for pay. Many of them had no shoes. In the camp, there was not one heavy cannon, and no artillery men were available to fire the few small cannon on site. The medical department lacked equipment and supplies. Few tents were on hand. The mood among the militia men was surly and insubordinate; the grumpy soldiers were loath to follow orders.[3]

While Van Rensselaer was under pressure from his superiors to mount an attack on the British forces at the earliest opportunity, Brock was en route from his triumph at Detroit. He sailed from Amherstburg on August 17 but, held up by contrary winds, he did not reach Fort Erie for six days. Many of Van Rensselaer's men actually saw Brock across the river, as well as the dispiriting spectacle of the U.S. prisoners from Detroit being marched past Queenston en route to Montreal.[4]

A few days before Brock reached the Niagara Frontier, Major General Roger Hale Sheaffe, who was in command during his absence, negotiated an armistice with Van Rensselaer. The armistice initiative went back to Prevost's hope that an end to the war might be possible, since Britain had repealed the Orders in Council. On

August 21, Sheaffe and Van Rensselaer agreed to "a cessation of all acts of hostility between the troops and vessels of all descriptions under our command, until we shall receive further orders; and the party who shall first receive orders for the renewal of hostilities, shall give four days' notice, computing twenty-four hours to each day, before any offensive operation shall take place." They further agreed not to take advantage of the temporary armistice to bring forward men or supplies of ammunition.[5] Sheaffe did have the advantage of knowing about the British victory at Detroit a few days earlier, while his American counterpart was unaware of the disaster. But Van Rensselaer did manage to get the best of Sheaffe by ensuring that the U.S. forces could be supplied by water. During the hiatus in fighting, the Americans shipped heavy guns to Niagara from Oswego, at the eastern end of Lake Ontario.[6]

Van Rensselaer received orders from General Dearborn, who commanded U.S. forces in the Northeast, to end the armistice. In light of these instructions, Van Rensselaer sent a letter to Brock on September 4, informing him that "having now received orders to terminate the armistice . . . I have the honour to transmit you this notice, that the armistice will be terminated at twelve o'clock, at noon, on Tuesday, the eighth day of September, inst."[7] The U.S. commander was scrupulous in living up to the four days' notice embodied in the armistice agreement.

With the armistice over and the Americans committed to taking the offensive, Van Rensselaer received reinforcements. Troops from the 5th, 12th, 13th, and 14th U.S. Infantry Regiments and from the 2nd U.S. Artillery vastly increased the number of troops available to the Americans on the Niagara Frontier. By September 29, when a new senior officer reached the camp to share command with General Van Rensselaer, the United States had six thousand soldiers available. A regular army officer, Brigadier General Alexander Smyth, was under instructions from the War Department to place his own units at the disposal of Van Rensselaer. A forty-seven-year-old former lawyer, Smyth had opted for a military career in 1808, when he took command of a newly formed U.S. rifle regiment. Although lacking real military experience himself, the headstrong Smyth took an instant dislike to Van Rensselaer, whom he regarded as a political general. Smyth refused to attend the senior officers' meetings that Van Rensselaer held on a regular basis.[8] This forced Van Rensselaer to go ahead with his own planning, not knowing whether Smyth would coordinate an attack with his own forces when the time came.

In a book that recorded the bickering between the two senior officers, Solomon Van Rensselaer, the major general's cousin, charged Smyth with a general unwillingness to act in concert with his superior. "It is plain that his second in command [Smyth] had no cordial disposition to act in concert with him [Van Rensselaer]. And in . . . confirmation of the fact, is his letter reporting his arrival from Buffalo, dated 29th Sept.; in this, although an entire stranger to the country, he goes out of the way to obtrude his advice upon his commanding officer, touching movements and localities of which he knew nothing . . . All who were aware of his conduct, and many, among whom I was one, were of opinion that coercive measures should be resorted to, to bring him to a sense of duty." If Solomon Van Rensselaer had any criticism of his cousin Stephen, it is that he chose not to bring matters to a head with Smyth.[9]

Despite the lack of cohesion in the American camp, Van Rensselaer pushed ahead with his plans for an attack. His soldiers at Lewiston outnumbered Brock's, who were spread out along the opposite shore. Counting on that advantage, Van Rensselaer planned to seize a foothold in Upper Canada before the onset of winter. Hot on his back were his superiors, pressing for action. In a letter to Van Rensselaer on September 26, General Dearborn wrote, "The enemy may be induced to delay an attack until you will be able to meet him, and carry the war into Canada. At all events, we must calculate on possessing Upper Canada before winter sets in."[10]

Brock did not know when and where an American blow might fall. He deployed his main forces at Fort Erie, located at the southern junction of the Niagara River and Lake Erie, and at Chippawa, just upstream from the Falls. At Queenston, where a crossing would be more difficult, he positioned only the flank companies of the 49th Regiment and an equivalent number of militia.[11]

At Lewiston, the Americans had about 2,300 regular soldiers and 4,000 militia. Brock's force numbered 1,200 British army regulars and 800 Canadian militia. In addition, he had on hand a force of five or six hundred warriors from the Six Nations settlement at Grand River (near present-day Brantford, Ontario), along with Mississaugas, Delawares, and Ojibwas. Brock deployed the native warriors as a fast-moving light force, which he dispatched across the Niagara River to Grand Island to scout the enemy and skirmish with them.[12]

Prior to the war, Brock had regarded the Grand River warriors as a potentially important source of military strength to shore up border defences in the vulnerable Niagara sector. But his initial efforts to raise a force there had been met with a very cool response. When the war did break out, most of the Iroquois chose to remain neutral or to quietly back the Americans. Brock also had to cope with the fact that Iroquois from New York State were actively pressing the Six Nations on the Grand River to decline invitations to rally to the British side. In early June 1812, before the United States declaration of war, a council on the Grand River considered the options. Those who favoured neutrality left the meeting, allowing the pro-British Mohawks to prevail.[13] It was from the pro-British elements that Brock drew his present complement of warriors.

Van Rensselaer decided to move. On October 10, he ordered Smyth to march his force at once to Lewiston. He issued unequivocal instructions: "Immediately on the receipt of this you will please give orders to all the United States troops under your command to strike their tents, and march, with every possible despatch, to this place."[14] The next day Van Rensselaer again wrote to Smyth, informing him that the failure of the latter's troops to arrive swiftly meant that an opportunity to attack the British batteries at Queenston had lapsed. "In the interim," he wrote, "the United States troops under your command will remain at their encampment near Buffalo."[15]

To this Smyth replied a day later that "the badness of the weather and roads" had "harassed" the progress of his troops. They would now have to spend the next day washing themselves and their clothing, and 1,200 men should be prepared to march the day after that, on October 14.

Van Rensselaer decided to proceed with his plans despite his problems coordinating the American forces. Not only was he not working effectively with Smyth, he had failed to act in concert with U.S. commanders farther afield—Captain Isaac Chauncey on Lake Erie and William Henry Harrison, who had been named by Madison to replace the disgraced Hull as commander in the Northwest. It was the usual set of problems the Americans encountered early in the war. The commanders got on badly and seldom hesitated to express their feelings. Instead of a coordinated series of attacks on Upper Canada, bringing their superior numbers to bear, the Americans made do with a feint here and a feint there against a more agile opponent. Justifying his actions after the battle, Van Rensselaer wrote: "On the morning of the 12th, such was the pressure upon me from all quarters, that I became satisfied that my refusal to act might involve me in suspicion and the service in disgrace."[16]

For Van Rensselaer, the days leading up to his attack could not have been worse. Instead of a well-coordinated operation, the attack was to be made without all the available units being prepared to participate.

At 3:00 a.m. on October 13, three hundred U.S. regular soldiers boarded embarkation vessels and set out for the Canadian shore. Major General Van Rensselaer had put his cousin Solomon in command of these lead troops. To cover the U.S. crossing, two 18-pounders in Fort Grey, in the hills above Lewiston, and a mortar in the adjacent woods opened fire on the British positions across the river. Only thirteen vessels made the initial assault, which meant that too few troops were deployed to make the attack fully effective. Again, American disorganization was a factor. Thirty-nine vessels were

available not far away at Fort Schlosser, but they were not commandeered to give the first assault more punch.

The roar of the American guns alerted the defenders at Queenston
that an assault was underway. On duty for a fifth consecutive night,
Lieutenant George Ridout, a Canadian officer in the 3rd York Militia,
later wrote to his father that when he heard the gunfire, "I went down
to our battery from whence the view was truly tremendous, the darkness of the night, interrupted by the flash of the guns and small-arms."
Ridout could see the Americans struggling against the swift current
to make it to the Canadian shore. Three of the vessels were driven too
far downstream and headed back to the point of embarkation. The
other ten boats succeeded, however, in coming ashore upstream
from Queenston, as intended.

The 49th Grenadiers and the Canadian militiamen opened fire
on the Americans. Following a fierce engagement, the 160 soldiers in
the 13th U.S. Infantry, led by Captain John E. Wool, drove off the
defenders toward Queenston. Captain Wool and Colonel Van
Rensselaer suffered severe wounds in the firefight, but the Americans
were lodged on the Canadian side of the river. The wounded Van
Rensselaer was ferried back to the American shore. Wool carried on,
leading his men up the winding path to the summit of Queenston
Heights, 106 metres above. There the Americans drove off the British
gunners, who were directing the fire of their 18-pounder and mortar
at the U.S. embarkation point.

The initial bellowing of the American cannon warned Brock at
Fort George that the anticipated U.S. attack had commenced. He
mounted his horse and rode approximately one kilometre to the
scene of the attack. By the time Brock arrived, Captain Wool and his
men had reached the summit. Downstream from Queenston at
Hamilton's Point, where the whole invasion force was supposed to
have landed, four American vessels came ashore. There the soldiers
of the 49th's Light Company raked the U.S. force with a relentless
series of volleys. The members of the 49th had been repositioned
from the Heights as soon as the attack began, in order to meet the

Americans at the riverbank. In this they were successful. Only one American vessel escaped. The rest of the U.S. soldiers in this second offensive attack were killed or captured.

Twenty-one-year-old Lieutenant John Beverley Robinson of the 3rd York Militia later described the American survivors from the botched landing: "The road was lined with miserable wretches suffering from wounds of all descriptions and crawling to our houses for protection and comfort."[17] Robinson, later knighted as Sir John Robinson, went on after the war to enjoy a distinguished career in Upper Canada.*

At the summit, where the small American force under Captain Wool was installed, two companies of Canadian militia commanded by Brock's aide-de-camp, Lieutenant Colonel John Macdonell, counterattacked. The Canadians initially succeeded in forcing the Americans back. But U.S. reinforcements arrived from below, driving the militia back down the hill and in the process fatally wounding Macdonell.

Alarmed that the Americans were once more installed at the summit and regretting the earlier decision to move the Light Company from the Heights, Brock prepared a new attack. He assembled all the men he had available to him in the village. Riding on his horse, he led the men southward. Just before reaching the foot of the Heights, he shouted, "Take a breath, boys—you will need it in a few moments." Dismounting from his horse, Brock led his men up the hill.[18]

Outfitted in his scarlet uniform with gold epaulettes and the ornamental scarf that had been Tecumseh's present to him after Detroit, the general led his horse by the bridle. He had taken only a

---

* Born in Berthier, Lower Canada, in 1791, the son of a United Empire Loyalist, the infant Robinson was moved with his family to Kingston, Upper Canada, and then to York. As a child he was sent to Kingston to pursue his studies. When he was twelve years old, his family dispatched him to Cornwall, where he lived and studied with Reverend John Strachan. Later to be the first Anglican bishop of Toronto, Strachan was a staunch supporter of the British Empire. He became a key member of the Family Compact and a fierce opponent of American republicanism and the institution of slavery in the United States.

few steps when a ricocheting bullet hit the wrist of his sword arm. It was a slight wound and did not deter Brock, who waved his sword and urged his men forward.

As Brock was leading the charge to battle, a scout from Ohio saw the tall general in his resplendent scarlet, took aim, and felled him with a shot that tore through his left breast.[19] According to the account from George Jarvis, a fifteen-year-old gentleman volunteer in the 49th's Light Company who was close to Brock when he was hit, "Our gallant General fell on his left side, within a few feet of where I stood. Running up to him I enquired, 'Are you much hurt, Sir?' He placed his hand on his breast and made no reply and slowly sunk down."

A legendary account has it that, with his last breath, Brock uttered the words, "Push on, brave York volunteers," to rally the York militiamen. Another man who saw the general fall, militia private John Birney, recounted, "With the help of others, he was laid on the grass and the surgeon called out, but he was past human aid and never moved or spoke."[20]

Following the death of General Brock, the counterattack he had led against the Americans faltered. With about four hundred soldiers in place at the summit, the Americans fought off British assaults and managed to capture twenty-one soldiers, including the young George Jarvis. Abandoning Queenston Village by about 9:00 a.m., the British retreated to the north. Now in a position to cross the river unimpeded, the Americans managed to send reinforcements to the scene of the battle, and a 6-pounder along with them. Disorganization and lack of will hampered the American effort at this crucial moment. Boats were still in short supply and some of the U.S. troops wandered off to plunder the village, while others who wanted no more of the fight returned to the American shore.

With the Americans established on the Canadian shore and occupying the heights above the river, swift action could consolidate their position and give them the edge in the next phase of what remained a very fluid battle.

~

The British command shifted to Major General Roger Hale Sheaffe, who quickly mobilized his forces to drive the Americans from Canadian soil. He dispatched the 41st's Light Company, under the command of Captain William Derenzy, and about 160 Grand River warriors from Fort George, commanded by John Norton, William Kerr, and John Brant, in the direction of Queenston. The latter were a remarkable trio. John Norton, whose parents were Iroquoian Cherokee and Scottish, and who had spent his early years in Britain, was a fully accepted member of Mohawk society. William Kerr was an Indian Department officer and was married to Joseph Brant's daughter, Elizabeth. John Brant was the son of Joseph Brant.[21] This force was equipped with two 6-pounders and a 5.5-inch howitzer. Sheaffe left Fort George for Queenston. Behind him, taking the same route, were 140 men from the 41st Regiment and some militiamen, including the Corps of Artificers, also known as the "Company of Coloured Men," commanded by Captain Robert Runchey.[22]

While the British garnered their forces for an effective attack, the American commanders dithered. Without the counsel of his wounded cousin, Stephen Van Rensselaer was unsure what to do. At the onset of daylight, he ordered a massive artillery bombardment of Fort George and Newark from Fort Niagara. The rounds fired had been heated in a shot oven until they were nearly red-hot. The barrage soon had the courthouse, the jail, a brewery, and a number of homes in flames. The British managed to quell panic by bringing the fires quickly under control and launching their own artillery bombardment to silence the American guns. The dozen heavy guns at Fort George did not manage to knock out the American artillery but did succeed in reducing their volume of fire.

Having learned that the Americans had mounted to the Heights, Norton led his force into the woods, though half of them left, fearing for their families at Niagara. The remaining eighty warriors climbed the heights, using the forest to keep themselves concealed from enemy view. At about 11:00 a.m., they launched an assault on the American rearguard, quickly pushing the militiamen back to the main U.S. line. The Iroquois kept themselves low in the brush and were largely unaffected by the volleys the Americans fired at them. As was not unusual at this stage of the war, the inexperienced American soldiers often aimed too high.

The warriors soon charged out of the woods in a direct attack. This drew heavy return fire from the U.S. troops, and the Grand River men took some casualties and fell back. Norton's force managed to get to the south of the Americans and threaten their line, but the U.S. troops, under the command of Lieutenant Colonel Winfield Scott, counter-attacked and drove them back. Although this counterattack was partially successful, volleys from the warriors continued to harass Scott's troops, who were also subject to British artillery fire from below.

The fighting paused while Sheaffe led his 650 regulars and militia inland on a circular route up the Heights so that he would be in posi-tion to assault the enemy across flat ground. "Revenge the General!" the British shouted as they attacked the panicked Americans. Once Sheaffe charged, supported by the Iroquois on the flank, Scott's force collapsed. Having methodically mobilized his force and positioned them to the rear of the foe, Sheaffe had all but assured victory for the British side.

Aware of the vise closing in on his troops, Major General Van Rensselaer crossed the river to the Canadian side to hold a brief council with his officers. As he prepared to cross the river again to summon reinforcements, a number of panic-stricken American sol-diers stormed his vessel and shoved off. When they reached the U.S. side of the river, they fled.

Meanwhile, as the British regulars, Canadian militiamen, and native warriors closed in on the U.S. troops on Queenston Heights, a fierce firefight erupted. The Americans resisted, but some of their officers were quick to favour retreat. After a final stand, the remnants of the American force that had crossed the river in the early hours of October 13 had no choice but to lay down their weapons.[23]

It took some time to halt the mopping-up by British forces, which in places was degenerating into slaughter. Some of the U.S. troops threw down their arms and ran for the boats on the shore, while others jumped off the cliff. Three times, the Americans sent forward men carrying a flag of truce in a desperate bid to get the message across that the fight was over. Some U.S. soldiers dove into the swift current of the Niagara River to try to swim to the other side as British troops and native warriors kept up a sporadic fire. At last, around 4:00 p.m., a British bugle call, repeated a number of times, stopped the shooting. The victorious British took a cache of American muskets and ammunition, as well as a 6-pounder, and sent a captured stand of New York militia colours to Britain to celebrate the triumph at Queenston.

Just two months after the fall of Fort Detroit, the battle along the Niagara River dealt a further blow to the American cause, not least to American national pride. Although no fully accurate numbers were available on the American side, Major General Van Rensselaer reported to Major General Dearborn that 60 U.S. soldiers died and 170 were wounded. During the following week, between eight hundred and one thousand Americans deserted their units across the river in New York.

Sheaffe's force suffered nineteen casualties, including five warriors. Eighty-five were wounded; among those, between seven and nine were warriors from Grand River.[24] In his dispatches, Sheaffe singled out the Iroquois, John Norton in particular, stating that they merited "the highest praise for their good order and spirit."[25] Later, as civil and military leader of Upper Canada, Sheaffe bestowed on Norton the rank of "Captain of the Confederate Indians," the same rank held by Joseph Brant during the American Revolutionary War.[26] Following the Battle of Queenston Heights, most of the Six Nations warriors returned to Grand River. Norton and a small party stayed at Niagara until the end of 1812. During this time, the Americans tried several attacks that came to nothing.[27]

Taken prisoner along with the other Americans at Queenston, Winfield Scott and the regulars were marched to Lower Canada, while the militiamen were released. A year later, Scott was sent back to the United States in a prisoner exchange. Known as "Old Fuss and Feathers," Scott rose to hold the position of commanding general of the United States Army for twenty years, longer than any other officer to hold the rank. After the War of 1812, he wreaked havoc on the Cherokee Nation in 1836, during the administration of President Andrew Jackson. This exercise in ethnic cleansing became known as the Trail of Tears. During the Mexican War of 1846–48, Scott commanded the southern arm of the two U.S. armies. At the end of that conflict, he was appointed military commander of Mexico City. Following an unsuccessful run for the U.S. presidency in 1852, Scott stayed on as general-in-chief of the U.S. Army. He held that position at the beginning of the Civil War in 1861, and devised the Anaconda Plan to defeat the Confederacy, a strategy that would be used by succeeding commanders of the U.S. Army. Finally, in November 1861, suffering from gout and rheumatism, weighing over three hundred pounds, and unable to mount his horse, Scott resigned his military office.

The day after his defeat, Van Rensselaer, with an eye on his future career, sent a lengthy letter from his headquarters at Lewiston to General Dearborn, setting out the best possible case for himself. He explained that on October 5 he had written to General Smyth "requesting an interview with him . . . for the purpose of conferring on the subject of future operations." By October 10, he had learned that "General Smyth had not yet then agreed upon any day for the consultation." The following day, Van Rensselaer wrote, "Orders were . . . sent to General Smyth to send down from Buffalo such detachment from his brigade as existing circumstances in that vicinity might warrant." Following his extensive review of the course of the battle, which he claimed had resulted in victory for American arms until the very end, he concluded, "The enemy succeeded in repossessing their battery, and gaining advantage on every side. The brave men who had gained the victory, exhausted of strength and ammunition, and grieved at the unpardonable neglect of their fellow-soldiers gave up the conflict . . . I can only add, that the victory was really won, but lost for the want of a small reinforcement; one-third part of the idle men might have saved all."[28] But for lack of cooperation with Smyth and the consequent fail- ure to maintain enough troops to finish the job, the day would have been Van Rensselaer's, according to his own account.

Brock had celebrated his forty-third birthday a week before he rushed to Queenston to counter the American thrust across the Niagara. The body of the slain general lay in state prior to his inter- ment at Fort George alongside Lieutenant Colonel John Macdonell, his aide-de-camp. On October 16, three days after the battle, a funeral procession conveyed the bodies of Brock and Macdonell from Government House to Fort George, where the caskets were lowered into graves prepared at the northeastern corner of the fortress. Lining the route of the procession were British soldiers, Canadian militiamen, and native warriors. In three salvos, the British fired a twenty-one-gun salute. The American garrison across the river at Fort Niagara fired its own salute out of respect for the fallen general. More than five thou- sand people were present for the funeral, a striking number considering the small population of Upper Canada in 1812.

The *Quebec Gazette* described the loss of General Brock as a "public calamity." In Montreal, a newspaper warned darkly that the Americans "have created a hatred which panteth for revenge."[29]

Brock was knighted in recognition of his leadership in the cap- ture of Detroit. However, the news that he had been bestowed such an honour did not reach Fort George until a few days after he was killed. Thus he is known today as Sir Isaac Brock, though he himself was never aware that he bore the title.

Brock never set out to make himself a Canadian hero, but that is what he became. Along with Tecumseh, he changed the course of the history of the British colonies. The victories at Detroit and Queenston Heights refuted the American conceit that the capture of Canada would require no great military effort. While the populations of the Canadas would have to endure further invasions and periods of occupation in some regions until the end of the war, Canada's connection to the British Empire was much more durable than the War Hawks had anticipated. That connection would endure, and out of it a new transcontinental country would emerge.

Chapter 12

York in Flames

DETROIT AND QUEENSTON HEIGHTS threw Washington into turmoil. The Americans had started the war confident that their armies could seize Canada, or a large enough piece of Canadian territory that the British would be forced to the bargaining table and Tecumseh's native confederacy would be pushed out of the war.

The Madison administration had staked its political fortunes on the war. The president and his supporters could not allow two unexpected defeats to determine the outcome. Remaining firm in his commitment to the war, Madison led the United States through a political exercise that had been hitherto unknown in the history of the world, a democratic wartime election. It was a significant test of the durability of the United States Constitution, which had been drafted a quarter of a century before.

A month before the U.S. declared war on Great Britain in June 1812, a Democratic-Republican congressional nominating caucus picked Madison as its presidential candidate. A few days later, a caucus of dissident Democratic-Republicans chose DeWitt Clinton, the mayor of New York City and the lieutenant-governor of New York, as its standard-bearer. In September, a Federalist nominating caucus, meeting in New York City, decided after much wrangling to endorse Clinton for the presidency, seeing him as their best chance to defeat Madison.

During the election campaign, Clinton presented himself as an anti-war candidate in the Northeast, the region most opposed to the war, and as a pro-war candidate in the South and West, the regions where the war was popular. Madison carried eleven states, winning 128 electoral votes, while Clinton carried seven states. With the exception of Vermont, Clinton took all of New England, and prevailed in New York, New Jersey, and Delaware, winning a total of 89 electoral votes.

The military disasters at Detroit and Queenston Heights forced the Americans to rethink their approach to the war. In November 1812, from his estate at Monticello, former president Thomas Jefferson wrote a brief letter to President Madison, regretting that commanders in the field had sold Americans short. "Two of them have cost us a great many men," he commented ruefully. "We can tell from his plumage whether a cock is dunghill or game. But with us, cowardice and courage wear the same plume. Hull will, of course, be shot for cowardice and treachery. And will not Van Rensselaer be broke for cowardice and capacity?"

On a more hopeful note, he reckoned that Dearborn and Harrison could fare better. They, at least, would have "no longer a Brock to encounter." He concluded acidly, "If we could but get Canada to Trois rivieres [sic] in our hands we should have a set off against spoliations to be treated of, and in the mean time separate the Indians from them and set the friendly to attack the hostile part with our aid."[1] No longer in office, Jefferson understood just how lethal the combination of Brock and Tecumseh had been to the initial war plans of the United States.

In Washington, someone had to pay the price for the calamitous course of the war. In mid-December 1812, Secretary of War William Eustis's offer to resign was swiftly accepted by President Madison. To temporarily fill the gap, Madison added the position of acting secretary of war to James Monroe's duties as secretary of state. John Armstrong Jr. soon replaced Monroe as the secretary of war. As was the case with so many of the appointments made by the Madison administration in the early phase of the war, Armstrong, who had served in the militia during the American Revolutionary War, was widely distrusted in political circles. With his reputation for intrigue, Armstrong's nomination as secretary of war was confirmed by the narrow margin of 18 to 15 in the U.S. Senate.[2] With a new secretary of war in place, the administration could hope for a favourable turn in American military fortunes.

The year 1812 sputtered to its end with failed and relatively minor U.S. attempts to return to the offensive along the Niagara Frontier and an effort to launch an offensive toward Montreal that went nowhere. In December 1812, there was some speculation in the American press that Napoleon Bonaparte, whose Grande Armée had invaded Russia in June, was likely dictating peace terms in Moscow.[3] In fact, despite having suffered huge casualties in the Battle of Borodino near Moscow in September, Czar Alexander I refused to capitulate. The overstretched French army faced a reinvigorated Russian force and began a disastrous retreat westward. In December, Napoleon abandoned his ravaged army and rushed back to Paris to secure his political position at home. Although much fighting still lay ahead in Europe, Napoleon's Russian disaster was very good news for the British, who would now be able to send additional troops to fight the Americans. For that reason, Napoleon's calamities dealt a blow to the United States.

While the Americans were drawing up plans during the winter of 1813 for the war campaign that would begin in the spring of 1813, there was action on the diplomatic front. On February 24, 1813, news reached Washington that the Russian government was offering to mediate an end to the war between the Americans and the British. In fact, the Russian effort had been underway for a number of months, but President Madison and Secretary of State Monroe were unaware of this because of slow communications. On March 8, Count Andrei Daschkov, the Russian minister to the United States, formally transmitted the offer to Monroe. Three days later, Monroe accepted the initiative, without consulting Congress.[4] The president then appointed commissioners to negotiate with the British under the mediation of the Russians. The commissioners were Senator James A. Bayard, Treasury Secretary Albert Gallatin, and John Quincy Adams, who was then serving as the American minister to Russia.

The Madison administration was well aware that any initiative to end the conflict could take a very long time to yield results. In the meantime, Secretary of War John Armstrong crafted a military strategy with a multi-pronged attack on Upper Canada as its centrepiece. American military ambitions faced south as well as north. In February 1813, the U.S. Congress secretly approved the occupation of the Spanish territory of West Florida, east of New Orleans. On April 15, in a bloodless operation, the Americans seized Mobile and Fort Charlotte, on the Gulf of Mexico. West Florida turned out to be the only permanent acquisition of territory by the United States during the War of 1812, and there the foe was Spain, not Britain.

Turning to the more important northern front, on February 10, 1813, Secretary Armstrong sent a letter to Major General Henry Dearborn, commander of the U.S. Army's Northern Department, outlining the president's orders, "which you will immediately institute against Upper Canada." Seven thousand troops were to be assembled for the attacks, just over four thousand of them at Sackets Harbor and three thousand in the vicinity of Buffalo.[5]

The first target was Kingston. The U.S. fleet on Lake Ontario was to transport the soldiers from Sackets Harbor to Kingston, whose "garrison and the British ships wintering in the harbor of that place, will be the first object." The second object of the campaign was "York, the stores collected and the two frigates building there." The posts on the Upper Canadian bank of the Niagara River, "Forts George and Erie, and their dependencies," were to be the third object, and for its attainment there was to be "co-operation between the two corps." The assaults were to begin with the opening of Lake Ontario to vessels, "which usually takes place about the first of April."[6]

An essential part of the U.S. plan was to gain control of Lakes Ontario and Erie. Building local fleets on both lakes would allow the Americans to move men and supplies by water, which was much more manageable than travel by land — there were few roads, and the ones that existed were of poor quality. U.S. fleets could tie up the British in their ports. A few weeks after the fall of Detroit, U.S. Secretary of the Navy Paul Hamilton chose Isaac Chauncey, a highly experienced forty-year-old naval captain, "to assume command of the naval force on Lakes Erie and Ontario, and to use every exertion to obtain control of them this fall."[7]

Born in Connecticut in 1772, Chauncey had run away to sea at the age of twelve, and since then ships had been his life. He commanded vessels for John Jacob Astor's fur trade empire when he was only nineteen. In 1798, he was commissioned as a lieutenant in the newly established U.S. Navy. As the executive officer on the USS *President* and then on the USS *Chesapeake,* he saw action during the American war against the Barbary pirates, North African pirates whom the United States fought between 1801 and 1805 to halt attacks on American merchant vessels. In addition to his naval experience, Chauncey was a skilled shipbuilder, a talent that Hamilton was counting on when he picked him for the task on the Great Lakes.[8]

As soon as Chauncey arrived at Sackets Harbor in mid-November 1812, he took vigorous control of the U.S. fleet there and reported to Hamilton that his ships had driven British vessels into harbours on Lake Ontario. "We have now the command of the lake," Chauncey wrote, "and that we can transport troops and stores to any part of it without any risk of an attack from the enemy."[9]

The Americans soon dropped the idea of beginning their assault on Upper Canada at Kingston. Armstrong received reports from General Dearborn that the British had been moving companies of the 1st Royal Scots, the 8th Regiment, and the Voltigeurs Canadiens west to Kingston. Armstrong had reckoned the British force at Kingston at no more than two thousand men. Dearborn convinced him that the enemy had concentrated six or seven thousand men, three thousand of whom were British regulars, at the strongpoint at the eastern end of Lake Ontario. The general feared that the British could launch an assault on the American post at Sackets Harbor, which lay on the eastern shore of Lake Ontario just across from Kingston. Instead, the Americans decided to attack York first.[10]

Apart from its symbolic significance as the capital of Upper Canada, York was not of much military value. The only real prize was the warship *Sir Isaac Brock*, which was being slowly and rather ineffectually built, in part from the remains of the dismantled *Duke of Gloucester*, which had been damaged in a naval engagement against a U.S. ship the previous July.

Sir Roger Sheaffe, the general who had replaced Brock at Queenston, commanded the British forces at York. The seven hundred men at his disposal comprised a company of the Glengarry Light Infantry Fencibles, a company-sized unit of the Royal Newfoundland Regiment, the 3rd York Regiment of Militia, and about fifty Mississauga and Chippewa warriors. In addition, there were three hundred dockyard workers.[11]

York's defences were only partially developed, with Fort York still under construction. At the time of the attack, two 12-pounders were mounted in the fort. Sentries on the Scarborough Bluffs, located in what is now the east end of Toronto, sighted a fleet of fifteen American vessels, carrying about two thousand U.S. regular troops, close to the Lake Ontario shore. On the evening of April 26, 1813, the sentries flashed the warning by semaphore that York was about to be attacked.

Adverse weather delayed the American landing until the morning of April 27, by which time a strong east wind had carried the U.S. force more than ten kilometres to the west, placing them adjacent to a point now called Sunnyside, in the west end of Toronto. The landing area was heavily wooded but its long beach made it an ideal place to come ashore.

The best chance for the British to parry the attack was to meet the invaders at the water's edge. There they could take them out in detail and prevent them from concentrating and taking advantage of their superior numbers. But Sheaffe sent only about sixty Glengarry Fencibles and about twenty-five native warriors to counter the Americans at the beach. Some of his forces arrived after the main landing had been carried out, and some of his men were posted uselessly farther back. Later, Sheaffe was heavily criticized for his tepid initial response to the attack.[12]

Leading the Americans into combat was Brigadier General Zebulon Montgomery Pike, a career soldier who had been named after his father, a veteran of the War of Independence. Earlier in his career, the young Pike had been put in charge of expeditions to explore the source of the Mississippi River, and later to attempt to locate the headwaters of the Arkansas and Red Rivers in the territory acquired by the United States in the Louisiana Purchase. During this latter exploration, Pike and his party came upon a great mountain range that soared above the plains. Decades later, the grand peak that had fascinated the young officer was named Pike's Peak.

The night before setting out on the expedition to attack York, Pike wrote to his father, "I embark tomorrow in the fleet, at Sackett's [sic] Harbor, at the head of a column of 1,500 choice troops, on a secret expedition. Should I be the happy mortal destined to turn the scale of war, will you not rejoice, oh my father? May heaven be propitious, and smile on the cause of my country. But if we are destined to fall, may my fall be like Wolfe's — to sleep in the arms of victory."[13]

Pike's troops, to whom he had lectured that the inhabitants of Canada were innocent victims of the war and that any looting of their belongings would be punishable by death, came ashore following the landing of a party of U.S. riflemen. Briefly, a British counterattack pushed the Americans back. But the U.S. troops used their greater numbers to regain the initiative. As the British retreated, some of the native warriors abandoned the fight. Pike's three companies pushed the 8th's Grenadier Company back in the direction of Fort York.

Although historians differ about the size of the American expeditionary force, it likely numbered about two thousand soldiers, which, when added to the crews of the vessels, brought the aggregate force to just under 2,800 men.[14] Along for the attack was General Dearborn, the top U.S. soldier in this theatre of war.

The defenders of Fort York mounted a half-hearted defence, soon giving up the fight there and running for cover at nearby Government House, General Sheaffe's dwelling. Sheaffe huddled with his senior officers and concluded that he could not hold York. He decided to retreat to Kingston. The British had lost sixty-two men, and ninety-four were wounded. Before pulling the British regulars out of York, Sheaffe set fire to the warship *Sir Isaac Brock* to prevent it from falling into the hands of the enemy. In the aftermath of the battle, the inhabitants of York complained bitterly that Sheaffe had failed to inspire the troops to defend the town. Although York was not populous, it was the provincial capital, already inhabited by influential men who were beginning to develop the town that would grow into a Canadian metropolis.

Although Sheaffe had decided to withdraw from York, the Union Jack still flew above the fort, signalling that the fight was not yet over. General Pike was sitting on a stump nearby, questioning a wounded British sergeant who had been captured in the woods, when a huge explosion erupted from the remains of the fort.[15] The retreating British had set alight the underground powder magazine, which contained two hundred barrels of gunpowder and shot. The stone structure blew apart, catapulting chunks of rock into the air. Pike's prisoner died instantly. Bending forward to protect himself, the general was struck by a boulder. In a letter to his wife, U.S. General George Howard reported that Pike had been hit "on the forehead [with a blow] that Stamped him for the Grave."[16]

Pike was carried to the lake and taken on board the USS *Madison*. In great agony and uttering not a word of complaint, the brigadier general was laid down with his head on a captured Union Jack, the fruit of the day's victory, and that is where he died.[17]

Next to the fallen general, Dr. William Beaumont, the expedition's surgeon, "waded in blood cutting off arms, legs and trepanning [drilling holes in skulls to relieve excruciating pressure]," as he later recalled. "My God!" he wrote after forty-eight hours of non-stop ministering to the maimed. "Who can think of the shocking scene where his fellow creatures lye [sic] mashed & mangled in every part, with a leg — an arm — a head, or a body ground to pieces without having his heart pierced with the acutest sensibility & his blood chilled in his veins."[18]

Following the explosion, a young boy named Patrick Finan later recounted the arrival of the wounded at the hospital: "One man in particular presented an awful spectacle: he was brought in a wheel-barrow, and from his appearance I should be inclined to suppose that almost every bone in his body was broken; he was lying in a power-less heap, shaking with every motion of the barrow from which his legs hung dangling down, as if only connected with his body by the skin while his cries and groans were of the most heart rending description!"[19] The explosion, and the subsequent death of General Pike, infuriated the Americans, who saw the action as an act of treachery.*[20]

One resident of York needed no weapons to express his wrath to the Americans for their behaviour during their occupation of the town. Reverend John Strachan was already becoming a pillar of the Upper Canadian establishment. Born in Aberdeen, Scotland, in 1778, he was the youngest of six children; their father was a quarry worker. Strachan emigrated to Kingston in Upper Canada in 1799. On the eve of the War of 1812, he moved to York, where he became the rector of St. James Cathedral and headmaster of the Home District Grammar School.

In a lengthy letter to his friend Dr. James Brown in St. Andrews, Scotland, Strachan described in detail his experience during the

---

* The historian Gilbert Auchinleck, who leaned strongly to the British side in his mid-nineteenth-century history of the war, wrote that "a vast amount of nonsense, relative to this affair, has been penned by American historians who do not seem to reflect that this was an invading force, and that the mine has always been a legitimate mode either of attack or defence."

American occupation of the town. He started writing the letter on April 26, on the eve of the attack, and did not complete it until June 14, nearly six weeks after the American invaders had departed.

Strachan got up at 4:00 a.m. on April 27, the morning of the American attack, sighted the U.S. ships, mounted his horse, and rode to the location of the British garrison. From there he advanced toward the point, about three kilometres away, where the ships were approaching the shore. He counted fourteen vessels, and through a spyglass he could see that their decks were "thickly covered with troops — from which I infer, that they are come prepared to land in great force."

His letter goes on to excoriate the lacklustre, poorly planned defence of the town. Hearing two explosions, the second — the detonation of the powder magazine — vaster than the first, Strachan went home to "find that Mrs. Strachan had been terrified by the explosion" and had "run with the children to one of the Neighbours."

After sending his wife to the home of a friend a short distance out of town, Strachan headed back toward the British garrison, where he came upon General Sheaffe and his troops, holed up in a ravine. Members of the militia were scattering, and the general had decided to retreat with the regulars to Kingston. Strachan told the general that he was willing to help negotiate "the best possible conditions . . . for the town" with the enemy.

Over the next few days, Strachan devoted his efforts to trying to win the release of the militiamen being held prisoner, and at every opportunity he complained to the American commanders about the plunder and destruction being unleashed in York by U.S. troops. He demanded to be taken aboard the principal U.S. ship to discuss the terms of surrender directly with General Dearborn. As it happened, he met the U.S. general, who was clearly in a furious state of mind, just as he was coming ashore. Strachan presented Dearborn with a copy of the articles of capitulation, requested "to know when he will parole the officers & men," and demanded "leave to take away our sick & wounded." According to Strachan, Dearborn read the articles "without deigning an answer." "He treats me with great harshness," he wrote, and "tells me . . . not to follow him as he had business of much more importance to attend to."

Strachan then turned his attention to Commodore Chauncey and accused the Americans of holding up their signature of the capitulation "to give the riflemen time to plunder." The officers and men in the Canadian militia were eventually released on their own parole. But then U.S. troops ransacked the church and set fire to the provincial parliament and Government House. The invaders took with them provisions and military supplies and 2,500 pounds from the treasury. Although they did not manage to capture the British ship *Brock*, they did take the dismantled parts of the *Duke of Gloucester*. The invaders also carried off books from the library. Chauncey returned most of the books, some of them later that year and some after the war. The government mace, also taken by the looters, was not returned until 1934.[21] Strachan wrote that when he confronted Dearborn with the facts of these depredations, the general was "greatly embarrassed."

Penelope Beikie, a York resident, recalled that "every house they found deserted was completely sacked." Another resident, Ely Playter, wrote that the "Town thronged with the Yankees, many busy getting off the public stores. The Council office with every window broke & pillaged of every thing that it contained. The Government building, the Block House and the building adjacent all burned to ashes."[22] Local York residents also participated in the looting.

Strachan, furious at the British commanders for their failure to defend York and Upper Canada with greater vigour, concluded his letter with the retort that, "If this country" were to fall, "Sir Geo Prevost & he only is to blame."[23]

General Prevost, in his report to London on the Battle of York, made it clear that the military consequences would be serious. "The ordnance, ammunition and other stores for the service on Lake Erie," he wrote, "were either destroyed or fell into enemy hands when York was taken."[24]

Sheaffe was not a target of criticism in Prevost's report to London, but Prevost showed his displeasure by transferring him to Montreal within a few weeks of the fall of York. Baron Francis de Rottenburg replaced Sheaffe as commander-in-chief and administrator of Upper Canada.[25] Again Strachan's voice, along with those of six other prominent residents of York, was heard in a stinging rebuke they wrote of Sheaffe's conduct during the battle. Their letter to Prevost played a role in the dismissal of Sheaffe, who was recalled to Britain in November 1813.

The Americans did not plan a lengthy occupation of York. They intended to leave the despoiled capital to carry out the next in their series of attacks — on Fort George at Niagara.

Just after the fall of York, Sir James Yeo arrived at Quebec. A former commander of the frigate *Southampton*, Yeo had been appointed commodore and commander-in-chief of British naval forces in the Canadas. He set out at once for Kingston, where he energetically undertook the task of fitting out and manning British ships to take on the Americans on Lakes Ontario and Erie.[26]

While the Americans were fully engaged with their offensive against York and then Fort George, the British seized the chance to carry out an attack of their own against the U.S. base at Sackets Harbor. General Prevost oversaw the operation in conjunction with Yeo, who ran the naval side of the affair. On May 29, the British landed 750 soldiers west of Sackets Harbor. From there, they intended to go after the U.S. force at Fort Tompkins after laying waste the shipyard. The plan was thwarted, however, by a quick-thinking brigadier general in the New York State Militia. Jacob Brown swiftly assembled four hundred U.S. regulars and five hundred militiamen, spreading them out in the forest adjacent to the British beachhead. From there, the Americans poured a withering fire on the attackers, forcing them to retreat to their ships. Prevost's command to withdraw the British forces brought considerable criticism down on him for being excessively cautious.[27] Yeo, who opposed breaking off the attack, disapproved of Prevost's decision to retreat. The two men loathed each other ever after.[28]

The American victory was soured, however, by an event behind the lines. Believing that the British attack was going to succeed, a lieutenant in the U.S. Navy ordered the demolition of the naval stores and provisions that had been captured at York.[29]

While the British attacked Sackets Harbor, the Americans were busy at the other end of the lake. A fierce gale held up the departure of the ships under Chauncey's command from York. When his schooners did set sail, there were so many U.S. soldiers on board that only half of them could get below decks to seek shelter from the tempest. The bedraggled American force arrived off Fort George on May 8.[30]

Three weeks were consumed by the Americans' sending their wounded back to Sackets Harbor and bringing reinforcements forward to join in the assault on Fort George.[31] On May 27, General Winfield Scott, who had been released in a prisoner exchange following his capture at Queenston Heights, led four hundred Americans onto the Canadian shore of the Niagara River just west of Fort George, hoping to succeed where Van Rensselaer had failed the previous October. Several thousand U.S. troops on the American shore were waiting to follow up the initial foray.

Brigadier General John Vincent was in command of a force of about 1,100 British regulars and Canadian militia inside Fort George. He had a further 750 regulars and 200 militiamen on the ground along the Niagara River from Fort George to Fort Erie. Vincent's attempt to contain the American beachhead failed when fire from Chauncey's vessels drove back his men. That retreat sealed the fate of Fort George, which fell into American hands following demolition of the powder in the fort's magazines.[32] From there the British retreated upriver toward Fort Erie, which also fell to U.S. forces.

Once the Americans were installed on the Canadian shore of the Niagara Frontier, parties of officers and soldiers visited local farms to carry out a security check on the male residents. Those who seemed peaceably inclined were let off with a simple parole, and those who seemed unhappy with the American presence were warned that at the first sign of opposition they would be transported across the Niagara River and jailed.³³

Once Scott's force had taken Fort George, Chauncey sailed his fleet away from the western end of Lake Ontario to return to Sackets Harbor, to secure that base against further British attacks from Kingston. While General Prevost was lambasted for his weak effort at Sackets Harbor, his failed attack did have the effect of drawing Chauncey away from the fighting near Niagara. Now it was the turn of the British to bring their naval assets into the fight.

With U.S. Commodore Isaac Chauncey's Lake Ontario fleet back in Sackets Harbor, the British fleet sailed up the lake from Kingston to bring pressure to bear on the U.S. forces on the western shore of Lake Ontario. Commodore Yeo's ships carried close to 220 British regulars of the 8th Regiment, as well as provisions and ammunition to reinforce and outfit Brigadier General John Vincent's soldiers stationed at Burlington.³⁴

On June 5, 1813, after reconnoitering the American position at nearby Stoney Creek, Lieutenant Colonel John Harvey alerted Vincent that, "the Enemy having dared to pursue this Division by moving a Corps of 3,500 Men with 4 Field Guns and 150 Cavalry to Stoney Creek," the conditions were right for the British to "make a forward movement for the purpose of beating up this encampment." Harvey informed Vincent that the Americans had posted few sentries, and those few were badly placed.

Vincent concurred with the proposed attack and outfitted Harvey with seven hundred regulars of the 8th and 49th Regiments, close to half his force. The surprise nighttime attack began well for the British, who had learned the American password and used it to approach and bayonet the sentries, and then to burst into the camp. U.S. Brigadier General William H. Winder and a colleague of the same rank, John Chandler, were taken prisoner. General Dearborn had dispatched the two inexperienced generals, who had been appointed to their rank for political rather than military reasons, to the fight. At dawn Harvey ordered his men to retire into the woods. In addition to capturing the two brigadier generals, he came away with one hundred additional prisoners of all ranks, three cannon, and a brass howitzer.[35]

Following the fight at Stoney Creek, U.S. Colonel James Burn ordered his troops to fall back to their former position at Forty Mile Creek. But the next day, that fort was bombarded by Sir James Yeo's naval squadron, which intercepted a large shipment of supplies being transported from Niagara. The Americans were forced to fall back to Fort George.

Vincent advanced with his troops to Forty Mile Creek. There, in his words, he hoped to "give encouragement to the Militia and Yeomanry of the Country who are everywhere rising upon the fugitive Americans, making them Prisoners & withholding all Supplies from them and lastly (and perhaps chiefly) for the purpose of sparing the resources of the Country in our rear and drawing the Supplies of the Army as long as possible from the Country immediately in the Enemy's possession."[36]

In June 1813, the Americans suffered one more misfortune in Niagara. Under the command of Lieutenant Colonel C. G. Boerstler, a U.S. force set out to launch a surprise attack on the advance post of Brigadier General Vincent's troops near Beaver Dams. News of the planned American attack was conveyed to the British in one of the most celebrated incidents of the war. Laura Secord, a Queenston housewife, overheard loose talk among the Americans about the coming assault. At dawn on June 22, she began her journey on foot to alert the British. While the precise route she took and the time of her arrival at Beaver Dams are not established, she did arrive sometime that evening and conveyed her intelligence to Lieutenant James Fitzgibbon, who commanded one company of the 49th Foot.

While Secord's warning did not provide the Americans' timetable and detailed plan of attack, it alerted the lieutenant that the enemy was coming. At midday on June 23, an American force set out for Beaver Dams, numbering 575 cavalry and infantry and outfitted with two field guns. The next morning, native scouts sighted the U.S. troops and reported their position to Captain Dominique Ducharme of the province's Indian Department. About nine o'clock that evening, three hundred Caughnawaga warriors, under Ducharme's command, assaulted the rear of the U.S. force. One hundred Mohawk warriors under the direction of Captain William Kerr reinforced the attack. During a three-hour fight, the Americans fired uncertainly into the woods, and eventually their morale collapsed. The unnerving sound of war whoops in the woods drove them to the point of surrender. Afraid to give up to the warriors, they finally laid down their arms when Lieutenant Fitzgibbon arrived with fifty men from the 49th Regiment. Fitzgibbon had been alerted by a messenger from Ducharme. "Not a shot was fired on our side by any but the Indians," Fitzgibbon reported. "They beat the American detachment into a state of terror, and the only share I can claim is taking advantage of a favourable moment to offer them protection from the tomahawk and the scalping knife." It seems that Ducharme would have called on the Americans to surrender earlier, except for the fact that he did not speak fluent English.[37] At Beaver Dams, the Iroquois inflicted a major defeat on the Americans with the help of very few white troops. It was the most significant victory won by the Six Nations during the war.[38]

With the fighting centred between Burlington and Niagara, the Americans took advantage of the paltry number of British defenders at York to carry out a second assault there. On July 31, 1813, Captain Chauncey's squadron landed a small force of sailors and soldiers. Virtually unopposed, they destroyed provisions, captured five cannon and eleven boats, and proceeded to burn the British barracks and public warehouses. But they were unable to sustain their position in York and once again abandoned the capital of Upper Canada.

The course of the war on Lake Ontario and along the Niagara Frontier during these months was tit-for-tat, with both the Americans and the British claiming victory in various battles. Within a few months, decisive events farther west would have fateful consequences for Tecumseh and the native confederacy.

Chapter 13

Tecumseh's Last Days

FOR TECUMSEH AND THE NATIVE confederacy, 1813 was a tragic year. The essential fight took place where it always had, on the edge of the Ohio country, in what for the Americans was the northwest theatre of war. It was on this terrain that the struggle to regain native land from the Americans would ultimately be won or lost. Brock's death meant that Tecumseh would no longer have a British partner who saw the war the way he did, with native objectives built into the strategy.

Deadly combat in the west began in January 1813, when the opposing armies could move their forces back and forth across the frozen Detroit River. William Henry Harrison, in command of U.S. forces in the Northwest after replacing the disgraced General Hull, prepared to launch an assault to retake both Detroit and Amherstburg, across the river in Upper Canada. He divided his force, sending Brigadier General James Winchester, a veteran of the Maryland Militia during the Revolutionary War, north from the Maumee River, which flows into Lake Erie from the south. Winchester dispatched Colonel William Lewis with a strong contingent to attack Canadian militia and native warriors at Frenchtown (the present-day city of Monroe, Michigan, forty kilometres south of Fort Detroit), on the River Raisin. The first skirmish, known as the First Battle of the River Raisin, took place on January 18. Lewis's force charged across the frozen river and quickly drove back a combined force of British soldiers and native warriors, clearing Frenchtown of the enemy.

Harrison was pleased with this initial success. Even though he feared a British counterattack, he ordered Winchester and Lewis, who had joined the force at Frenchtown, to hold fast to the territory.

Brock's successor in the southwestern corner of Upper Canada was Major General Henry Procter, a career officer who had served in the British army from the age of eighteen. Contemporaries regarded him as a man of limited ability who tended to play things by the book. Procter had been named governor of Michigan following the triumph of Brock and Tecumseh at Detroit. He kept his headquarters at Fort Malden, however, which was a more defensible position in the event of a new American offensive.

When Procter learned about the British defeat at Frenchtown, he acted swiftly. From the Canadian shore, he led a force of six hundred British regulars and Newfoundland militia, along with eight hundred native warriors from the Shawnee, Potawatomi, Ottawa, Chippewa, Delaware, Miami, Winnebago, Muscogee, Sauk, and Fox tribes, across the frozen Detroit River. Although Tecumseh was in the area and was the pre-eminent leader among the native allies of the British, he was not present for the ensuing battle.

On January 21, Procter's combined force halted its advance about eight kilometres north of the River Raisin to organize for the coming fight. In the darkness before sunrise, the soldiers and warriors sneaked up to the American camp, which was poorly guarded, and unleashed a devastating attack. General Winchester was quickly captured by warriors and handed over to the British. While the Americans held out in some places for a time, they were eventually defeated and forced to surrender across the battlefield. Dozens of Americans were shot down; warriors tomahawked many of them as they tried to surrender. Others tried to flee in their stocking feet across the snow. Over four hundred U.S. troops died in the fight, and five hundred others were taken prisoner, having been ordered by General Winchester to surrender. The last American holdouts very reluctantly laid down their weapons on condition that their wounded would be protected. Members of the Kentucky Rifle Regiment, who had held out the longest, were in tears, cursing their commander, as the British soldiers collected the arms they had abandoned. The British lost 182 soldiers and 100 warriors in the fight.

Fearing an attack by Harrison's troops in the south, Procter decided to pull his troops back to Fort Malden, a short trek away across the frozen Detroit River. He marched the able-bodied American prisoners with him. The wounded Americans were housed in wooden buildings, awaiting the arrival of sleds to take them to the British fort. The morning after the battle, a number of native warriors — not those who had fought alongside the British — set the buildings on fire and murdered the wounded U.S. troops as they tried to flee. Some of the Americans who were marched north proved to be too badly wounded to keep up and were left behind to be murdered. Between thirty and one hundred Americans were slaughtered in what became known as the River Raisin Massacre. For miles along the route to the north, the bodies and bones of the dead lay strewn. The heads of a few had been severed and mounted on a picket fence not far from Detroit as a warning to other Americans. So as not to offend their native allies, the British left the heads in place for many days, as the wintry weather froze them in hideous grimaces.

The massacre, mostly of men from Kentucky, provoked fury among Americans, especially in the victims' home state. Later recruiting efforts among Kentuckians were fuelled by the rallying cry "Remember the Raisin."*

Following the disaster, Harrison reorganized his army and undertook the construction of Fort Meigs, in northwestern Ohio (present-day Perrysburg) on the Maumee River, near the southwest corner of Lake

---

* The Battles of the River Raisin are commemorated in annual re-enactments in Monroe, Michigan. The U.S. National Park Service operates the River Raisin National Battlefield Park along with an interpretive centre.

Erie. Shrewdly, he positioned the fort on a height of land overlooking the rapids. British vessels could make it upriver only to the edge of the rapids. On the other side of the river were the decaying remnants of Fort Miami, a long-abandoned British post near the site of the Battle of Fallen Timbers.

Tecumseh understood just how vital the bloody combat in this small area had become. The war to re-establish native control of lands would be won or lost here, and that was the war to which Tecumseh was committed. Unless Fort Meigs could be captured by Tecumseh and Procter, Harrison would use it as a base to build his reserves in the coming months and the fort could serve as a springboard for an assault on Upper Canada. Tecumseh pressured General Procter to undertake a joint native–British assault on Fort Meigs.

Twice the natives and the British tried to take the fort, first in April 1813 and again in July. In the first assault, which began with the landing of troops at the mouth of the Maumee River on April 26, the British deployed one thousand troops and Tecumseh mobilized twelve hundred warriors. During the siege, which continued for several weeks, the British fired thousands of rounds of cannonballs at the fort. With their bare hands, the American defenders dug "traverses," earthen barriers that could shelter them during the shelling. Harrison received reinforcements from Kentucky, who had to fight their way to the gates of the fort. As the siege continued, a large number of warriors drifted away.*

On May 5, several parties of Americans ventured outside the safety of the fort to assault British artillery batteries. In driving rain, the Kentuckians found themselves in a fight against British soldiers and Tecumseh's warriors. Believing they had gained the upper hand, they pursued some of the warriors deeper and deeper into the thick woods that surrounded the fort. Tecumseh, a master of this kind of combat, was deliberately pulling his men back to draw the Americans

---

* It was not uncommon for native warriors, who served as they wished, to grow weary of a lengthy siege and return to their homes.

into a trap. When the Kentuckians ventured too far from the safety of their fort and pushed ever closer to the warrior encampment, where more of Tecumseh's men could join the fight, the warriors suddenly sprang into action against their opponents, terrifying them into headlong flight. While some of the Americans managed to escape, hundreds of them were forced to surrender, desperate to hand themselves over to the British rather than the natives.

Fifty British soldiers sent the captured Americans to the remains of Fort Miami, where they were to be secured temporarily. A large number of warriors, who were in a deadly mood, gathered at the enclosure where the Americans were being held, forcing some of the prisoners to run the gauntlet and flaying them with tomahawks as they passed. Other prisoners were put to death.

The British urgently sent a messenger to find Tecumseh, who was not far from the scene of mayhem. He rushed back to Fort Miami. He arrived to see several warriors shooting prisoners and scalping them. Tecumseh dismounted from his horse and plunged into the milling warriors, loudly ordering the attack on the captives to cease. Although most of the angry natives were not Shawnees and understood but few of his words, they knew who he was. Their anger was quelled and the warriors dispersed.

Later, when the American prisoners were paroled and returned to their homes, they told the story of the native leader who had saved their lives when the British failed to do so. One oft-repeated version of the story, whether true or not, has it that Tecumseh turned on General Procter, condemning him for allowing the killings to take place, and shouting, "Begone! You are unfit to command; go and put on petticoats!"[1]

While the fighting outside Fort Meigs had been won by Tecumseh's warriors, overall the British and their native allies were not making much progress against the fort itself. It was well constructed and Harrison's men had the supplies they needed to hold out. A sufficient number of reinforcements had reached the fort, and the Americans had a greater troop strength than those mounting the siege.

Procter drew the conclusion that the siege was hopeless. On May 7, the two sides arranged for an exchange of prisoners, and two days later, Procter abandoned the fight and withdrew along with Tecumseh's warriors.

Again, in July, a smaller force of British troops and native warriors returned to assault Fort Meigs. Again the siege failed. Procter decided to lead his force against the less formidable Fort Stephenson, at Lower Sandusky, but his attack failed there as well. The Americans at Fort Stephenson numbered only 160 regulars and were equipped with one artillery piece, which they used to great effect to inflict casualties on a British storming party.*

Tecumseh had been all too right about the need for the native confederacy and the British to capture Fort Meigs. It was a strongpoint to which the Americans were sending reinforcements, and soon they would be in a position to take the offensive.

In September 1813, the Americans managed to gain ground in the fight around Lake Erie, first by winning a decisive naval battle on the lake and then by following it up with a land invasion of Upper Canada.

After the U.S. strategists decided in the winter of 1813 to focus on winning naval control of Lakes Ontario and Erie, and the British reached the same conclusion about the importance of the lakes, both sides began a feverish shipbuilding race. On Lake Ontario, the Americans and British constructed ships at Sackets Harbor and Kingston respectively, with neither side gaining a decisive advantage. At Presque Isle, Pennsylvania, master shipwright Noah Brown headed up the U.S. effort to outfit its naval force on Lake Erie.

---

* Fort Meigs has been rebuilt as an historical site. Along with an interpretive centre, the fort is open to the public. Operated by the Fort Meigs Society on behalf of the Ohio Historical Society, the Fort Meigs Center presents annual re-enactments of the battles fought around the fort. Participants with period costumes and muskets portray the U.S., British, and native forces in the battle. Canadians, dressed in the attire of the 41st Foot, participate with the Americans, who portray the U.S. units.

In September 1813, Commodore Oliver Perry, the twenty-seven-year-old officer who had been transferred from Rhode Island to take command of the U.S. naval fleet on Lake Erie, sailed forth from Presque Isle in command of two new twenty-gun brigs, seven schooners, and other smaller vessels, to meet the British squadron. At daylight on September 10, Perry's squadron closed with the British ships. A deadly exchange of carronade fire erupted. In the early going, the British had the advantage. At one point, Perry's flagship, the *Lawrence*, was being pounded on both sides, and in the bloody wardroom below the deck a young surgeon tended to the wounded, amputating dangling limbs and staunching the bleeding.

Perry left the ship and rowed under fire to the undamaged *Niagara*. There, he continued the fight for an additional forty-five minutes, until the British commodore struck his colours and surrendered.[2] In the absence of British vessels, with their ships free to sail the lake uncontested, the Americans could threaten British forts at will. Perry's victory had dire consequences for the British and grave implications for Tecumseh's confederacy.

Procter was panicked by the American control of the lake. In the aftermath of Perry's victory, he prepared to abandon Fort Malden, while Harrison readied his troops for yet another invasion of Upper Canada.

Encamped with his warriors on Grosse Ile, in the Detroit River, Tecumseh did not hear directly from Procter about the British defeat on Lake Erie, but he soon saw indications that the British were planning to give up Fort Malden.[3] Procter, who was obviously intent on falling back up the Thames River, had not consulted the Shawnee chief about his decision to retreat. The British commander imposed martial law over the western portion of Upper Canada so that he could husband the meagre supply of provisions still left to him.

When it became clear to him what Procter was up to, Tecumseh tried to stiffen his ally's spine. Assembling his warriors at Amherstburg, Tecumseh met with Procter and his officers in a large council room. Speaking in Shawnee, he summoned wit, ridicule, and his rhetorical powers to pour scorn on the British commander's decision to withdraw. He wore a fitted leather suit, and in his hair was a plume of white ostrich feathers. He held a wampum belt of many colours that had been arranged to set out the story of his people.

Tecumseh reminded Procter that two summers earlier, "When I came forward with my red brethren, and was ready to take up the hatchet in favour of our British father, we were told not to be in a hurry—that he had not yet determined to fight the Americans.

"When war was declared, our father stood up and gave us the tomahawk, and told us that he was now ready to strike the Americans; that he wanted our assistance; and that he would certainly get us our lands back, which the Americans had taken from us."

"Listen!" the Shawnee chief lectured the British general. "You told us *that* time, to bring forward our families to this place; and we did so, and you promised to take care of them, and that they should want for nothing, while the men would go and fight the enemy."

Then he turned to ridicule. "You always told us, that you would never draw your foot off British ground; but now, father, we see you are drawing back . . . We must compare our father's conduct to a fat animal, that carries its tail upon its back, but when affrighted, it drops between its legs, and runs off." When the interpreter rendered these words into English, the British officers laughed.

Tecumseh concluded by telling Procter that if the British intended to retreat they should leave their weapons and ammunition for the native warriors to use. "Our lives are in the hands of the Great Spirit—we are determined to defend our lands, and if it is his will, we wish to leave our bones upon them."[4]

Following his peroration, the natives on hand rose to their feet, shouted, and shook their tomahawks. Procter took in the message. Fearful that the British alliance with the natives was about to come apart, he requested another council in two days, at which time he would respond to the case made by Tecumseh. This was far from forthright. It was Procter's resolve to retreat, but so far he had been unwilling to share his plans, not only with his native allies but also with subordinate British officers. During the next two days, Tecumseh's warriors watched the British transport weapons, ammunition, and supplies from Fort Malden en route to the Thames.

At the second meeting, two days after the first, the mood was initially stormy. The natives brought with them a great wampum belt that had the figure of a heart woven into its centre. They planned to cut the belt, which symbolized their alliance with the British, to illustrate the breaking of that alliance.[5] Procter decided that only a direct appeal to Tecumseh could salvage the situation. He sent a message to Tecumseh to meet with him and his senior commanders at the quarters of his staff adjutant.

Tecumseh stood at a table with the British officers with a large map of the region around Detroit spread before them. With Colonel Matthew Elliott, one of Procter's officers, serving as translator, the British general explained to Tecumseh the military implications of Perry's victory on Lake Erie.[6] Tecumseh saw clearly the problem the British faced, and when Procter explained that his intention was to fortify Chatham at the Forks of the Thames and to make his stand there against the Americans, the Shawnee chief appeared reassured.

Tecumseh said he needed time to discuss the plan with the other chiefs. Within two hours, as Procter later reported, he had won over most of the chiefs and their warriors to the idea of making their stand at Chatham. In the council that followed, the natives agreed to accompany the British to the Forks of the Thames.

Even though Tecumseh had convinced most, but not all, of his followers to accept the retreat, the physical labour of the move to the new site would have to be endured. Native women and girls packed up most of the possessions from the houses they had constructed on Grosse Ile. They would be the ones who would have to do the principal work of establishing the new homes. Tecumpease, Tecumseh's sister, was one of the women charged with the back-breaking ordeal of departing from one settlement en route to another. In addition to her brother, the move involved her husband, Wahsikegaboe, and the nephew she had raised, Paukeesaa, who was seventeen years old. As she laboured to take possessions to the new site where she would help build new dwellings, she had to think about the members of her family who would fight in the upcoming battle.

On the day after the council, the natives crossed the Detroit River to the Canadian shore and started up the trail to Sandwich. About twelve hundred warriors and their families — including Kickapoos, Winnebagoes, Ojibwas, Ottawas, Senecas, and a few Creek warriors, in addition to Shawnees — set out on the journey. Several hundred native followers of Tecumseh's confederacy refused to join in the move. Disillusioned with what they saw as a faltering British alliance, they crossed over to the American shore.[7]

As the British and their native allies retreated up the Thames, the Americans marshalled their forces to take the offensive. William Henry Harrison merged his own units with troops from Kentucky. They served under the command of the state's governor, Isaac Shelby, who at age sixty-six had raised three thousand volunteers, many of them still in their teens, with no military experience.[8] In addition, one thousand Kentucky soldiers on horseback, under the command of Colonel Richard Mentor Johnson, set out from Fort Meigs to reinforce Harrison's expedition.

Their route took them past the River Raisin, the site of the massacre of Kentucky troops the previous January by native warriors. They saw the bones of the slain strewn over a distance of close to five kilometres. This stoked the anger of the soldiers and their commander, who had been a War Hawk when he sat in Congress, beginning in December 1810. Johnson had accused the British of inciting their native allies to commit atrocities against American settlers. "If Great Britain would leave us to the quiet enjoyment of independence; but considering her deadly and implacable enmity, and her continued hostilities, I shall never die contented until I see England's expulsion from North America and her territories incorporated with the United States," he declared in a speech in the House of Representatives.[9]

On the afternoon of September 27, 1813, two and a half weeks after Perry's victory on Lake Erie, Harrison led his troops ashore on

Lake Erie, just five kilometres from Fort Malden. To mark the
return of U.S. forces to this corner of Upper Canada for the first
time in over a year, the troops played "Yankee Doodle" on their
fifes and drums.[10]

As the Americans entered Amherstburg and came upon the
burned-out remnants of Fort Malden, Tecumseh sat on his horse on
a high point overlooking the scene. Mounted beside him was Colonel
Elliott, who was well over seventy years old. As the British agent in
the Indian Department, Elliott had known Tecumseh for years, and
the two had become friends. Watching the Americans march into
Amherstburg was a bitter and sad moment for both men. It had been
at Fort Malden that the Shawnee chief had cemented his alliance
with the British, the alliance that was crucial to his goal of creating a
native state. Elliott was looking down on the place that had been his
home. Finally, the two turned, putting the hopes of the past behind
them, and rode north to join the retreating British forces.[11]

Over the next three days the British moved slowly along muddy paths
in heavy rain. Tecumseh and Elliott stayed at the rear of the force,
often close to the advancing Americans, urging the natives who had
fallen behind to stay ahead of the invaders. When they reached
Chatham, at the forks of the Thames River, Tecumseh was disgusted
to find that Procter and the British had done next to nothing to ready
themselves for a possible battle there. Elliott was reduced to tears as
the Shawnee chief berated the British for their lack of serious preparation. By this point, Procter had lost the confidence of his own men,
and the native allies had little faith that the general would stand and
fight. Some were deserting, intent on coming to terms with the
advancing Americans.

As native warriors loyal to Tecumseh skirmished with the
advancing U.S. units, Procter left the army behind to survey the area
around Moraviantown and see where he could make a stand. His
absence from his troops contributed to the low morale.

On October 2, Harrison's men began a rapid passage across the wet countryside in pursuit of Procter's army and Tecumseh's warriors. The American advance forced Procter to make a stand just downriver from Moraviantown, in a place not of his own choosing. Unless he fought there, U.S. mounted troops would overtake the British, whose progress was slowed by the presence of the wounded and the women and children.

Only five hundred warriors remained with Tecumseh on October 5, the day of the battle. A thousand men had deserted him over the previous month. That morning, the Shawnee chief reconnoitered the American troops to see if they planned to march toward Moraviantown. He then rode across the Thames to join his warriors. Tecumseh had reasons for being downcast about the coming fight, but he did not show any such emotion to his followers. Dressed in deerskin leggings and a hunting shirt, Tecumseh inspected his men, well aware that they drew inspiration and courage from him. Later, he walked down the British line and shook hands with each officer. He addressed words of encouragement to them in Shawnee. While there are different accounts about Tecumseh's last words to Procter, the general's aide-de-camp reported that he said, "Father! Have a big heart!"[12]

With Harrison at Moraviantown was Richard Johnson, the Kentuckian who commanded one thousand U.S. troops on horseback (though they were not in fact a cavalry unit). Some of the first Americans to attack the enemy line were quickly cut down. After Harrison and Johnson consulted about tactics, Harrison ordered the Kentuckian to attack the native warriors on the left while he mustered his troops to attack the British on the right. Johnson urged his superior to allow him to ride forward with his mounted soldiers in a frontal assault on the British line.

The attack ruptured the right side of the British line, and only three of the Kentuckians were wounded. Johnson's troops dismounted, turned, and seized the British position, forcing those on the first line and then the second to lay down their arms. Effectively, that was the end of the British in the battle.

Tecumseh and his men fought long and hard, on swampy ground and in the woods, against Harrison's army. The warriors could see Tecumseh firing his musket and rallying his men. His face was painted black and red. He had a bandage around one arm, worn as a result of a slight wound he had received a couple of days earlier in a skirmish with the Americans. Around his neck, he wore the King George III medal. Both Johnson's men and Tecumseh's warriors undertook charges, only to be repulsed. Then Tecumseh rushed forward to rally his men to mount another charge. An American soldier raised his loaded gun, aimed it, and fired in the direction of Tecumseh's left side. The bullet struck the Shawnee chief in the chest, killing him.

The news quickly spread among the warriors that their great leader was dead.[13] By then, the British had withdrawn. The warriors slipped away from the battlefield into the woods.* Thirty-three warriors died, eighteen British soldiers were killed, and twenty-five of the British were wounded. On the American side, only seven were killed and twenty-five were wounded, five of them dying after the fight.[14]

Despite the low casualty rate, one death was enormously significant. When they killed Tecumseh, the Americans knocked a major foe out of the war. Although the British sorely missed Brock, who had died a year earlier, their state and military structure allowed for an orderly succession of command. The death of Tecumseh was different. There was no succession of command within the native confederacy. With its towering leader gone, the confederacy disintegrated.

While the longer-term implications of the loss of Tecumseh would soon be felt, an immediate consequence was squalid behaviour by trophy-hunters. A number of Kentuckians spied a native corpse decorated with plumes and war paint and assumed that this was the fallen Tecumseh. They cut strips of flesh from his back and thighs as souvenirs.

---

*Near the spot where Tecumseh fell, the Government of Canada has erected a monument to his memory.

Some American soldiers rushed to claim to have fired the shot
that killed Tecumseh. The most prominent of these was Colonel
Johnson. After the war, Johnson used this supposed deed to demonstrate his fitness for political office. In 1836, when he successfully ran
for the vice presidency of the United States, supporters of his chanted:
"Rumpsey dumpsey! Colonel Johnson killed Tecumseh!"[15]

To Americans, the death of Tecumseh meant they had finally
succeeded in breaking the native peoples' resistance to the westward
march of the settlers. In his celebrated history of the naval battles of
the War of 1812, Theodore Roosevelt, writing in the early 1880s,
summed up the Battle of Moraviantown: "Tecumseh died fighting,
like the hero that he was."

On its wider significance, he concluded, "The battle ended the
campaign in the Northwest. In this quarter it must be remembered
that the war was, on the part of the Americans, mainly one against
Indians. . . . The American armies . . . were composed of the armed
settlers of Kentucky and Ohio, native Americans, of English speech
and blood, who were battling for lands that were to form the heritage
of their children. In the West, the war was only the closing act of the
struggle that for many years had been waged by the hardy and rest-
less pioneers of our race, as with rifle and axe they carved out the
mighty empire that we their children inherit; it was but the final
effort with which they wrested from the Indian lords of the soil the
wide and fair domain that now forms the heart of our great Republic.
It was the breaking down of the last barrier that stayed the flood of
our civilization; it settled, once and for ever, that henceforth the law,
the tongue, and the blood of the land should be neither Indian, nor
yet French, but English."[16]

Tecumseh was not the only leader to envision a union of native
peoples living on their òwn land. Others came before, and still others
tried after him. But in his time, he was peerless — a man of enormous
energy whose political gifts and willingness to work with others,
whether they were native or white, made him singular in his determination to change the history of the continent. When Tecumseh fell, the

War of 1812 had reached its midpoint, but the combat in the northwest theatre had effectively come to an end. The whole of Tecumseh's life was devoted to the struggle to hold on to native land in the Ohio country, in the Indiana Territory, and indeed along the western edge of American settlement to the Gulf of Mexico. With his death on a battlefield on the Thames River in Upper Canada, a chapter in the Endless War to defend native peoples and their lands was closed.

Chapter 14

The Creek War

F AR TO THE SOUTH of the Great Lakes where Tecumseh had fought, another native struggle was underway. The great Shawnee chief had helped sow the seeds for what came to be known as the Creek War.

Tecumseh's journey to Tuckhabatchee in September 1811 won a militant Muscogee faction called the Red Sticks to his cause. The war of the Muscogees was waged in the land now known as the Old Southwest. This region, in which Spain, France, and Britain had had imperial interests, was a magnet for settlers, especially wealthy land-owners who hungered to create a new cotton kingdom to replace the land farther east, where the soil had been depleted by intensive agriculture.

To make sense of the Creek War, the stage needs to be set for the southern theatre of conflict. The influence of the Red Sticks, who drew their name from the red war clubs that they carried as a symbol of justice, spread rapidly through Upper Creek settlements in the early months of 1812. The movement was one of resistance, not only to the encroachment of settlers on Muscogee land but also to the increasing influence of American ways upon Muscogee society. Adherents of the Red Stick movement attacked and intimidated those who did not share their views, in some cases murdering them.[1]

The great earthquake that struck the area around New Madrid, Missouri, on December 16, 1811, reinforced support for the rebel movement. So too did the sight of a comet in the heavens in the autumn of 1811. Some Muscogees associated the comet with the words Tecumseh had spoken at their council, when he said, "You shall see my arm of fire stretched athwart the sky."[2] The Shawnee chief had prophesied events that would shake the world. His prophesy seemed to many to carry great meaning. As elsewhere among native peoples, the earthquake and the comet were interpreted as a signal of the Great Spirit's displeasure with the native peoples' adoption of the European lifestyle.

By June 1812, when war erupted in the North against Great Britain, the Americans were also embroiled in a conflict across their southern border in Florida, with the Seminole natives and with runaway blacks who had escaped from slavery in Georgia. With the tacit support of Washington, freelance military operations were mounted from Georgia to seize territory in Florida from the weak Spanish administration. For the Seminole natives, resistance to the American intruders was similar in character to movements elsewhere on the continent to protect native land and sovereignty. For the blacks (known as the Maroons), the prospect of an American occupation threatened them with no less than enslavement. In July and August 1812, the two groups resisted an incursion of self-proclaimed U.S. Patriots and drove them back across the border.[3] Subsequent U.S. attacks were also rebuffed. The pattern on the southern frontier was the same as on the western and northern frontiers of the United States: where American settlers and their political backers saw opportunities for expansion, they acted on them, and the native population resisted.

In 1810 American freelancers had seized Baton Rouge and adjacent parts of Spanish West Florida and had called on the U.S. Congress to annex the area. On October 27, 1810, President James Madison proclaimed that the portion of West Florida between the Mississippi and Perdido Rivers was now U.S. territory.[4] In February

1813, the Madison administration took action to acquire another piece of territory on the Gulf Coast, instructing the commander of the U.S. Seventh Military District at New Orleans to seize Mobile from Spain. Two months later, General James Wilkinson, who later commanded American units in the northern war against the British, led the landing of six hundred American troops against the Spanish bastion near Mobile. The Spaniards surrendered without firing a shot. Thus the Americans obtained Mobile, gateway to much of the Alabama interior.

On the road to their own war with the United States, the Red Sticks were involved in the fighting between the British and the Americans as backers of Tecumseh's native confederacy. Fanning the flames of American resentment against the militant Muscogee faction, a number of Red Sticks allied with Tecumseh participated in the January 1813 battles at the River Raisin.

The following month, another incident incited rage among Americans. Red Sticks returning south from the River Raisin murdered members of seven white families in the Ohio Valley. When he received word of the murders, Indian agent Benjamin Hawkins called on the leaders of the Muscogee National Council to punish the perpetrators. A party led by William McIntosh, an influential mixed-blood Muscogee, set out to hunt down the killers, ambushing them in the house where they slept. When the culprits ran out of ammunition and refused to lay down their weapons, McIntosh had the house set alight and five of the murderers were either burned to death or died trying to get away. The next day the leader of the Red Stick group was also hunted down and killed.

Following this episode, the Muscogee leaders who sided with the United States wrote to Hawkins to underline their loyalty to the American cause. "You think that we lean to the Shawnee tribes because you saw Tecumseh and his party dance in our square, around our fire," they wrote, "and some of our people believed their foolish talk . . . You need not be jealous that we shall take up arms against the United States: we mean to kill all our red people that spill the blood of our white friends."⁵ As was the case with many other native peoples, the Muscogees were riven with deep, fratricidal divisions about how to respond to the American threat.

In July 1813, the Red Sticks took fateful steps that transformed their conflict with the United States into all-out war. Several Red Stick leaders, accompanied by a party of at least one hundred warriors, rode south to Spanish Pensacola, where they expected to receive arms from the Spaniards for their struggle against the Americans. The Red Sticks were particularly anxious to acquire muskets and rifles,⁶ but the Spanish governor at Pensacola, Gonzalez Manrique, told the Red Stick leader, the mixed-blood Peter McQueen (also known as Talmuches Hadjo), that he had no arms to give them. The Red Sticks insisted belligerently that they had come to be supplied with weapons. Eventually Manrique provided McQueen and his followers with one thousand pounds of gunpowder, some lead, and food and blankets.

While the expedition to Pensacola was underway, other Red Sticks mounted a siege of Tuckhabatchee, where the Muscogee council leaders who supported the Americans were based. The Red Sticks were not well armed but they maintained their siege for eight days, at which point the council leadership abandoned the town and the Red Sticks proceeded to torch it. In response, the state of Georgia mobilized fifteen hundred militiamen to guard against any attacks across the state's frontier. Tennessee and the Mississippi Territory also placed their militias on alert.⁷

Meanwhile, McQueen's party, returning from Pensacola, set up camp at Burnt Corn Creek. There, on July 27, they were discovered by a U.S. militia unit led by Colonel James Caller, who had recently written to his commander to say that decisive action was needed to stop the Red Sticks from endangering communities in the territory. When Caller came upon McQueen's camp, the men were cooking and eating and had posted no guards.

The militiamen burst out of the woods and opened fire on the Red Sticks, who returned fire and raced for cover. Instead of pursuing them, the militiamen halted to inspect and divide the baggage McQueen's men had left behind on their pack horses. This delay gave the Red Sticks time to organize a counterattack, even though only about a dozen of them had guns. They managed to drive off some of their attackers, but others remained, and the two sides exchanged fire for close to an hour. The militiamen then withdrew and the Red Sticks recovered their pack horses. Those who fell at Burnt Corn Creek were the first casualties in the Creek War.[8]

The victory at Burnt Corn Creek against better-armed and more numerous opponents convinced some of the Red Sticks that they could take on the Americans and win. But in the aftermath of the fight, the political divisions among the Muscogees burst into violence, fomenting attacks and reprisals between the two sides and splitting families. One mixed-blood, who until now had stood in the middle, decided to throw in his lot with the Red Sticks. William Weatherford (Red Eagle), who had refused to side with Tecumseh in 1811, was descended from a Scottish trader and a mother who belonged to the Wind clan. Fluent in Muscogee and English, Red Eagle was a gifted military strategist who had considerable political influence among the Muscogees.

As the Red Sticks mobilized, their fight taking on the character of a national struggle, the settlers, both whites and mixed-bloods, grew increasingly fearful, and many of them abandoned their homes to seek protection in wooden stockades that had been thrown up during the crisis. One of these was Fort Mims, north of Mobile and close to the Alabama River.

The Red Sticks chose Fort Mims as their next target, charging Red Eagle with planning the operation. They mobilized a force of 750 warriors, including a number of black fighters, and sent a smaller force of about 125 men to assault a small stockade nearby, hoping that this secondary operation would confuse their opponents about where the main blow would fall.

Just after noon on August 30, Weatherford led the surprise attack. The people in the fort were eating their lunch, and the main gate of the stockade was wide open. In the first minutes, many of the shocked defenders were killed, but others managed to repel several assaults. After three hours of fighting, in which the houses in the fort were torched, the Red Sticks paused. Their chief had died early in the engagement, and they held a brief council to choose a successor, naming Weatherford to take command.

Weatherford urged the warriors to resume the attack so that they could claim a complete victory. The warriors soon overcame the last resisters. Then came a wanton spree of destruction and mayhem. Although Weatherford tried his best to halt them, many of the Red Sticks set about massacring the men, women, and children who had fallen into their hands. Victims were hacked to pieces and their bodies burned along with the remnants of the fort.

A relief column of the Mississippi Militia arrived on the grisly scene ten days later. Its commander, Major Joseph P. Kennedy, wrote to Brigadier General Ferdinand L. Claiborne, his superior, that "Indians, negroes, white men, women and children, lay in one promiscuous ruin. All were scalped, and the females, of every age, were butchered in a manner which neither decency nor language will permit me to describe. The main building was burned to ashes, which were filled with bones. The plains and the woods around were covered with dead bodies . . . The soldiers and officers with one voice called on divine Providence to revenge the death of our murdered friends."[9]

The massacre at Fort Mims ignited an appetite for revenge among Americans far and wide. It drew into the struggle a Tennessean by the name of Andrew Jackson. After moving to Jonesborough, Tennessee, the young Jackson had become a public prosecutor, dealing with issues of petty crime, debt, and drunkenness. Outfitted with a brace of pistols, which he kept in his desk, Jackson was prepared to settle his own disputes by fighting duels. In 1796, he was elected to the House of Representatives, then briefly was named to a vacant

Senate seat and spent a short time as a member of the Tennessee Supreme Court. Jackson dabbled in ventures both commercial and political.

The massacre at Fort Mims generated a political shock wave in Tennessee, where the state legislature passed an act on September 25, 1813, calling up thirty-five hundred volunteers to counter the Red Stick threat. This mobilization followed the mustering of fifteen hundred militiamen earlier in the summer. Andrew Jackson learned about the Fort Mims massacre when he was at his home, the Hermitage, near Nashville, recovering from a bullet wound suffered in a street fight. Jackson declared to Tennessee volunteers, "The horrid butcheries . . . can not fail to excite in every bosom a spirit of revenge." Arriving at Fayetteville, near the Alabama border, on October 7, Jackson took direct command of one thousand infantrymen and a further force of thirteen hundred cavalrymen and mounted riflemen, to be led under Jackson's overall command by Brigadier General John Coffee. Coffee was Jackson's best friend and business partner, a man in whom the future president of the United States had complete confidence.[10]

Jackson's foray into Muscogee territory began inauspiciously. The militiamen were supplied with insufficient provisions. At one point, members of his party threatened to defect, and only Jackson's gift for profane bombast brought them back into line.[11] Pushing into the heart of Muscogee country in late October, the members of the expedition were desperate for food. They came upon a native village and attacked it solely to make off with the cattle and corn of the villagers. That expedient netted Jackson and his party food for an additional three days. In addition, Jackson's men took twenty-nine Muscogees prisoner, including a number of women and children, and burned the village of Littafuchee, located on Canoe Creek in the present-day Alabama county of St. Clair.[12]

One member of Jackson's force was a twenty-seven-year-old Tennessean by the name of David Crockett, who had signed up with the expedition to avenge the Fort Mims massacre. A self-styled sharpshooter, Crockett would become famous to millions of children through a mid-twentieth-century television series that portrayed him as displaying all the virtues of the plain-spoken American frontiersman. Before departing with the troops, Crockett explained to his wife why he had to go on the expedition. "I knew that the next thing would be, that the Indians would be scalping the women and children all about there, if we didn't put a stop to it," he told her. "I reasoned the case with her as well as I could," he wrote in his memoir, "and told her, that if every man would wait until his wife got willing to go to war, there would be no fighting done, until we would all be killed in our own houses."[13]

Jackson led his troops east from Littafuchee to launch an attack on the small Muscogee town of Tallushatchee, located not far from present-day Jacksonville, Alabama. Having learned that a large number of Red Stick warriors were positioned in the town, Jackson ordered Coffee to attack it with nine hundred members of his mounted force. The troops were shown the way to the town by a party of Cherokee warriors and two Muscogees who had sided with the Americans.

As Davy Crockett described the attack, the soldiers approached the town in two columns and "then closed up at both ends, so as to surround it completely." When the Red Sticks saw one of the soldiers approaching, "they raised the yell, and came running at him like so many red devils." With the Americans surrounding the town and pouring volleys of fire into it, some of the natives surrendered. Others were chased into the dwellings. Crockett recounted an attack on forty-six warriors he saw taking cover in a house. When Crockett and his fellow soldiers got near the house, "We saw a squaw sitting in the door, and she placed her feet against the bow she had in her hand, and then took an arrow, and raising her feet, she drew with all her might, and let fly at us, and she killed a man . . . His death so enraged all of us, that she was fired on, and had at least twenty balls blown through her." Then the soldiers dealt with the warriors: "We now shot them like dogs; and then set the house on fire, and burned it up with the forty-six warriors in it. I recollect seeing a boy who was shot down near the house. His arm and thigh was broken, and he was so near the burning house that the grease was stewing out of him . . . He was still trying to crawl along; but not a murmur escaped him, though he was only about twelve years old. So sullen is the Indian, when his dander is up, that he had sooner die than make a noise or ask for quarters [sic]."[14]

To finish off the Red Sticks, the soldiers torched the remaining houses. The warriors trapped inside burned to death and those who tried to flee were gunned down when they tried to make their escape.

Coffee's force killed and captured 186 warriors, and 5 members of the Tennessee contingent were killed. Following their destruction of the town, Coffee's men rejoined Jackson's force and discovered that no new food supplies had arrived. The next day, some of the men who had been involved in the attack returned to the burnt-out ruins of Tallushatchee to scavenge for something to eat. Despite the stench of the corpses and the appalling sight of the dead, one of the men uncovered a potato cellar beneath one of the burnt dwellings, and the soldiers helped themselves to its contents. "For we were all hungry as wolves," Crockett recorded.[15]

In the midst of the ruins, soldiers heard the crying of a small infant, who was found near the body of his dead mother. They picked up the baby and took him back to Jackson's camp. When Jackson saw the baby he asked some of the Muscogee women who had been taken prisoner if they would look after the infant. They refused, telling the general that all the baby's relatives were dead and that the soldiers should kill him too.[16] Jackson felt a surge of compassion for the baby, who was about ten months old, about the same age as his own adopted son, Andrew Jr. The general decided he would adopt the boy, and send him back to the Hermitage in Tennessee to live with his family there. To make sure he could be cared for, Jackson took a Muscogee woman as a slave.[17]

Whatever the range of emotions he experienced during his campaign, Jackson was developing a taste for war and for the glory it could win him.

∿

Jackson's next target was Talladega, a Muscogee trading post east of the Coosa River that was outfitted with a stockade. The Tennesseans tried to use the same tactics that had worked so well for them in their previous engagement. They advanced on the town and attempted to surround it. The resourceful Red Eagle, however, knew the enemy was coming. He had moved his warriors to the nearby woods, where he waited to launch a surprise attack of his own.

From their concealed position, the Red Sticks rushed forth at a portion of the Tennessee force. In Crockett's lurid account of the attack, the Red Sticks were "all painted as red as scarlet, and were just as naked as they were born." He described them as "being like a cloud of Egyptian locusts, and screaming like all the young devils had been turned loose."[18]

Many of the mounted militiamen fell from their horses in their rush to make it to the relative safety of the fort. Militiamen in the woods opened fire on the Red Sticks, who turned in their direction and attempted a charge that was broken by a further volley of fire. Trapped by militiamen on both sides, the Red Sticks fought a desperate twenty-minute battle, deploying muskets and bows and arrows against their foes. At last, the native warriors found a gap in Jackson's line and rushed through into the nearby woods. Coffee's mounted militiamen took up a hot pursuit and inflicted more casualties on the Red Sticks. The native allies of the Americans, who had been holed up in the fort, came out to slake their thirst at a nearby spring. The Red Sticks had been besieging them for days.

Three hundred Red Sticks died in the encounter, while only fifteen militiamen were killed and eighty-five wounded. Two more soldiers died later of their wounds. But seven hundred Red Sticks had made it through the gap to safety, prepared to fight another day. Jackson's troops had managed to kill or wound about one thousand warriors in the Battles of Tallushatchee and Talladega.

After the latter battle, Jackson ruefully concluded, "Had I not been compelled by the faux pas of the militia in the onset of the battle, to dismount my reserves, I believe not a man of them would have escaped."[19]

With insufficient provisions to feed his troops, and worried about the security of his base and supply lines, Jackson decided that he could not continue his pursuit of the remaining Red Stick warriors, and pulled back to the Coosa River. Meanwhile, another Tennessee force, commanded by Major General John Cocke, with whom Jackson had been attempting to coordinate, was experiencing its own supply problems.

Cocke determined that he and his men would carry on their own campaign against other Red Stick power centres. What he did not know was that the chiefs of the Hillabee towns (Muscogee settlements located on creeks and rivers not far from the Tallapoosa River in what is now northeastern Alabama) had decided they wanted to end their support for the Red Sticks and make peace with the Americans. In return for surrendering any Red Stick leaders among them and handing back property taken from white settlers, especially their slaves, the warriors in the Hillabee towns had secured a truce with Jackson.

The militiamen under Cocke's direction, along with their Cherokee allies — who had been won over to the American cause with the promise that they would be recognized as a people[20] — surrounded the settlement of Hillabee Creek in the pre-dawn hours. Among those in the town were sixty-five wounded warriors who had survived the attack at Talledega, along with their women and children. At dawn, the attack was unleashed on the unsuspecting men and women, who thought they were protected by the truce. The Cherokee warriors went in first, followed by the troops. Guns and bayonets cut down those in the cabins. In less than fifteen minutes, the slaughter was complete. Two hundred and fifty-six prisoners, most of them women and children, were taken, and the town was burnt to the ground. The prisoners were dispatched to the Hiwassee Garrison of the Cherokee Nation, located in southeastern Tennessee, a post where federal U.S. troops were stationed.

The massacre at Hillabee Creek extinguished any hope of a quick end to the Creek War. The Hillabee Muscogees held Jackson responsible for what they saw as a betrayal. In the struggles to come, they aligned themselves fiercely on the side of the Red Sticks, holding out until the end.*[21]

While Cocke was launching the ill-fated assault on the Hillabee settlement, Jackson faced a problem within his own ranks. The supply issues had not been resolved, and in mid-November 1813, a large faction of the Tennessee Militia decided they had had enough and that they were going to head home. The crisis came to a head on November 10, at Fort Strother, when the rations for Jackson's soldiers ran out. Over the previous five days, his men had eaten less than two meals. Not only were the soldiers on the verge of starvation, the nights were growing longer and colder as autumn advanced, and many of them did not have proper clothing to cope with the rapidly dropping temperatures.

Jackson was determined to carry on the war against the Red Sticks until victory was achieved. His quest for glory or triumph was so strong that it overcame his personal ills. He suffered from persistent diarrhea and from the bullet that remained in his shoulder as a result of the brawl he had been involved in just prior to the expedition. The militiamen under his command were in an increasingly mutinous state. A number of his officers presented him with a petition urging him to march to Fort Deposit, eighty kilometres over mountainous country north of Fort Strother. There, the men would

---

* Before the attack on Hillabee Creek, Jackson and Cocke had had their problems coordinating what was supposed to be a joint operation. Now the two fell out. Jackson was determined to shift the blame for the massacre and the consequent prolongation of the Creek War onto the shoulders of Cocke. Eventually, this led to Jackson preferring charges against Cocke and the calling of a court martial to judge the conduct of the major general. Although Cocke thought Jackson supporters had stacked the court martial against him, he was acquitted.

In fact, Cocke had let Jackson know prior to the massacre that he intended to launch an attack on the Hillabee towns. When Jackson, who was thus aware of the planned assault, wrote back to Cocke to inform him of the offer to surrender made by the Hillabee chiefs, he did not mention Cocke's plan to attack the towns.

find food. But that would lead Jackson's force away from the heart-land of the Red Sticks. He urged the officers to wait a little longer for a relief column carrying provisions.

But many of the men could endure no more. Jackson had to mobi-lize his volunteers to stop some of the militiamen from leaving, but the following day, the volunteers decided they too could take it no more. Jackson urged them to wait two more days for the supplies. Then the men in his three brigades voted on what to do. One brigade voted to remain with the general; a second voted to remain for two more days; and the third, the volunteers, voted to depart. This time Jackson did not try to stop them. He did get them to agree to return to Fort Strother as soon as they could and to bring provisions with them. Davy Crockett was among the volunteers who left, and after going home to obtain a new horse, he returned once more to take up the fight against the Red Sticks. Most of the volunteers did not come back.[22]

Two days passed, but the relief column did not arrive. Forced to march north, Jackson convinced just over 100 men to remain behind and safeguard Fort Strother. Twenty miles into their march, Jackson's soldiers ran into a supply column heading south from Fort Deposit with a herd of 150 cattle and 9 wagons laden with flour. The ravenous troops slaughtered the cattle at once and ate decently for the first time in days.

Jackson was now determined to lead his force back to Fort Strother, but one company resumed the march north. The general confronted the men and threatened to open fire on them if they did not follow his order and return to camp. Reluctantly, they did so. The mutinous mood had not passed, however. Another brigade began preparations to depart for the North. The general wielded a musket with his good arm and aimed it at the disobedient troops. "You say you will march," he declared. "I say by the Eternal God you shall not march while a car-tridge can sound fire." The standoff continued for some moments, until several officers and loyal soldiers joined the general, their weap-ons bristling. The rebellious soldiers backed down.[23]

～

While Jackson had spent much time and energy keeping his own force in the field, other American units were carrying on the fight against the Red Sticks. In late November, a force of about 950 Georgia militiamen and 400 Cherokee warriors, under the command of General John Floyd, launched an attack on the Red Stick stronghold of Autossee, located on the eastern bank of the Tallapoosa River.[24]

On a cold morning, with frost covering the country around the town, the Georgians attacked Autossee and a small settlement a few hundred yards away. The fight was long and fierce. In the end, the Georgians prevailed, their artillery particularly effective in smashing the homes where their foes were holed up. Many of the Red Stick warriors died in the flames, while others carried on the fight from the brush surrounding the town. Two hundred Red Stick warriors were killed, according to the count carried out by the Georgians, who lost eleven men and had fifty-three wounded. Among the Muscogee dead was the venerable chieftain Big Warrior.[25]

As had been the case at Talladega, despite their victory and the destruction of Autossee, the Georgians failed to prevent most of the Red Stick warriors from escaping. Short of supplies, Floyd decided to lead his Georgians east to Fort Mitchell, their supply base on the Chattahoochee River, on the border of Georgia. As they set out on their march, the Red Sticks launched their own surprise attack. Four or five Georgians died, but Floyd's men repelled the assault and continued to Fort Mitchell.[26]

The fighting between the Americans and the Red Sticks continued into 1814. Reinforced with eight hundred new recruits, Jackson decided to launch an assault on a key Red Stick position called Tohepeka, or Horseshoe Bend. The Red Sticks did not wait for Jackson's troops to reach their base. They struck the Tennessee force, attacking the Americans in three places simultaneously, the very tactic the U.S. troops had been using against them. Jackson's soldiers just managed to hold their ground against the attack, and the general concluded that he needed more men to win at Horseshoe Bend. He led his troops in a retreat back toward Fort Strother and was once again struck by a Red Stick attack, which he fended off.[27]

A few weeks after the American troops were driven back to Fort Strother, volunteers from eastern Tennessee and the 39th Regiment of U.S. Infantry reached the fort. This infusion of fresh blood brought the general's numbers back up to make good the loss of those who had left when their enlistment times were up. On March 14, 1814, Jackson led the bulk of his troops south while leaving a covering force behind at the fort. The general's army numbered about four thousand men, including Cherokee and Choctaw warriors and Muscogees who had sided with the United States. Their target was Horseshoe Bend, about 160 kilometres to the south, on a loop in the Tallapoosa River. Here the Red Stick warriors numbered about one thousand, and about three hundred women and children were at the site. The Red Sticks had chosen a defensive position on a peninsula and had constructed breastworks made of logs to shield them against attack. In the breastworks were portholes through which the warriors could fire.

On March 27, 1814, Jackson launched his attack, which opened with an ineffectual artillery bombardment during which the Americans and their native allies managed to make it over the barricade and drive back their foes. While a few Red Sticks got away, the rest fought to the finish, unwilling to surrender when Jackson sent forth a flag of truce. In its latter phases, what happened at Horseshoe Bend was a slaughter. In one incident, a young soldier saw his officer rubbing his eyes. The officer told him that a Red Stick bullet had hit a tree and deflected bark into his eyes. "I want you to kill an Indian for me," the officer said. The soldier saw an old Muscogee sitting on the ground, pounding corn, refusing to acknowledge what was happening around him. He took deliberate aim and shot the old man dead. Another soldier beat a small Muscogee boy to death with the butt of his weapon. When an officer reprimanded him, the soldier explained that the little boy would one day have grown up to become a Red Stick.[28]

In a letter he later wrote to his wife, Jackson conceded that "the carnage was dreadful." When the Americans made their count of the fallen Red Sticks, they concluded that close to 900 had died — 557 lay dead on the ground and an estimated 300 had perished in the river.

Following the bloody victory, Jackson declared to his men that "the fiends of the Tallapoosa will no longer murder our women and children, or disturb the quiet of our borders."[29] He then led his force south to the junction of the Coosa and Tallapoosa Rivers, the heart of the Muscogee territory, and constructed Fort Jackson. Having fought his way through the Muscogee country, Jackson sent word to Muscogee settlements that they faced a stark choice: surrender or destruction. Many agreed to surrender. To complete his triumph, the general demanded that the Muscogees turn William Weatherford, Red Eagle, over to him. Red Eagle did not wait for others to come for him. He walked into Jackson's camp and declared, "My warriors can no longer hear my voice. Their bones are at Talledega, Tallushatchee, Emuckfaw and Tohopeka . . . I now ask for [peace] for my nation, and for myself." With this, Red Eagle went about the task of talking the remaining Red Sticks into giving up.

Jackson's war against the Creeks was over. The general returned to Nashville to a hero's welcome. That summer, he came back to Fort Jackson to dictate the terms of the Treaty of Fort Jackson to the shattered Muscogee nation. The United States took more than half the territory of the Muscogees, twenty million acres of land.[30] The Muscogee chiefs were astonished by the harshness of the terms. Those who had remained allies of the Americans anticipated generosity in return. They had expected land to be taken from the areas in which the Red Sticks had been strongest, but they did not imagine that the Americans would seize the heart of the territory of the whole Muscogee people.

The general's rejoinder was that the whole Muscogee nation had to pay the price for the Red Stick rebellion. He told the chiefs that the Muscogees should have taken Tecumseh prisoner when he came to draw them into his confederation. Now the Muscogees would suffer for the choice they had made.[31]

Andrew Jackson built his career, which culminated in two terms as president of the United States, on his reputation as a warrior on behalf of the new West. He stood up for the settlers west of the Appalachians and defied the established ways and institutions of the East. He fought against the power of eastern banks and championed a financial system in which local banks would meet farmers' and industry's need for capital.

In the conventional version of American history, Jackson is recorded as a leader who broadened the concept of democracy. He is the author of so-called Jacksonian democracy. Every year, the Democratic Party of the United States holds its annual Jefferson-Jackson dinner, named in honour of two of its greatest champions, the first a slave owner, the second a man who won his spurs in the systematic destruction of an entire people. The Creek War was one more chapter in the Endless War, the war to which Tecumseh had dedicated his life.

Chapter 15

Out of the Furnace of War, an Upper Canadian Identity

W HEN THE WAR OF 1812 ERUPTED, political identities were fluid on both sides of the border. The Americans did have their revolution behind them, as well as the founding documents of the civil religion of American patriotism: the Declaration of Independence and the U.S. Constitution of 1787. Although the United States was on the way to a national identity, it was not there yet. The political divisions between Democratic-Republicans and Federalists were more than schisms between parties; they expressed dangerous regional chasms, most importantly that between New England and the rest of the country.

Unlike French Canada, with its firm and long-established identity, the settler communities in Upper Canada at the turn of the nineteenth century were fragmented. Some were Loyalist, some were American, some were British. A rainbow of loyalties was on offer. The war would change that.

For French Canadians, the threat from the south called up vivid memories of the invasions of the past, most recently the one undertaken by American Patriots in 1775, one year before the Declaration of Independence. They did not view the Americans as liberators but rather as descendants of those who had waged bloody struggles against them for nearly two centuries. Preserving their language,

religion, and way of life meant halting the invader, even if it meant
fighting under the folds of the Union Jack, a flag that provoked mixed
feelings, at best, among the Canadiens.

On the eve of the war, the Lower Canada legislature unanimously
passed the Army Bills Act, which approved funding for the local military effort.[1] The legislature also passed an act that authorized the
establishment of an "incorporated militia" to number two thousand
men. The governor-general-in-council — made up of the governor
general and his appointed advisors, in effect his cabinet — increased
the number to four thousand, which remained the official size of this
militia until the end of the conflict.

Married volunteers were not encouraged to join this force, whose
members had to serve for two years. Half the members of the militia
could be discharged each year, with new recruits topping up the
strength of the corps. Men who had served and been discharged
formed a trained reserve that could be recalled to active duty in the
event of an emergency. By law, all able-bodied men between the ages
of sixteen and sixty were required to enroll with the local militia captain during the month of April. They were also obliged to attend four
muster parades, where they learned the basic elements of drill. Once
a year, they were mustered for an inspection carried out by a superior
officer assigned by the commander-in-chief.

Of Lower Canada's total population of 330,000, 52,000 were
enrolled in the militia.[2] In Upper Canada, only 11,000 men were
enrolled, out of a population of under 100,000. From this total enroll-
ment, called the "sedentary militia," members were activated when
they volunteered or were selected by ballot.

The local British North American regulars played an important
role in the defence of the territory. Among them were the Canadian
Fencibles, the Voltigeurs of Lower Canada, the Royal Newfoundland
Regiment, the New Brunswick Regiment, the Royal Veterans, and
the Glengarry Light Infantry Fencibles. Drawn from Roman
Catholics from the Scottish Highlands who had migrated to
Glengarry County, in Upper Canada on the St. Lawrence River, the

Glengarrys numbered eight hundred men. The manpower of the six corps totalled about four thousand soldiers.[3]

On the eve of the war, Brock worried that the Upper Canadians' response to an invasion might be tepid, with most settlers waiting to see which way the wind would blow. When U.S. General William Hull set foot on Canadian soil in the summer of 1812, he was gratified that several hundred Canadian residents answered his call to support the United States, and that several dozen Canadian militiamen deserted from Fort Malden to join the American forces. But much of the initial Canadian enthusiasm for the American invaders was soon put to rest at Detroit and Queenston. And in the aftermath of the burning of public buildings in York and later atrocities on Canadian soil, public opinion turned sharply against the Americans. The fires of war were forging an identity in Upper Canada, whose elements would be evident for many decades to come. Indeed, the contemporary political culture of Ontario has its roots in the war.

While the Upper Canadian identity would one day embrace democrats as well as political and social reformers, its bedrock was Tory. Loyalty to the British Crown was its central point of reference. That hard truth was driven home by the American invasions. John Strachan, the Anglican cleric who did so much to annoy American military leaders during their brief occupation of York, personified Upper Canadian Toryism. Unlike Brock and Tecumseh, who fought on Canadian soil by happenstance rather than design, Strachan was in Canada for the duration. Not surprisingly, he was a staunch admirer of Brock and the military alliance with the native confederacy.

Even before the U.S. attack on York, John Strachan had become a constant critic of the government, cheering on those he thought were putting up a valiant fight against the American invaders and writing scathing attacks on those who he thought were weak-kneed in their defence of the Canadas, particularly Upper Canada. On September 30, 1812, he wrote to the Honourable John Richardson, an influential Montreal merchant, to rail against "the languid manner in which the war is carried on." He outlined a long series of steps that the military should take to pursue the war more vigorously, and he set out the political benefits that would flow from taking the offensive. "We are told that some wise acres," he concluded, "find fault with General Brock for employing the Indians, but if he had not done so, he and all his men must have perished."[4]

A few weeks later, in a lengthy missive to the Honourable William Wilberforce, the British politician renowned for his campaign against the slave trade, Strachan set out the case for an alliance with the native peoples in the prosecution of the war against the United States. Rehearsing the historic mistreatment of native peoples in the U.S., Strachan said, "The Americans drive them [natives] from their hunting ground . . . and the American government makes fraudulent purchases of their lands from Indians who have no power to sell — one or two insignificant members of a village for example." He referred to the reasons for the war of the native peoples against the Americans as given "by the Famous Chief Tecumseh to General Brock when he was lately at Detroit on his expedition against General Hull. This Indian Chief unites the most astonishing wisdom to the most determined valour — he has been employed for several years in uniting all the Indians against the Americans."[5]

In another letter to Richardson, Strachan made the case that despite the other stated causes of the war, the true object of the United States was Upper and Lower Canada. "The importance of this country to them is incalculable," he wrote. "The possession of it would give them the complete command of the Indians who must either submit or starve within two years and thus leave all the Western frontier clear and unmolested. The Americans are systematically employed in exterminating the Savages, but they can never succeed while we keep possession of this country. This my Dear Sir is the true cause of the war."[6]

Strachan's distaste for the invaders was captured in a letter to the Marquess Wellesley in November 1812, in which he advocated the establishment of a University of Upper Canada. He hoped to create a university "upon an extensive and liberal plan so as to prevent in future our young men from going to the United States to finish their education, where they learn nothing but anarchy in Politics and infidelity in religion."[7]

Strachan was an authentic voice of the Upper Canada to come, an Upper Canada in which loyalty to the Crown and distance from the republic to the south were deeply embedded values.

For the balance of the war, the people of the Canadas and their defenders carried on the gruelling fight against a succession of American invasions, and many Upper Canadians had to put up with the misery of occupation by U.S. troops. Occupation brought with it the horrors of day-to-day intimacy between occupiers and occupied: destruction of property, the commandeering of farm animals and crops, guerilla warfare, treason, the naming and punishment of traitors.

But the Americans did not limit their forays north of the border to Upper Canada. In late September 1813, a few weeks before Tecumseh died at Moraviantown, Sir George Prevost transferred his headquarters from Kingston to Montreal on receipt of the news that U.S. Major General Wade Hampton — a veteran of the Revolutionary War, a former member of the U.S. House of Representatives, and a fierce defender of states' rights[8] — had led a force north up the shore of Lake Champlain, crossing the border into Lower Canada near Odelltown. That placed the Americans just off the northwest corner of Lake Champlain and about seventy-five kilometres due south of Montreal. U.S. attacks on Upper Canada, particularly west of Kingston, posed a threat, but nothing like the threat that a descent on Montreal would represent. If the Americans could take Montreal and choke off British access to the St. Lawrence River, all points west under British control would eventually fall into their hands.

On October 8, Prevost wrote to Lord Bathurst, the secretary of state for war and the colonies, that after receiving news of the American buildup on the frontier, he had moved his headquarters to Montreal, where he had learned that General Hampton's force numbered about five thousand regulars. He informed Bathurst that after crossing the border near Odelltown, Hampton had led his troops westward and was now encamped near the Chateauguay River. The U.S. force assembled for the invasion of the province, said Prevost, was greater than any other so far mounted during the war.[9]

Hampton's drive on Montreal was undertaken in conjunction with a related push up the St. Lawrence from Sackets Harbor. In the opinion of military historian Donald E. Graves, the "offensive was possibly the largest military operation mounted by the United States before 1861."[10]

The second American pincer, the one driving north from Sackets Harbor, was led by Major General James Wilkinson, one of the most notorious characters to command a U.S. force during the war. Wilkinson was associated with multiple scandals during his long career. After serving in the Continental Army during the American Revolution, he was appointed governor of the Louisiana Territory in 1805. By then he had exchanged communications with Aaron Burr, who had been vice president of the United States during Thomas Jefferson's first term; some observers believed Wilkinson was associated with Burr's conspiracy to establish a state in the west, independent of the U.S. A megalomaniac given to hatching geopolitical schemes, Burr was eventually charged with treason. After he was acquitted, he lived for a time in Europe before returning to spend the latter years of his life in the U.S. Decades after Wilkinson's death, documents were unearthed that exposed him as having been a paid agent of the Spanish Crown.

If Wilkinson's reputation was not shady enough, there was the additional problem that Wilkinson and Hampton hated each other. Their enmity predated the war; Hampton was one of many officers who had long distrusted Wilkinson. When Hampton became a general in 1808 during an expansion of the U.S. Army, the officer corps was divided between those supporting Wilkinson — the larger group — and those backing Hampton.

In 1811, Hampton believed his problems with Wilkinson would be resolved by a court martial President Madison convened, to consider charges against Wilkinson for conspiring with Aaron Burr against the United States and for being on the payroll of the Spanish government. Although the court discovered questionable transactions on the general's part, he was found not guilty on all charges and was restored to his command.[11]

In addition to his personal antagonism toward Hampton, Wilkinson did not favour giving first priority to the attack on Montreal. He preferred an attack on Kingston, which would be launched if Commodore Chauncey could establish clear U.S. naval superiority on Lake Ontario. His second choice was to redouble efforts near the Niagara Frontier, an offensive he believed would have the secondary advantage of striking a blow at the native peoples allied against the United States. In the end, the Americans implemented the double-pronged assault on Montreal from Lake Champlain and Sackets Harbor, with Secretary of War Armstrong hoping that Wilkinson and Hampton could coordinate their efforts at critical points.

With the Americans marching north, Prevost rallied his forces to defend Lower Canada. Under Prevost's orders, Lieutenant Colonel "Red George" Macdonell led his 1st Light Infantry Battalion from Kingston to Montreal. Roger Sheaffe, having been redeployed in Lower Canada, had already mobilized three thousand members of the Lower Canada sedentary militia. Prevost called up five thousand more militiamen.

During his journey by road from Montreal to Upper Canada to join the 89th Regiment of Foot, Dr. William Dunlop saw several units of Lower Canada's French-speaking militia and wrote of them: "They had all a serviceable effective appearance — had been pretty well drilled, and their arms being direct from the tower [of London], were in perfectly good order, nor had they the mobbish appearance that such a levy in any other country would have had. Their capots and trowsers [sic] of home-spun stuff, and their blue tuques (night caps) were all of the same cut and color, which gave them an air of uniformity that added much to their military look.

"They marched merrily to the music of their voyageur songs, and as they perceived our [scarlet] uniform as we came up, they set up the Indian War-whoop, followed by a shout of Vive le Roi along the whole line. Such a body of men in such a temper, and with so perfect a use of their arms as all of them possessed, if posted on such ground as would preclude the possibility of regular troops out-maneuvering them, and such positions are not hard to find in Canada, must have been rather a formidable body to have attacked."[12]

Delayed by defenders in outposts and by a dearth of drinking water for both men and horses during a dry summer, the Americans decided to take a roundabout route toward Montreal, along the Chateauguay River, where they would have plenty of water. Hampton received approval for his altered route from the U.S. secretary of war, along with his request for additional soldiers. He led his force back into New York State and then in a northeasterly direction along the Chateauguay River and again into Canada.

On October 8, in a letter to Bathurst, Prevost outlined his decision to concentrate more forces on the defence of Montreal, making the point that the city had to be held, not least because of the need to guard the supply route and the men marching westward to Upper Canada. He noted that "His Majesty's [French-]Canadian Subjects have a second time answered the call to arms in defence of their Country with a zeal and alacrity beyond all praise."[13] The British defence of the region was the responsibility of the Swiss-born Major General Louis de Watteville, who had led his own foreign-raised regiment to Lower Canada the previous spring.

When Hampton's forces crossed the border back into Lower Canada on October 21, they numbered four thousand infantry and two hundred dragoons, and they were outfitted with ten field guns. The two brigade columns moved slowly — they included a large number of farm wagons and had to cross small streams where the bridges had been destroyed.

Two units of active militia from the Canadian Fencibles (a regiment with Scottish origins, consisting mostly of Scottish commissioned and non-commissioned officers and French-Canadian rank and file) and the Canadian Voltigeurs (a light infantry unit raised in Lower Canada), as well as sedentary militia and a small number of native warriors, were in place to meet the attackers. Lieutenant Colonel Charles de Salaberry, a French-Canadian officer in the regular British army, commanded the force. The thirty-five-year-old de Salaberry was the son of the seigneur of Beauport. His grandfather, Michel de Salaberry, had fought on the side of France in the war against Britain that resulted in the conquest of Canada. At the age of fourteen, Charles de Salaberry joined the British army and served in the West Indies, Sicily, and Ireland before returning to Canada in 1810, after an absence of sixteen years.

De Salaberry set up his defences at a sharp bend in the Chateauguay River. The men prepared a line of breastworks and abatis (created by cutting down trees and crossing them over one another to block the progress of the enemy) at the edge of the forest and constructed a blockhouse. De Salaberry deployed his force, totalling just over three hundred men, in two places. About half of them were posted behind the erected defences and the other half were placed on the other side of the river, near a shallow ford where U.S. troops could cross. About two and a half kilometres to the rear was a further force commanded by "Red George" Macdonell, consisting of about 300 Canadian Voltigeurs, 480 men from the 2nd Battalion, additional militia, and about 150 native warriors.

On the afternoon of October 25, an American patrol informed Hampton that the defensive position ahead of the U.S. troops was lightly held, and mostly by militia. The U.S. commander ordered about fifteen hundred men, under the direction of Colonel Robert Purdy, to march forward at night through dense forest and surprise the enemy. The idea was to march down the river past the defences, then cross at the ford and take the defenders from the rear. Many of the Americans got lost in the woods, and by the time they reached the point across the river from de Salaberry's defences, it was broad daylight.

De Salaberry's troops opened fire. When an advance unit of Purdy's force finally approached the ford, it too came under fire, from the three Canadian militia companies on the right bank of the river. The members of the U.S. force discovered that covering the rear of de Salaberry's men was Macdonell's contingent. Their flanking attack was about to be flanked in turn. The Americans gave up the fight and withdrew in good order.[14] Hampton led his men back across the border to the village of Chateauguay, New York.

The Battle of Chateauguay was a political as much as a military triumph. It sent a clear message that the French Canadians would not be enticed to side with this latest invasion from the south.

On November 1, General Hampton wrote an extensive letter to U.S. Secretary of War Armstrong to explain why the American forces had broken off their attack at Chateauguay and retired. To reinforce the decision to retreat, Hampton informed Armstrong that he had polled the commanding officers of brigades, regiments, and corps, and the heads of the general staff, and they had unanimously agreed that the U.S. force should "immediately return by orderly marches to such a position as will secure our communications with the United States." The letter combined apologia with bravado, making it appear that Hampton's army was ready either to retire into winter quarters or to return to the attack if ordered to do so.[15] In fact, Hampton had already made the decision by crossing the border into New York State.

Less than three weeks later, another deadly engagement was fought on Canadian soil. This time, British regulars and Canadian militia countered the American invasion on the St. Lawrence River, in the eastern reaches of Upper Canada. The Battle of Crysler's Farm on November 11, 1813, was supposed to be coordinated with the advance of Hampton's troops up the St. Lawrence from Sackets Harbor, the push that failed at the Battle of Chateauguay. On the night of October 17, Major General James Wilkinson led an army of between seven and eight thousand men from Sackets Harbor. The plan was to proceed down the St. Lawrence and attack Montreal.

Wilkinson's considerable force consisted of fourteen infantry regiments, two regiments of dragoons, and three artillery regiments, as well as a contingent of riflemen to lead the advance. Three hundred bateaux, as well as twelve gunboats and some smaller vessels, had been mobilized to transport the army. Hampered by gales and snowstorms, Wilkinson's force was held up in the Thousand Islands on the St. Lawrence until November 5, when more clement weather allowed them to move forward.[16]

By the time Wilkinson's men were able to resume their advance, Hampton had already been rebuffed at Chateauguay and had pulled his troops back to New York State. In addition, U.S. Secretary of War John Armstrong had by then concluded, without informing Wilkinson, that with winter coming on, it was too late to attack Montreal. On October 16, Armstrong dispatched an order that the U.S. force should establish winter quarters on Canadian territory upriver from Montreal.[17]

As the Americans advanced, their commander was often giddy with ague and fever. To deal with the ailment, he took large doses of laudanum, a compound laced with opium. A friend of Wilkinson's concluded that the major general was often high, which would account for his erratic judgement, his delusions about the enemy, and the completely unrealistic strategic suggestions he frequently made.[18]

When the British at Kingston learned that the Americans were on the move, General Francis de Rottenburg sent the 49th and 89th Regiments in pursuit, as he had been instructed to do by Prevost in the event of an American attack down the river. Leading the force was Lieutenant Colonel Joseph W. Morrison of the 89th. His force, numbering only 680 soldiers and a few artillerymen with two 6-pounder field guns, embarked on two schooners, seven gunboats, and a few bateaux.[19]

Canadian farmers took potshots at the Americans on the river. As Morrison's force pursued them, the Americans had to work their way around British artillery housed in Fort Wellington, at Prescott. On the morning of November 9, Morrison's men landed at Prescott, where they were reinforced by a detachment of 240 soldiers, made up of two flank companies of the 49th Foot, some men from the Canadian Fencibles, three companies of Canadian Voltigeurs, a few artillerymen in charge of a 6-pounder gun, and a few Provincial Dragoons, who acted as couriers. This brought Morrison's numbers up to about nine hundred.[20]

As rain and sleet pelted the men in both armies, the American force advanced close to the Long Sault Rapids on the St. Lawrence with the British close behind them. On the night of November 10, Morrison picked a farmhouse belonging to John Crysler, a business-man and politician in Upper Canada who served in the local militia, as his headquarters. He calculated that he was well positioned, with his advance force established with its flank against the river and his main units just over five hundred metres behind them. If the Americans decided to turn and attack his men, thought Morrison, this was good ground on which to fight.

After a native warrior fired at an American reconnaissance patrol on the morning of November 11, Wilkinson decided it was time to assault the pursuers. He ordered Brigadier General John P. Boyd to advance on the enemy with his two thousand regulars arrayed in three columns. The Americans easily pushed back the thin skirmish line of Canadian Voltigeurs, but when they came upon the main British force, they were stopped in their tracks by volleys fired by the men of the 49th and 89th. A U.S. attempt to turn Morrison's left flank was successfully parried when the British commander turned the companies of the 89th nearly ninety degrees. The experienced British soldiers stood their ground as the Americans attacked, then countered with devastating volleys and well-directed cannon fire. The Americans broke and ran, some of them deeply distressed when they learned that the opponents in grey greatcoats were not militia but the men of the famed 49th.[21]

The Americans lost 102 men. They managed to retreat with 237 of their wounded but had to leave the more seriously injured behind. It was a stunning defeat for an American force that outnumbered its opponent.[22]

Behind Wilkinson were Morrison's troops, who had won the fight at Crysler's Farm, and looming ahead of him were the forces of General Prevost, who were mobilizing to block any attack on Montreal. On November 12, after his men had succeeded in getting past the Long Sault Rapids, Wilkinson received a letter from Major General Hampton stating that he could not press on to Montreal and would not lead his men to St. Regis, on the south shore of the St. Lawrence just downstream from Cornwall, to join forces with Wilkinson's men.[23]

In his letter in reply, Wilkinson made Hampton's refusal to march on Montreal a reason for breaking off the campaign. "Such resolution defeats the grand objects of the campaign in this quarter," Wilkinson wrote rather grandly, "which, before the receipt of your letter, were thought to be completely within our power, no suspicion being entertained that you would decline the junction directed, it will oblige us to take post at French Mills, on Salmon River, or in their vicinity for the winter."[24]

Had the Americans proceeded to carry out an attack on Montreal, they would have encountered a well-appointed enemy force of about six thousand men that had been put into place by Prevost. Instead, the contending parties went their separate ways into winter quarters. Morrison's men retired to Prescott or Kingston. Wilkinson's men wintered at French Mills, on the south shore of the St. Lawrence, just three kilometres inside U.S. territory. In this miserable location, named Fort Covington after the war, the U.S. troops suffered through the winter months. Rations were in short supply, and some regiments had no bread for up to four days. Medical care for the sick was very poor. Many soldiers suffered from pneumonia, diarrhea, typhus, and dysentery.[25] At Crysler's Farm as at Chateauguay, American armies were beaten by superior generalship on the British side.

For the rest of the war, Lower Canada was safe from American occupation. In Upper Canada, however, U.S. troops occupied the southwest and much of the territory on the Canadian side of the Niagara Frontier. The occupation provoked treason on the part of some, reprisals on the part of others, and ugly incidents against settlements on both sides of the border.

Just prior to the outbreak of the war and in its early days, Brock had expressed concerns about the loyalty of many of the recent American immigrants to Upper Canada. A number of these new arrivals did indeed go over to the American side, some of them taking up arms. The most notorious turncoat was not an American, however. Irish-born Joseph Willcocks, who had led the vocal opposition to Brock in the Upper Canada Legislative Assembly before the war, supported the British in the early days of the conflict but later switched sides.

Anxious to control Willcocks and to keep him on side, Brock enlisted him to generate support for the British cause among the Six Nations natives. At the Battle of Queenston Heights in October 1812, where Brock fell, Willcocks fought as a gentleman volunteer in a contingent of Six Nations warriors. While still a member of the assembly, Willcocks grew deeply disturbed by Upper Canadian measures against those who expressed disloyal views in the wake of the 1813 U.S. invasions. Had Willcocks been born a couple of decades later, he would have fought on the side of the failed rebellions against British rule led by William Lyon Mackenzie and Louis-Joseph Papineau in the 1830s. In July 1813, he went over to the American side, where he was given the rank of major and assigned the task of recruiting a Company of Canadian Volunteers to fight under the Stars and Stripes.

During the American occupation, Willcocks and the Volunteers participated in the burning and looting of farms. They arrested well-known Loyalists and dispatched them to U.S. prisons across the river. Most notoriously, Willcocks supported and participated in the burning of the village of Newark on December 10, 1813.

Early that year, U.S. Secretary of War John Armstrong had decided that if British troops threatened to take cover in Newark, which was adjacent to the U.S.-occupied Fort George, the Americans could take the pre-emptive step of destroying the village. During the first week of December 1813, Lieutenant General Gordon Drummond replaced the cautious Major General Francis de Rottenburg as the commander of British forces in North America. Drummond, the youngest officer to serve in Canada during the period, ordered the British units at Burlington Heights to advance toward Niagara.

On December 10, U.S. Brigadier General George McClure, who had emigrated to the United States from Ireland in 1790, become a businessman, and risen through the ranks in the New York Militia,[26] decided that his under-strength complement, which included one hundred members of the Company of Canadian Volunteers, was insufficient to hold Fort George. He pulled his men out of the fort and moved them across the river to Fort Niagara. The retreating Americans threw the cannon from Fort George into the surrounding ditch. Then McClure gave the order to burn the village of Newark to the ground.

With the active participation of the Company of Canadian Volunteers, that order was carried out, leaving only one of the 150 houses in the village standing. Given little warning to retrieve their belongings from their houses, the inhabitants of Newark, who were mostly women and children, were rendered homeless in the bitter cold of a mid-December night. Left destitute in the snow with only a few of their possessions, the four hundred townsfolk desperately sought shelter, some finding it in Fort George and in a nearby barracks. Others built makeshift shelters by leaning partially burnt boards against the chimneys of gutted houses. When the sun rose the next morning, the bodies of women and children were found in the snowdrifts.

The Company of Canadian Volunteers was created to win wavering Upper Canadians over to the American side. The depredations of the unit, climaxing in the burning of Newark, had exactly the opposite effect, driving inhabitants sharply to the British side and leaving them thirsting for revenge.

Vengeance came quickly. Having retaken Fort George, the British were in a position to threaten Fort Niagara and the surrounding region on the American side of the river. On the night of December 18, Drummond sent a force of over five hundred men across the river. Having forced a U.S. picket to reveal the American challenge and password, the British approached the fort's gate and used this intelligence to gain entry. Resistance was soon overcome, except for a stout defence put up by U.S. troops in one of the fort's buildings. After the Americans refused a British demand to surrender, the attackers forced their way inside. The order was then given to "bayonet the whole."

Only six British soldiers were killed and five wounded in the attack. Sixty-five Americans were killed, and fourteen were wounded and taken prisoner, along with three hundred and forty-four others. The American toll did not include those bayoneted, who numbered at least eighty.

From Fort Niagara, the British marched through the American settlements along the Niagara, dispensing destruction and death along the way. Much of Lewiston and the villages of Manchester and Schlosser were laid waste. Several days later, the British again crossed the Niagara River to assault Black Rock and Buffalo. British soldiers torched the buildings in Black Rock and then meted out the same punishment to Buffalo before destroying the naval yard at Buffalo Creek. They left more than forty Americans dead, losing close to that number themselves, and took ninety prisoners back with them to the Canadian side of the river.

Brigadier General McClure's order to burn Newark, which started the round of destruction on both sides of the border, was later disavowed by the U.S. government. In the spring of 1814, in what came to be known as the Ancaster Bloody Assize, Upper Canadians were tried in absentia for high treason. John Beverley Robinson, the attorney general of Upper Canada, was the prosecutor. Fifteen Upper Canadians, including Joseph Willcocks, were convicted. Eight of them were later captured and hanged at Burlington Heights on July

20, 1814. Willcocks met his death when he was shot in the chest during the siege of Fort Erie on September 4, 1814. He is buried in an unmarked grave in Buffalo's Forest Lawn Cemetery.

Chapter 16

Bloody Niagara

W HILE THE TWO SIDES were inflicting atrocities on one another along the Niagara Frontier, cooler heads on the other side of the Atlantic were once again considering ways to bring the war to an end. In the later months of 1813, hopeful for a victory over Napoleon and the end of decades of fighting in Europe, the British government was also in a mood to seek peace with the Americans. In November 1813, Lord Castlereagh offered to begin direct negotiations with the United States to end the war.

By the time the British took this initiative, the earlier Russian offer to mediate the conflict had come to nothing. In May 1813, the Madison administration had dispatched Treasury Secretary Albert Gallatin and Senator James Bayard on a journey to St. Petersburg to serve as American negotiators. When the two reached Russia, they soon found that their mission was doomed to failure. The British were not interested in having the Russians mediate the war in North America. In January 1814, Gallatin and Bayard left Russia with nothing to show for their efforts.[1]

On January 5, 1814, the Madison administration accepted the offer from the British government to open direct negotiations, and the president added two additional members to the roster of American commissioners: Henry Clay and Jonathan Russell, a New

Englander, who had been U.S. chargé d'affaires in Britain when the war broke out.[2]

The American commissioners travelled first to Göteborg, Sweden, where talks with the British were initially scheduled, and from there to Ghent, in present-day Belgium. The British, confident that the war with Napoleon was over, dragged their feet, hoping that the veterans dispatched to North America might achieve victories that would strengthen their hand in the talks.

The British commissioners, men of lower political stature than their American counterparts, were not selected until May 1814, and they departed for Ghent on August 2. Moreover, they were close enough to home that they could quickly consult their government, which the Americans could not. Leading the British commissioners was Admiral Lord James Gambier, who had participated in the bombardment of Copenhagen in 1807 and had served in Newfoundland during the American Revolutionary War. William Adams, LL.D., a distinguished maritime law expert, was also on the negotiation team, as was Henry Goulburn, a young undersecretary for war and the colonies who went on to have a successful career in politics (a town in New South Wales is named after him). The final member was Anthony St. John Baker, who was to serve as secretary to the commission.[3]

John Quincy Adams, the future secretary of state and president, was infuriated that the British were delaying the start of talks, leaving the Americans to cool their heels. "They have kept us waiting nearly four months since the arrival of Mr. Clay and Mr. Russell in Europe," he complained in a letter, "and their commissioners are not yet here to meet us. In the mean time they have sent to America formidable reinforcements . . . and I can imagine no other motive for their studied and long protracted delays to the commencement of the negotiation, than the intention of waiting for the effect of their forces upon our fears. Whatever they may do, I trust in God that they will find in our country a spirit adequate to every exigency."[4]

While the fighting continued on the other side of the ocean, talks proceeded at a glacial pace. There were two broad ways a territorial settlement could be reached, and two other large questions that had to be resolved. On the territorial issue, one way forward would be for both sides to keep the territory they held when the fighting ceased, according to the doctrine of *uti possidetis*. Alternatively, the two sides could restore the boundaries that had existed between them when the war started, with each agreeing to withdraw as speedily as possible from its positions on the other side's territory.

In addition to resolving this fundamental question, each side had a major issue it intended to press on its adversary. The Americans were determined to push the British to end the impressment of American ships in their quest for runaway British sailors. For their part, the British were concerned about the question of the creation of a native state between Canada and the United States. This was a means of both securing Canadian territory against American attack and meeting the commitment they had made to their native allies.

Negotiators on both sides acted on the instructions they received from their home governments, the Americans having to wait several months to send a missive to Washington and receive a reply, while it took the British only a couple of days to hear from London. Secretary of State James Monroe had given the U.S. commissioners a series of instructions on the opening positions they were to adopt. "On impressment," he primed Henry Clay before he departed for Europe, "the sentiments of the President have undergone no change. This degrading practice must cease." A few weeks later, on February 14, 1814, Monroe wrote that he hoped that Britain's recent triumphs against Napoleon would cause the British to ease up on the issue of impressment. John Quincy Adams wrote back that he feared that Britain's victories in Europe could have precisely the opposite effect and could prompt the British to harden their stance in North America. Their winning hand on the continent, he replied, "has undoubtedly made the continuance of the war with America, a purpose of policy with them, as much as it is a purpose of passion with their nation."[5]

In June 1814, Albert Gallatin reinforced the anxieties expressed by Adams in a note to Monroe. "You may rest assured of the general hostile spirit of this nation [Great Britain]," he wrote, "and of its wish to inflict serious injury on the United States; that no assistance can be expected from Europe; and that no better terms will be obtained than the status quo ante bellum."[76] With talks to resolve the conflict proceeding slowly, the miseries of the war continued.

By the summer of 1814, the war was in its climactic phase. British veterans freed from the Napoleonic Wars were on their way to Canada to take up arms against the Americans. Along the Canadian-American frontier, the fighting continued, with engagements won by both sides. But there as well, the conditions of the war were changing. The injection of British regulars would fortify the defence of the Canadas. And American regulars, under a new generation of commanders such as Brigadier General Winfield Scott, were much more fit to fight their British counterparts than they had been two years earlier.

The rapidly evolving war in Europe had direct implications for the related struggle in North America. Buoyed by Napoleon's catastrophic defeat in Russia, a new coalition of powers — which included Great Britain, Russia, Prussia, Austria, Sweden, Spain, and Portugal — took shape to combat the French Empire. While Napoleon's armies achieved some successes, the heavily outnumbered French were defeated at the crucial Battle of Leipzig in October 1813. Napoleon retreated into France, his once-dominant Grande Armée badly depleted. In March 1814, the coalition forces captured Paris. On April 11, with his top marshals no longer supporting him, Napoleon abdicated and was exiled to Elba, an island off the coast of Tuscany.

With Napoleon safely exiled, Lord Bathurst wrote Prevost to let him know that large numbers of foot soldiers and artillerymen were on their way to Canada. During the winter of 1814, Bathurst had written to the Duke of Wellington to seek his views on the conduct of the war in North America. On February 22, the Iron Duke replied candidly that he was not well informed about the affairs of the continent or its topography, but he did have some sound points to make. "I believe that the defence of Canada, and the co-operation of the Indians," he ventured, "depends upon the navigation of the lakes ... Any offensive operations founded upon Canada must be preceded by the establishment of a naval superiority on the lakes.

"But even if we had that superiority, I should doubt our being able to do more than secure the points on those lakes at which the Americans could have access. In such countries as America, very extensive, thinly peopled, and producing but little food in proportion to their extent, military operations by large bodies are impracticable, unless the party carrying them on has the uninterrupted use of a navigable river, or very extensive means of land transport, which such a country can rarely supply.

"I conceive, therefore, that were your army larger than the proposed augmentation would make it, you could not quit the lakes; and, indeed, you would be tied to them the more necessarily in proportion as your army would be large."[7]

With the promise of more British troops on the way, Prevost had to conceive a plan to deploy and support these forces. A major ship-building effort on the lakes would be a basic part of the strategy.

As it had been over the previous two years of fighting, the narrow strip of land between Lakes Ontario and Erie along the Niagara River was the vortex of action. On the morning of July 3, 1814, American forces commanded by Winfield Scott crossed the Niagara River, landing near Fort Erie on the Canadian shore.[8] Realizing its position was hopeless, the small garrison at the fort surrendered. In preliminary fighting on July 4 and a major battle at Chippawa, upriver from Niagara Falls, on July 5,[9] the Americans were victorious. Leading the British was Major General Phineas Riall, who made the foolish assumption that he could take the Americans lightly as inferior fighters. In truth, the quality of the American army was dramatically better by the summer of 1814 than it had been as recently as a year earlier. The soldiers were better trained, and the leadership was vastly more competent.

When the British advanced on Chippawa, Scott set up his three battalions to meet the attack with his troops facing obliquely forward to prevent them from being flanked and to allow him to concentrate his fire on the centre of the British line. Taking heavy casualties and facing an assault from the American lines, Riall ordered his men to retreat. Later, accounting for his defeat, Riall explained that he "immediately moved up the Kings Regiment to the right while the Royal Scots and 100th Regt. were directed to charge the Enemy in front, for which they advanced with the greatest Gallantry, under a most destructive fire. I am sorry to say, however, in this attempt they suffered so severely that I was obliged to withdraw them, finding that their further Efforts against superior numbers of the Enemy would be unavailing." In fact, Scott's U.S. troops were slightly fewer in number than Riall's forces, but they prevailed.[10]

After losing the engagement, the British soldiers in the 1st and 100th fell back in orderly fashion. With the support of dragoons, they made it back across the wide Chippawa River, taking their artillery with them. Once across, the engineers deftly dropped the central span of the bridge into the water.[11]

Absorbing the hard lessons learned at Chippawa and confronting the fierce new effectiveness of the American regulars, the British prepared for the next round of the campaign. On July 24, Lieutenant General Gordon Drummond left York to sail across the lake to Fort George and take personal command of the campaign along the Niagara.

Having prevailed at Chippawa, Scott's brigade moved north along Portage Road to Niagara Falls. On July 25, the two sides encountered each other at Lundy's Lane, a road running at right angles from Portage Road, alongside the Niagara River. As the U.S. troops advanced toward the lane, they came upon the British force commanded by Riall. Drummond, who had arrived from York that morning with additional soldiers, countermanded Riall's initial order to his men to withdraw. The British deployed along Lundy's Lane with their artillery positioned on a slope above the road. Scott's men, who had arrived in the area the previous evening, moved out of the thick woods to the south of Lundy's Lane and readied themselves for the fight. Fearing that he was outnumbered and that he would have a tough time of it along Portage Road if he was forced to withdraw, Scott threw caution to the wind and attacked.

U.S. assaults on the British left and centre were met with fierce resistance. Repeated charges by Scott's men were countered with artillery volleys from British gunners. An American force did succeed in crossing Portage Road on the east side of the battlefield and swung through the woods so that they were able to outflank some militiamen and a small force of Royal Scots. In this attack, Major General Riall was hit in the arm and captured. The British managed to overcome their problems on the flank, however, by turning to face the enemy and refusing the line.

Neither side had gained a decisive advantage over its adversary. Both received reinforcements. As night fell, the Americans managed an attack up the slope in the direction of the British guns. With a desperate bayonet charge, they overcame the British artillerymen and seized the guns, opening the way for an American advance to the high ground. Drummond undertook repeated counterattacks but failed to take back his lost artillery.

In the end, the Americans withdrew from the field, leaving the bruising battle at Lundy's Lane a tactical British victory. According to the British account, British and Canadian losses at Lundy's Lane totalled 84 officers and men killed, 559 wounded, 193 missing, and 42 taken prisoner. The Americans compiled their losses at 173 dead, 571 wounded, and 117 missing.[12]

As historian Donald E. Graves points out in his history of the Battle of Lundy's Lane, the casualty numbers do not tell the full story: "Only the most primitive arrangements existed for the removal of the wounded — there were no ambulances; common supply wagons served instead. The wounded American enlisted personnel had to suffer the agonies of a nearly twenty-mile ride in unsprung and uncovered vehicles to Fort Erie, while the British wounded faced a similar tortuous journey to Fort George.

". . . The wounded collected by the British were taken to Fort George and placed in the charge of Surgeon William Dunlop of the 89th Foot. When Dunlop inquired where he was to put them, he was 'shown a ruinous fabric, built of logs' known as Butler's Barracks . . . The small buildings were so crowded that the wounded 'had to be laid on straw on the floor . . .'

"Conditions in these hospitals [at Fort George and elsewhere during the war] were appalling. Lacking any form of anaesthesia, medical personnel could do little to lessen the misery and had to leave the wounded in pain until they lapsed into unconsciousness or died. In 1814 military hospitals after a major battle resembled nothing so much as noisy charnel-houses . . ."[13]

At Lundy's Lane, the professionalism of the soldiers on both sides outpaced the professionalism of those running the medical facilities to treat the wounded. The ability of the soldiers to inflict mayhem was increasing more quickly than the ability of the caregivers to cope.

Following Lundy's Lane, the Americans withdrew to their remaining stronghold on the Canadian side of the frontier, Fort Erie. There, they offered fierce resistance against an assault mounted by three thousand soldiers under the command of Lieutenant General Drummond. Originally a British fort, the small, well-constructed structure had been improved and extended by the Americans to include an earth wall that extended seven hundred yards to the south, bringing it to within fifty yards of the lake.[14] The addition was needed to house the twenty-two hundred American troops at the site.

The prospect of unleashing a direct assault on the fort was a daunting one. Instead, Drummond launched a British raid across the Niagara River against Buffalo and Black Rock. If successful, the assault would threaten the American rear, cut off the Americans in

Fort Erie from supplies, and force them out of the fort. The raid failed, however, and the U.S. troops stayed put in the fort. On August 15, Drummond launched a three-pronged assault on the American position, with each prong intended to take out one of the American batteries. The British attacks on the fort were intense and bloody, and breakthroughs were nearly achieved at certain points. The siege continued until the middle of September, with fierce assaults launched by both sides. With many of his men suffering from illness and fatigue, and with heavy rain making the conditions even more miserable, Drummond ended the siege, pulling his troops back to the Chippawa River. Despite their success in repelling the British attacks, the Americans found their position untenable for the long term.

On October 15, the British launched the HMS *St. Lawrence* on Lake Ontario, which prompted Chauncey to pull his vessels off the lake to the safe haven of Sackets Harbor. With this shift in the naval balance, supplying the American force at Fort Erie became too difficult to contemplate. On November 5, Major General George Izard pulled the U.S. troops out of Canada and demolished the fortifications at Fort Erie.

From the beginning of the war until November 1814, the fighting in the Niagara campaigns went on for 125 days, with four major battles, two minor actions, and a large number of skirmishes. It was the toughest and most drawn-out campaign of the War of 1812.

By the time the Niagara campaign was over, Upper Canada had changed. While the U.S. troops still occupied the southwestern corner of the province, any idea that the Americans were liberators was long gone, a casualty of the bitter fighting and the experience of occupation. Upper Canadians were becoming a people in their own right, with that combination of British and American characteristics, filtered through the lens of Canadian experience, that has made the English-Canadian identity so infuriatingly difficult to comprehend.

Chapter 17

Rockets' Red Glare

T HE BRITISH MILITARY STRATEGISTS were well aware that
prevailing in ground initiatives alone would not win them the
war against the United States. Throughout the conflict, the Royal
Navy mounted a blockade along the American coast to deprive the
United States of the bounties of commerce with other nations. U.S.
exports and imports were both hard hit. For commercial interests
and for the country's port cities and towns, the blockade dealt a devastating blow. In commercial, seafaring New England, the blockade
heightened the sullen outlook. Other American seaports, from New
York to Baltimore and along the southern seaboard to New Orleans,
also felt the pain.

In the summer of 1814, the British decided to strike at the solar
plexus of the United States, in the vulnerable area of Chesapeake Bay.
The great bay extends from Baltimore, Maryland, in the north almost
to Virginia Beach in the south, and its lengthy coastline on both the
east and the west was a constant invitation to the British to deploy
their superior naval power. The bay also tempted them to strike at the
political heart of the enemy, Washington D.C., and in the process to
mete out reprisals for the burning and sacking of York and Newark
the previous year.

The Americans were slow to assess the threat and take steps to counter it. During much of 1813, with British ships in the Chesapeake,[1] a swift strike against the American capital was a live possibility. President James Madison perceived the risk, and on July 1, 1814, he convened an emergency meeting of his cabinet at the President's House. This mansion was a glittering architectural jewel, an imposing edifice amid the vast spaces of a national capital that was only in the initial stages of construction. Although it was sometimes called the "White House," that name only became official early in the twentieth century, during the presidency of Theodore Roosevelt.

News of Napoleon's abdication had reached Washington by the time Madison called the cabinet into session. At the end of June, the president received dispatches from American diplomats in Europe warning that Britain could soon send thousands of experienced veterans to fight in North America. Present at the cabinet meeting were Madison's confidants: Secretary of State James Monroe, Attorney General Richard Rush, and Secretary of the Navy William Jones. Also in attendance were the secretary of the treasury, the ailing George Campbell, and Secretary of War John Armstrong, a man whose strident manner repelled the others.[2]

At the time of the meeting, the national capital was much more an aspiration than an accomplished fact. In 1810, Washington's population numbered a mere 8,200 citizens. Among them were 5,900 whites, fewer than 900 free blacks, and 1,400 slaves. By then, the town boasted more inhabitants than long-established and better-appointed Georgetown, five kilometres away. Many congressmen preferred to reside in Georgetown and commute to the capital. In 1810, Georgetown was inhabited by just under five thousand people, and over eleven hundred of them were slaves.[3]

The District of Columbia had been carved out of the marshy low-lands adjacent to the Potomac River. In addition to the President's House on Pennsylvania Avenue, a mile away on a modest rise in the otherwise flat landscape, the magnificent Capitol was under construction.*

Madison, as he told the members of his cabinet, believed a British attack was imminent and recommended positioning several thousand men between the capital and the marine approaches to it along Chesapeake Bay. As a further precaution, he wanted ten to twelve thousand militiamen placed on standby in D.C., Maryland, and the neighbouring regions of Virginia. Those present at the emergency council agreed that the British were threatening to attack, but they had differing views on which city would be the primary target.

The problem for the U.S. was that few regular soldiers were available in the threatened region. Most of the regulars were deployed along the Niagara border and at various points as far south as New Orleans. The regulars were vastly better trained than the militia and would be a much more formidable match for British veterans should the time come for a serious battle.

The day after the cabinet met, the 10th Military District was created to cover the areas believed to be at risk.[4] The government appointed Brigadier General William H. Winder to organize the defence of the new military district.[5] A thirty-nine-year-old Baltimore lawyer whose uncle, Levin Winder, was the governor of Maryland, the brigadier general had landed the quintessential political appointment. His military experience was slight, though it did include having been captured at the Battle of Stoney Creek the previous year.

Winder rushed around his district, putting energy, if not effectiveness, into action. He badly needed troops and was not getting enough of them. The expiration of a military law in Pennsylvania deprived him of a potential force from that quarter. The new militia

---

* The new capital city, fit for a world power, was designed by the French planner Pierre L'Enfant. No one could work with L'Enfant for long, and eventually he was dismissed as the District's conceptual planner, but not before he had left his indelible mark on Washington.

law in that state was not to take effect until October, leaving a large hole in Winder's potential to mobilize effectively.[6]

To make matters worse, Winder was in constant conflict with Secretary of War John Armstrong, who dismissed the very idea that the British were planning an attack on Washington. On the afternoon of July 14, the lead ships of the British armada sailed into Chesapeake Bay. Even with this clear signal of aggression, the secretary of war scornfully told the head of the Washington militia, "By God, they would not come with such a fleet without meaning to strike somewhere. But they certainly will not come here! What the devil will they do here? No! No! Baltimore is the place, Sir. That is of so much more consequence."[7] To Armstrong, it seemed logical that the British would deliver a blow against the great commercial port rather than the country's capital, which was still a raw town.

Sir Alexander Cochrane, the fifty-six-year-old commander-in-chief of the North American Station, was in charge of the British expeditionary force. The British plan was to strike first at Washington and then to take aim at Annapolis and Baltimore. In a letter to his superiors in London, he asserted that the U.S. capital could be "either destroyed or laid under contribution."[8] For months prior to the arrival of the British fleet, Rear Admiral George Cockburn, Cochrane's subordinate, had acquired considerable experience commanding his own flotilla and laying waste to settlements in raids along the Chesapeake. He was so detested that one American offered a cash prize in exchange for his head and each of his ears.[9]

Cockburn's harsh unwillingness to spare settlements and homes that fell under his sway distressed even the officers who served under him. On one occasion, Cockburn, along with British soldiers who included fellow officer Sir Peter Parker, entered a Maryland village and encountered three young women who had remained at their home to beg for it to be spared. Cockburn, oblivious to their pleas, told the women he knew their father was a colonel serving in the state militia. He announced that their house would be burned down in ten minutes, and that they could remove their possessions within that time. While the sisters and their sixteen-year-old brother pleaded with Cockburn, Parker joined in to protest the demolition. Unmoved, the admiral counted down the minutes on his watch and called in his men to set the building alight. Parker wept along with the family members as the house burned to the ground.[10]

Cockburn believed that Washington could be taken easily. He wrote to Cochrane that seizing a capital city was "always so great a blow to the government of a country."[11] He recommended landing at Benedict, on the Patuxent River, located less than eighty kilometres southeast of Washington. He reasoned that the British could live off the bounties of the countryside by commandeering the food they needed and acquiring horses to haul their cannon to Washington.

"To distract and divide the enemy" as the British army marched on Washington from the east, Cockburn favoured sending ships up the Potomac River to threaten the capital and devastate its approaches from the south.[12] The assault was aided by local residents, including runaway slaves, who could be bribed or cajoled into providing pertinent information. During their campaign in the Chesapeake, the British issued proclamations declaring that slaves who joined their ranks would be set free and resettled on British territory.[13]

In mid-August, Cochrane's ships anchored close to the mouths of the Patuxent and Potomac Rivers so he could hold a council of war with his subordinates. Cockburn would direct operations on the water. On land, Major General Robert Ross, an Irish-born forty-eight-year-old seasoned officer who had been picked for his role in North America by the Duke of Wellington, would direct the armed forces. Respected, even beloved, by his soldiers for his valour in combat, Ross was preternaturally more cautious than his naval counterpart.

Once the mission shifted from water to land, Ross would outrank Cockburn, which could engender friction between the two, since Cockburn was far from deferential. Indeed, later in his career, Cockburn was chosen for the ticklish task of escorting Napoleon Bonaparte by ship to his second, and final, place of exile, the island of Saint Helena in the South Atlantic. Bonaparte discovered in his personal relations with Cockburn that the bristly British admiral had no problem standing up to the dethroned emperor. Napoleon and Cockburn paced the deck of the ship and played cards on their long voyage. "It is clear he is still inclined to act the sovereign occasionally, but I cannot allow it," Cockburn noted in his diary.[14]

Compounding American confusion about the true goals of the operation, the British made it appear as though they were primarily intent on crushing the minor American naval presence on the Chesapeake, under the command of Commodore Joshua Barney. A hero of the Revolutionary War, Barney specialized in harassing British ships on the Chesapeake.[15] Pursuing Barney's ships into the dead end of the Patuxent River would allow the British to make quick work of this persistent adversary. More important, it would position British troops not more than two days' march from Washington.[16]

The British conceived a two-pronged plan of attack. Four thousand troops, the strike force, would be on board the ships heading up the Patuxent River. Meanwhile, a squadron of vessels armed with rockets and bombs would venture into the Potomac. Under the command of Captain James Gordon, who had lost a leg during a naval engagement in the war against Napoleon, this latter force would attempt to destroy Fort Warburton, which guarded the approaches to the District of Columbia. Then Gordon's troops would provide cover for the British units during their withdrawal from Washington, after the planned seizure and destruction of the federal government's public buildings.[17]

The initial target of the flotilla that sailed up the Patuxent was the settlement of Benedict, which had been established to export tobacco to Britain from the earliest days of European settlement, and so was equipped with wharves and warehouses. Two frigates negotiated the shallow waters, drawing close to the village, while the heavier ships of the line had to drop anchor miles short. Beginning at 2:00 a.m. on August 19, boats were lowered over the side of the heavy ships to ferry the troops upstream. After rowing for a couple of miles, the soldiers boarded the lighter frigates.

Those who had long been penned up on the stiflingly hot ships were glad to come ashore. Disobeying their orders not to take anything from farmers without paying for it, many made off with pigs, chickens, and sheep. Some found fresh milk and cream abandoned in houses. Shooting wild birds and hares soon became great sport for men who were happy to stretch their legs and enjoy the fertile countryside.

To proceed with the attack on Washington, two hundred men dragged ashore the heavy assault equipment, which included rockets, ammunition, two 3-pounders, a 9-pounder, and a 5 1/2-inch howitzer.[18]

With members of the top American leadership still disagreeing about whether Washington or Baltimore was the first British target, Secretary of State James Monroe decided to scout the area himself that same day. Accompanied by a small party of men on horseback, the former cavalry colonel rode off in the direction of Benedict. To his alarm, he witnessed British soldiers advancing through the woods with no U.S. abatis to block them.[19]

By the afternoon of August 20, having encountered no American resistance, British soldiers were marching in three columns upstream toward Nottingham, about thirty-two kilometres distant. Each was equipped with three days' worth of rations, which amounted to three pounds of pork and two and a half pounds of biscuit. They were accompanied by small craft on the adjacent Patuxent. The stifling heat, the poor condition of the men after months on board ships, and a heavy thunderstorm during the first night of the advance made the going slow and difficult. On the late afternoon of August 21, the troops reached Nottingham. The hard-driving Cockburn was already there, and he set out the following day in pursuit of Barney's flotilla. Farther upstream, at Pig Point, Cockburn and his men came upon the sorry remains of the American naval unit. Sixteen of Barney's seventeen craft had been blown up under his orders, leaving only one to be captured.

Winder sent no troops forward to slow the British advance. He had managed to assemble a force of about two thousand soldiers, including three hundred regulars, at Bladensburg, a few miles northeast of Washington. In command there was Brigadier General Tobias Stansbury.

On August 22, panic hit Washington. Much of the citizenry abandoned the city, and by the following evening few women and children were still in residence. Uncertain about what course to follow, Winder pulled back the troops directly under his command to Old Fields. At this location, about thirteen kilometres from the capital and the same distance from Bladensburg, the brigadier general was reinforced by the arrival of Barney and his four hundred sailors, now without ships.

Having ordered most records of the federal government to be removed from Washington — they were taken in linen bags on carts and wagons to a house in Leesburg, Virginia, about fifty-six kilometres distant — President Madison decided to visit the troops to raise morale.[20] The diminutive chief executive looked anything but martial when he turned up at Stansbury's camp with two duelling pistols strapped around his middle.

The Battle of Bladensburg, which would determine who controlled the approaches to Washington, was fought on August 24, a miserably hot day. For hours, both American and British soldiers marched to the site of the coming fight. American militiamen, many of them attired in civilian clothing and looking distinctly unmilitary in black coats or shooting jackets, were exhausted by the time they reached Bladensburg. On the other side of the river, closing in on Bladensburg from the opposite direction, were British troops in their customary red coats. Buglers played marching airs to buoy the spirits of the soldiers, some of whom fell to the side when they were overcome by cramps and weakness.[21] A few dropped dead, struck down by dehydration. Six thousand, three hundred Americans equipped with twenty-six guns, including twenty 6-pounders, were assembled in a strong position on the heights above the town of Bladensburg. Facing them were twenty-six hundred British soldiers.

Stansbury placed his artillery and riflemen at the front of the line to oppose any river crossing by the British, and positioned his militia in the rear. Higher-ups could not resist the temptation to interfere with the deployment. Secretary of State Monroe arrived at the American lines and pulled the militia back, leaving the artillery and riflemen with no nearby reserves to support them. The British, throwing conventional military thinking to the winds, decided on an immediate attack.[22] Forgoing further reconnaissance and any attempt to outflank the Americans, the troops of the 85th Light Infantry ditched their packs and charged, some through the woods, some across a bridge, and others across the stream. Although the British encountered heavy fire and took casualties, the attackers held their ground. The 4th and 44th Regiments joined the attack. The Americans resisted for a time, but when the British set up wooden launchers and fired Congreve rockets against them, their first line broke and the militiamen took to their heels. The rockets created the shock and awe expected of them. While some Americans continued to hold, Winder ordered them to retreat. The effective resistance of the U.S. forces was at an end.[23]

In a letter to Secretary of War John Armstrong, written from Baltimore three days after the battle, Winder laid blame for the American defeat on the half-hearted effort of a part of his force. "The contest was not as obstinately maintained as could have been desired," he wrote, "but was by parts of the troops sustained with great spirit and with prodigious effect, and had the whole of our force been equally firm, I am induced to believe the enemy would have been repulsed notwithstanding all the disadvantages under which we fought."[24] It was the sort of letter, expressly penned to shift the blame for the defeat, that was written all too often by the politicians-turned-commanders who regularly led American troops during the war.

Uniquely in American history, much of the top leadership of the U.S. government was on hand to witness the debacle. In addition to Monroe, who had foolishly interfered with the placement of the militia, the president and the secretary of war arrived on the scene. As the commander-in-chief watched the beginning of the rout of his forces, he noted to Monroe and Armstrong, "It would be now proper for us to retire to the rear, leaving the military movement to military men."[25]

The redoubtable Commodore Joshua Barney managed to play his part in the losing cause at Bladensburg. Having lost their flotilla, Barney's naval men managed to tow some of their cannon with them and, acting as infantry, they used their guns to halt a British advance. Just as the American front was collapsing around him, Barney was severely wounded in the thigh. Losing a great deal of blood, Barney was forced to lie down. He ordered his officers to leave him, which they refused to do. When a British officer learned who he was, General Ross and Admiral Cockburn were brought to him. As Barney wrote a few days later, "Those officers behaved to me with the most marked attention, respect and politeness, had a surgeon brought, and my wound dressed immediately. After a few minutes [of] conversation, the general informed me (after paying me a handsome compliment) that I was paroled, and at liberty to proceed to Washington or Bladensburg."[26]

General Ross decided against any pursuit of the Americans, noting in a missive to London that "the rapid flight of the enemy and his knowledge of the country, precluded many prisoners being taken." The British victory against superior numbers — the U.S. militiamen could not hold their own against British regulars — opened the way to Washington. The British had lost 64 men and 185 were wounded, while their foes had suffered 26 casualties and 51 wounded.[27]

On the afternoon of the battle, the president's wife, Dolley, remained in the President's House, hoping for news of an American victory. By the time the president returned to the residence at around 4:30 p.m., however, his wife had departed for Virginia, insisting that Gilbert Stuart's portrait of George Washington must be brought along. Dolley was not willing to tarry while the portrait was being unscrewed from the wall; as she later noted in a letter to her sister, "I have ordered the frame to be broken and the canvas taken out."[28] A fifteen-year-old personal slave by the name of Paul Jennings was ordered to stop unscrewing the painting by Jean Pierre Sioussat, a French confidant of Dolley's. Sioussat proceeded to cut the painting free with a knife and insisted that it not be rolled up, for fear that it would crack. The painting was shipped to the home of a Virginia farmer, who safeguarded it for the next few weeks.[29]

After defeating the Americans at Bladensburg, a brigade of British troops, under the command of General Ross, set out along the road to the capital. Accompanied by Admiral Cockburn, the force arrived in Washington at twilight, proceeding into the square on the east side of the Capitol.[30] Gunfire erupted as American snipers took aim at the British. "Part of the enemy," Corporal David Brown of the 21st Fusiliers later wrote, "being Concealed in one of the houses, fired upon our approach, which killed two of our Corporals and General Ross got his horse shot from under him."[31]

After the snipers vanished, Ross ordered the house from which the shots were fired to be put to the torch. Next came the two wings of the Capitol, one for each house of the U.S. Congress, joined together by a wooden structure. Lieutenant George de Lacy Evans, the deputy quartermaster general of the British 3rd Brigade, and munitions expert Lieutenant George Pratt of the Royal Navy organized the burning of the stone edifice, which was not easily set alight. Eventually they launched Congreve rockets at the Congressional House, and flames shot forth from windows and doors.[32] On the western side of the Capitol, the Library of Congress was also torched.

Before the destruction of the Capitol, Admiral Cockburn visited offices on the ground floor of the House of Representatives and wandered into a room used as an office by the president when he visited Capitol Hill. There, Cockburn found a green leather volume — the president's own copy of the record of revenues and expenditures of the U.S. government in 1810. The admiral took the volume with him and later made a gift of it to his brother, the governor of Bermuda.[33]

That evening, Captain Thomas Tingey of the United States Navy diligently set alight the Washington Navy Yard, following the instructions of William Jones, the secretary of the navy. Tingey was determined to prevent the British from capturing the yard's munitions. He proceeded with the conflagration, despite the arrival of a number of people who feared that the fire would threaten their nearby property. As he reported to Jones several days later, these concerned citizens endeavoured "to prevail on me to deviate from my instructions." Tingey did not heed their pleas, but he did wait until 8:30 p.m., when the afternoon's breeze had subsided.[34] Tingey's demolition lit up the night sky. People saw the terrible glow from across the Potomac in Virginia and from as far away as Baltimore to the northeast.

At around 10:30 p.m., Ross and Cockburn assembled a force of about 150 men to take their assault to the President's House. Along the way, a man by the name of William Gardner called to Cockburn from the open window of his home on Pennsylvania Avenue: "I hope, Sir, that individuals and private property will be respected."

"Yes, Sir," replied the admiral, who guided his horse under the window. "We pledge our sacred honour that the citizens and private property shall be respected. Be under no apprehension. Our advice to you is to remain at home."[35]

The arrival of the unwelcome guests at the executive mansion was captured in Ross's journal: "So unexpected was our entry and capture of Washington; and so confident was Maddison [sic] of the defeat of our troops, that he had prepared a supper for the expected conquerors; and when our advanced party entered the President's house, they found a table laid with forty covers. The fare, however; which was intended for *Jonathan* was voraciously devoured by *John Bull*; and the health of the Prince Regent and success to his Majesty's arms by sea and land, was drunk in the best wines."[36]

The British commanders and a lucky few of their men savoured the food and enjoyed the fine wines. Then the victors explored the house. Some of them found pristine shirts, one belonging to the president, and put them on to replace the sweaty clothes they were wearing. A few more jocular games were played in the building before it was destroyed. Cockburn, who revelled in such scenes, picked up a cushion from Dolley Madison's chair to remind him of her "seat." As the British left the President's House, soldiers set beds, curtains, and other combustible materials on fire.[37] Near the mansion, the Treasury building was also torched, its valuable contents having been removed beforehand by the Americans.

The destruction continued the following day. The War Office and Navy Office in Georgetown were burned to the ground, and government supplies of cordage, hemp, and tar were set alight, spewing vast clouds of smoke into the air. The smoke was visible to members of the Virginia Militia, who decided to destroy the bridge across the Potomac to prevent it from falling into the hands of the British. On the afternoon of August 25, the day after the destruction of much of official Washington, the region was rocked by a violent wind and rainstorm that uprooted trees, tore up crops in farmers' fields, and felled houses. The storm served as a metaphor for the British descent on the capital of the United States — furious and brief. At 9:00 p.m., without fanfare, the British who had visited such devastation on Washington marched out of the city and back to their boats at Nottingham.[38]

In the aftermath of the burning of Washington, President Madison took up the issue in his report to the U.S. Congress: "Direct communication from the British commander indicates it is his avowed purpose to employ the force under his direction 'in destroying and laying waste such towns and districts upon the coast as may be found assailable' and subsequently British soldiers wantonly destroyed public edifices under the insulting pretext that it was done in retaliation for a wanton destruction committed by the army of the United States in Upper Canada when it is notorious that no such destruction was committed."

When Thomas Jefferson added his own criticism, John Strachan, who had witnessed the devastation of York the year before, addressed a letter to the former president: "In April 1813 the public buildings at York, the capital of Upper Canada, were burnt by troops of the United

States, contrary to the articles of capitulation. They consisted of two elegant halls with convenient offices for the accommodation of the Legislature and of the Courts of Justice. The library and all the papers and records belonging to these institutions were consumed; at the same time the church was robbed and the town library totally pillaged. Commodore Chauncey, who has generally behaved honourably, was so ashamed of this last transaction that he endeavoured to collect the books belonging to the library and actually sent back two boxes filled with them but hardly any were complete. Much private property was plundered and several houses left in a state of ruin. Can you tell me why the public buildings and the library at Washington should be held more sacred than those at York?"[39]

Jefferson did not reply.

The British foray in Washington against enemy formations three times their army's size was a considerable feat of arms. Not only did they leave the capital in ruins, they made off with two hundred cannon, five hundred barrels of gunpowder, and one hundred thousand musket cartridges. Admiral Cockburn later wrote in triumphalist terms that this achievement "for the extent of the ground passed over, the importance of its objects, the mischief done the enemy — ashore and afloat — in so short a space of time is scarcely perhaps to be paralleled."[40]

Madison and Monroe returned to Washington on August 28. With a British naval squadron at Alexandria, just across the Potomac, the American political leadership had reason to fear a second assault on the capital. The next evening, the president rode his horse over to the lodgings of Secretary of War John Armstrong. Earlier that day, Madison had been warned in the strongest possible terms by a militia general that his officers would not allow Armstrong, by then hated in the capital, to supervise them. In his meeting with Armstrong, the president said frankly that the British capture of the capital had ignited "violent prejudices" in the hearts of many against both of them. In light of the anger of the soldiers, Madison told Armstrong that it would be wise for the secretary to "have nothing to do with them."[41]

Ever haughty, Armstrong refused to shoulder any blame for the debacle. Although he had repeatedly made the case that the target of the British invasion was not Washington, he lashed out at his critics. To Madison's surprise, instead of agreeing to a temporary absence, the secretary of war offered his resignation, insisting all the while that he had done nothing wrong.

This was too much, even for the gentlemanly Madison, who told his colleague that he had failed to foresee the threat to the capital and all of the consequences that flowed from its capture. Earlier, Armstrong had suggested that he might go home to his family in New York. The president ended the tense meeting by saying that he would have no objection if Armstrong followed through on the suggestion. The next morning, Armstrong sent a missive to Madison announcing that he was leaving for New York.

A few days later, Armstrong sent a letter to the *Baltimore Patriot* that made the case for his actions during the siege of Washington. He ended the letter with a denunciation of the troops who had fled from the battlefield. "It is obvious," he declared, "that if all the troops assembled at Bladensburg had been faithful to themselves and to their country, the enemy would have been beaten and the capital saved."[42]

While the British forces' lightning attack on Washington was underway, their naval assault on the Potomac was proceeding according to plan. Captain Gordon's ships managed to reduce Fort Warburton and then continued upstream, where they forced the humiliating capture of Alexandria. Having been beseeched by the town's mayor and other notables to spare the municipality, Gordon issued an ultimatum. While a couple of demands were struck off the list as impractical, the town leaders pledged to hand over munitions, tobacco, flour, and cotton.

The British held on to Alexandria, plundering the town for the goods on the list, until September 3, when they finally withdrew.

Gordon was concerned about American threats vowing that his return voyage down the Potomac would be a living hell.[43] Rumours that the Americans were setting up ambushes to strike Gordon's ships as they navigated narrow stretches of the river were not ill founded. In the end, the Americans did manage a few attacks, even doing some damage to the vessels and wounding and killing a few British sailors.[44] But Gordon's fleet emerged largely unscathed at the end of the twenty-three-day sally. Many Americans were disgusted that Alexandria had offered no resistance to the invaders. Dolley Madison went so far as to tell friends that letting Alexandria burn would have been preferable to such a humiliating surrender.[45]

Baltimore, America's third largest city and a key commercial port, was the next obvious target for the British. When they learned the fate of the capital, many Baltimore residents were alarmed and pessimistic about what lay in store for them. Under the leadership of the mayor, a Committee of Vigilance and Safety was formed that included representatives from Baltimore's wards and precincts. Its job was to counter defeatism, prevent loose talk, and look out for suspicious strangers.

Hesitation on the part of the British proved costly. Cochrane, the man in charge, was skeptical of Cockburn's instinctive response to assault Baltimore. Indeed, Cockburn's squadron had just set sail for Bermuda when a message from Cochrane recalled him. After a week of reflection on the matter, Cochrane had decided that the British would proceed with an attack on Baltimore.

When the British fleet sailed north en route for Baltimore, it passed before the eyes of the residents of Annapolis. Panic ensued in the old town that had briefly served as the capital of the United States. The ships sailed up the bay and anchored twenty-two kilometres southeast of Baltimore, at the mouth of the Patapsco River.

During the early hours of September 12, landing boats conveyed the soldiers ashore. By 7:00 a.m. about five thousand men had disembarked at North Point, taking with them the horses needed to pull eight cannon, including two howitzers. The British plan was to defeat the American forces in a battle near North Point and then to swing around and take Baltimore from the north.[46]

Ross and Cockburn led the troops, with Ross in command of the forty-five hundred soldiers and the admiral leading six hundred seamen and Royal and Colonial Marines. Leading a party of about fifty men ahead of the main force, Ross and Cockburn ran without warning into a screen of American soldiers, who had been deployed to warn of the enemy's approach. U.S. cavalry and riflemen were directly in the path of the British commanders and their troops.

To frighten the Americans into believing the whole British force was upon them, the commanders and their small party charged and drove off the soldiers. In the brief melee, however, General Ross was shot and severely wounded. Two hours later, he died.[47] The death of the general, who was so highly regarded by his troops, had a dramatic effect on the critical events of the next twenty-four hours.

With Ross gone, command of the British troops passed to Colonel Arthur Brooke. The new commander led his troops toward the main American line, where three thousand men were deployed. With the two sides facing each other, most of the British soldiers calmly lay down to eat their lunch while sections of the 21st Fusiliers and Royal Marines launched an attack on the enemy's left flank. Lunch over, the British attacked along the whole American line. Following several exchanges of fierce volleys, the Americans broke and fled. The British won the engagement in less than half an hour.

Twenty-four Americans were killed, 139 were wounded, and 50 were taken prisoner. The British casualties numbered 46 dead (including General Ross) and 295 wounded.[48]

The British managed to win the battle that followed the death of General Ross. How they would fare under less seasoned leadership in the days to come was yet to be determined.

The morning after their victory at North Point, the British advanced to within 2.4 kilometres of Baltimore while their ships began the bombardment of Fort McHenry. Brooke had gone ahead of the main body of his troops to reconnoiter the defences the Americans had assembled around the northern approaches to Baltimore. British intelligence had concluded, quite accurately, that the Americans had about fifteen thousand men in position to protect the city. To mount an assault on Baltimore, Brooke would need ammunition and rations, including rum, to be sent to his lines from the HMS *Seahorse*. While Brooke was considering his options, the navy launched their attack on Fort McHenry. The British sent a squadron of seventeen vessels — frigates, sloops, schooners, bomb boats, and a rocket ship — into the Patapsco River. Admiral Cochrane took personal charge of the attack from the deck of the light frigate *Surprize*.[49]

The Americans had previously sunk twenty-four ships in the waters between Fort McHenry and Lazaretto Point to prevent the British ships from sailing in to make a direct assault. Major George Armistead commanded the one thousand soldiers guarding the fort.

Initially, the British ships were positioned just under 4.8 kilometres from Fort McHenry, out of range of the fort's guns. Congreve rockets were launched from the *Erebus* but did little damage. In their wake came a bombardment opened up by two frigates. When their initial volleys fell short into the water, the ships sailed forward into range. In response, Major Armistead ordered his gunners to fire their 24-pounders and long-range 42-pounders at the ships, which forced the frigates to shift back out of range.

Then the British bomb vessels sailed in and launched their own barrage. When the U.S. defenders replied, their cannonballs fell short of the targets. The British could now assail the fort at will.[50] While the British guns could fire far enough for their shots to hit Fort McHenry, the bomb vessels could not close in without making themselves choice targets for the fort's gunners.

The long-range shelling of Fort McHenry went on for hours. Over the course of the battle, Major Armistead estimated that between fifteen hundred and eighteen hundred 10- and 13-inch shells were fired. About four hundred struck within the walls of Fort McHenry, in the process killing four of the defenders and wounding twenty-four.[51]

While their gunners shelled the fort, the British commanders considered their options. Characteristically, Cockburn favoured going ahead with an assault on Baltimore, while Brooke had other views. He was no Ross. "If I took the place," he wrote in his diary, "I should have been the greatest man in England. If I lost, my military character was gone for ever." He was prepared to attack, but only if his ground assault could be reinforced by additional troops from the British ships.

Admiral Cochrane, who was already thinking ahead to an attack on New Orleans, had instructed his subordinates not to press on against Baltimore "unless positively certain of success."[52] When Brooke received a dispatch informing him that Cochrane had decided not to contribute to the attack on the city — "It is impossible for the ships to render you any assistance" — Brooke concluded that he could not proceed on his own.[53] His hopes of commanding British troops in a glorious victory were dashed.

While the commanders were still deciding what to do, twelve hundred Royal Marines were undertaking a diversionary attack on Fort Covington, located on the far side of the peninsula, near Fort McHenry. The plan was for boats to carry the force in stealth up the Patapsco so they could execute a surprise attack simultaneously with the shelling of Fort McHenry. But the American defenders detected the coming assault and opened fire on the marines with guns based in Fort Covington and Battery Babcock. Royal Navy Lieutenant Charles Napier, who was in command of the operation, decided to call off the assault at about 2:00 a.m. He pulled back the marines, whose boats were under a heavy barrage. As the sun rose, the dead bodies of marines could be seen floating in the river.[54]

On September 15, the British forces pulled back from their positions, boarded their boats, and returned to their ships. Cochrane was pre-occupied with the coming British assault on the port city at the mouth of the Mississippi, a campaign that would deliver a further blow to the commerce of the United States. The admiral knew that more British troops were on their way across the Atlantic. On September 19, his forces set sail for Halifax, where they would be refitted and prepared for the later descent on New Orleans. Cochrane meantime had dispatched Cockburn and a part of the fleet to block-ade the coasts of South Carolina and Georgia. The intention was to draw American forces away from the defence of New Orleans, the real target.[55]

For the Americans, the British assault on Baltimore and Fort McHenry took on a meaning that would be remembered long after the battles were waged. Francis Scott Key, a Baltimore lawyer, watched the bombardment of Fort McHenry from the vantage point of a truce ship. Days earlier, Key had paid a visit to the British com-mander, Admiral Cochrane, to seek the release of William Beanes, a medical doctor from Maryland who was a personal friend of U.S. President James Madison. Key went in the company of John Skinner, a United States agent for the release of prisoners. The two sailed on a sloop sporting a white flag of truce to make contact with the British fleet.

Skinner and Key were welcomed on board Cochrane's flagship, HMS *Tonnant*. But they were then not allowed to leave with Dr. Beanes until the coming engagement against Baltimore was com-plete. The two were invited to join the British officers for dinner. Cochrane informed his American guests that they would have to be held aboard the frigate *Surprize*, which was commanded by Cochrane's son. Even though they were quartered on the smaller ves-sel, the Americans continued to have dinner each evening with the British officers. In a letter he wrote three weeks later, Key expressed his feelings about those with whom he had spent time: "Never was a man more disappointed in his expectations than I have been as to the character of British officers. With some exceptions they appeared to be illiberal, ignorant and vulgar, seem filled with a spirit of malignity against everything American."[56]

Growing weary of being held by the British, Skinner eventually managed to convince Cochrane to let the Americans return to their own sloop, where they were to be guarded by British sailors and marines until the battle was over. Throughout the night when Fort McHenry was shelled, Skinner and Key remained on deck, anxiously awaiting the outcome of the encounter. At dawn, as the famous story recounts, the two men looked toward the fort to make out which flag flew above it, and Key spotted the huge star-spangled banner above the ramparts. As he later related the moment to his brother-in-law, Roger Taney, "Our flag was still there!"

Key began scribbling his feelings and reflections on the back of a letter he had in his pocket.[57] The resulting work, "The Star-Spangled Banner," was adopted as the U.S. national anthem in 1931.

The divisive war was being transformed into a patriotic crusade. The battles of Lake Champlain and New Orleans would put the finishing touches to this heroic recasting of the conflict.

Chapter 18

American Victories at Lake Champlain and New Orleans

THE CALAMITOUS REPORT that Washington had been occupied and devastated by the British came as a heavy blow to the American commissioners in Ghent and had the sobering effect of removing some of the more fanciful ambitions from the American agenda. Even Henry Clay, the War Hawk westerner whose goal was the conquest of Canada, expressed fears about what might lie ahead. In a letter he wrote in October 1814, he confessed, "I tremble indeed whenever I take up a late newspaper. Hope alone sustains me."[1]

By the summer and autumn of 1814, earlier hopes of acquiring Canada had faded. Gone was the sentiment expressed by Monroe to U.S. negotiators in June 1813 that "it may be worthwhile to bring to view the advantages to both Countries [Britain and the United States] which is promised, by a transfer of the upper parts and even the whole of Canada to the United States . . . The possession of it [Canada] by England, must hereafter prove a fruitful source of controversy which its transfer to the United States would remove . . . That these provinces will be severed from Great Britain at no distant day, by their own career, may fairly be presumed, even against her strongest efforts to retain them."[2]

President Madison's message to Congress in September 1814 presented an administration that hoped for peace. He noted with foreboding that the outcome of the war in Europe had removed "any check on the overbearing power of Great Britain on the ocean; and it has left in her hands disposable armaments with which, forgetting the difficulties of a remote war with a free people, and yielding to the intoxication of success . . . she cherishes hopes of still further aggrandizing a power already formidable in its abuses to the tranquility of the civilized and commercial world." The president went on to say that in the present campaign against the United States "enemy, with all his augmented means, and wanton use of them, has little ground for exultation." He referred to "a series of achievements which have given new luster to the American arms." It was a statement that balanced the prospect of peace with the willingness to fight on if necessary.[3]

The British took a tough line on territorial issues. They were intent on achieving the demilitarization of the Great Lakes and navigation rights on the Mississippi in return for American access to the fishery on the Grand Banks of Newfoundland. This was needed, the British insisted, so that the Americans would give up their determination to conquer Canada.

The Americans baldly replied that the annexation of Canada had never been the goal of the United States. The British scoffed, pointing to General William Hull's proclamation to the people of Upper Canada in the summer of 1812 that he was invading their province to protect them. The American rejoinder at Ghent was that Hull's bombastic proclamation had not been sanctioned by Washington. To claim that the acquisition of Canada was not a war aim of the United States was clearly disingenuous, given the letters sent by Secretary of State James Monroe to the American negotiators in 1813 and 1814, which repeatedly raised the prospect of the United States' gaining some or all of the Canadian territory at the conclusion of the conflict. In a letter to his government's negotiators in January 1814, Monroe referred to his letter of the previous June "in favour of a cession of the Canadas to the United States," which he said had "gained much additional force from further reflection." He went on to assert that "the inevitable consequence of another war, and even of the present, if persevered in by the

British Government, must be to sever those provinces by force from Great Britain. Their inhabitants themselves will soon feel their strength, and assert their independence. All these evils had therefore better be anticipated, and provided for, by timely arrangement between the two Governments, in the mode proposed."⁴

By the time serious negotiations got underway in the late summer of 1814, the conquest of Canada was falling off the list of achievements on which the Americans were intent. The same happened to their demand that the British stop the practice of impressment. Given the Americans' heated feelings on the issue, backing off on impressment was a major development. When President Madison met with his cabinet on June 27, 1814, he polled its members on whether they could contemplate a treaty that was silent on impressment. All responded in the affirmative. In a letter of instruction to his commissioners in Ghent, the president wrote, "You may omit any stipulation on the subject of impressment, if found indispensably necessary to terminate it. You will, of course, not recur to this expedient until all your efforts to adjust the controversy in a more satisfactory manner have failed."⁵

The British, meanwhile, opened with an apparently strong position on the creation of a native state. From England, Foreign Minister Castlereagh was constantly updating his commissioners in Ghent with fresh instructions. Through them, he advanced the initial propositions the British negotiators placed before the American team in mid-August 1814. As reported to Washington by the U.S. negotiators, the British maintained that their country sought no increase in territory on its own behalf. They did, however, insist that "the Indian allies of Great Britain" must be "included in the pacification and a definite boundary to be settled for their territory."

"The British Commissioners stated," the U.S. negotiators reported, "that an arrangement upon this point was a sine qua non: that they were not authorized to conclude a Treaty of peace which did not embrace the Indians . . . and that the establishment of a definite boundary of the Indian Territory was necessary, to secure a permanent peace, not only with the Indians but also between the United States and Great Britain."⁶

With this proposal, the British were putting Tecumseh's vision of a native state on the table. It would be established between the Ohio River and the Great Lakes, in a territory to be agreed on by the U.S. and Britain. It would encompass much of the region the Americans called the Old Northwest. In a memorandum addressed to the British commissioners, Canadian fur traders brashly suggested that the native state's boundary should be drawn south from Erie, Pennsylvania, on the southern shore of Lake Erie, south to Pittsburgh, and from there westward along the Ohio River.

For Henry Clay, who was committed to the cause of the settlers, the Canadian proposal was anathema, the negation of everything he had hoped for from the start of the war. The Canadian plan would have handed over the territory of Ohio, which was admitted as the seventeenth U.S. state in 1803. Even the less ambitious idea of creating a native state farther west along the Wabash River, which would cut through the present-day state of Indiana and along the boundary of Illinois, horrified Clay.

Over time, Clay had softened his position on the conquest of Canada. By the end of 1812, the discouraging course of the war had caused him to rethink. In a letter he wrote at the end of the first year of the war, he opined that "Canada was not the end but the means, the object of the War being the redress of injuries, and Canada being the instrument by which that redress was to be obtained."⁷ But he refused to surrender settler territory west of the Appalachian Mountains to the Native peoples.

In the end, just as the Americans gave up on their insistence that the British put an end to the practice of impressment, the British abandoned the idea of a native state.

The same week that the British unleashed their attacks around Baltimore and their salvos on Fort McHenry, they launched a second assault on the United States from the north. With peace talks under-way in Ghent, the British were determined to drive as hard a bargain as possible with the U.S. Facts on the ground were crucial to their negotiations. Eliminating American power on Lake Champlain would powerfully assist the British negotiators.

The thrust southward came a few days after the successful and nearly bloodless occupation of eastern Maine by the British, which began in July 1814 with the seizure of Eastport, the easternmost point in Maine. (Maine remained a part of Massachusetts until it was established as a separate state in 1820.) Because Major General Sir John Coape Sherbrooke, who had served as lieutenant-governor of Nova Scotia since 1811, had only twenty-five hundred soldiers avail-able to him, the plan was to advance into Maine from the New Brunswick border only as far as the Penobscot River. This would place a substantial portion of the Maine coast in the hands of the British without taking them farther southwest into the more popu-lous regions of Maine, which would be harder to secure with such a small occupying force.

Sherbrooke's attack went smoothly, with the Americans blowing up their installations as the enemy approached. From the coast, the British proceeded upriver and took the towns of Hampden and Bangor. Farther along the coast they occupied Machias. During the two-week operation, with only one of their soldiers killed and eight wounded, the British took 161 kilometres of coastal Maine and the adjacent backcountry, territory they held until the end of the war. Following the occupation, the male inhabitants of the region took an oath of allegiance to the British Crown.

The British hoped that by occupying territory in Maine, they would draw more of the commerce of New England, where enthusi-asm for the war was tepid at best, into their sphere. They established a customs post at Castine and appointed a military governor to administer the occupied region. Under this regime, Swedish and Spanish commercial vessels carried large shipments of British goods to Hampden, next door to Bangor. From there, they were distributed across New England. The arrangements fostered robust trade between New England and Nova Scotia.*[8]

By 1814, the British blockade was so effective that many New England communities suffered severe economic hardship and even sought ways to reach their own arrangements to end the war against Britain. For instance, the inhabitants of Nantucket Island met on July 23, 1814, to draft a petition to Admiral Cochrane to allow them to import food and fuel from the mainland during the following winter, pleading that without such an arrangement they could face starvation. In their petition, they stated that they had been "universally opposed" to the war.[9]

Having won eastern Maine, the British turned their attention to Lake Champlain. An expedition commanded by General Prevost set out to seize control of the area south of Montreal, just across the U.S. border.

On July 29, the eve of the offensive, substantial British reinforcements landed in Quebec: the 4th Royal Scots; the 97th Regiment, from Ireland; and a brigade drawn from British units that had been serving in Spain and had been dispatched from Bordeaux. The following week, a brigade drawn from the 3rd (East Kent), 5th (Northumberland), 57th (West Middlesex), and 81st Regiments, along with a brigade of artillery, arrived in Montreal, but these reinforcements were not earmarked for the descent on Lake Champlain — they were to form an army reserve, supplying manpower in Kingston and providing troops in the event of an attack on Sackets Harbor.

For his offensive, Prevost could muster about 10,300 regular soldiers and militiamen. In all, he had three brigades. Major General Sir Frederick Robinson commanded the first brigade, made up of the 3rd, 27th, and 39th (Dorsetshire), 76th, and 88th (Connaught Rangers) Regiments. At the head of the second was Major General Thomas

---

* In the aftermath of the British occupation of Maine east of the Penobscot, British commissioners at the peace talks, for a time, demanded that the hump of northern Maine be transferred to Britain. This would provide an easier passage on British territory between Quebec and the Maritimes.

Brisbane, whose units — the 2nd, 8th, 13th, 49th, and De Meuron Regiments and the Canadian Voltigeurs — were based in Lower Canada. Major General Manley Power led the third brigade, with soldiers from the 3rd, 5th, 1st, 27th, and 58th Regiments. A Royal Artillery brigade outfitted with five 6-pounders and one 5 1/2-inch howitzer accompanied each brigade. While the paper strength of these units totalled more than ten thousand men, the real number available for the attack was much lower after those who were sick or otherwise unavailable to their units were taken into account.[10]

It has not been uncommon for American historians to portray Prevost's force as larger than it actually was and comprising more veterans than it did. Moreover, such historians argue that the objective of his offensive extended well beyond Lake Champlain to Albany or even as far as New York City. In his book *Union 1812: The Americans Who Fought the Second War of Independence*, for instance, A. J. Langguth asserts that "commanding thirty thousand veteran troops in Montreal . . . Prevost took one third of his army over the border at the town of Champlain" and was "headed toward Albany."[11]

On September 1, the British forces crossed the border, pushing down the west shore of Lake Champlain in the direction of Plattsburgh. They moved slowly along extremely poor roads.

Key to the ensuing battle was the struggle between British and American naval squadrons on the lake. Ever cautious, Prevost regarded coordination with the British naval squadron on the lake as crucial to his success, just as he had previously focused heavily on supremacy on Lakes Ontario and Erie. The British and the Americans both had naval squadrons on Lake Champlain, where they had been conducting a race to outbuild each other.

In command of the British squadron was Captain George Downie. A new frigate, the *Confiance*, had been completed just in time for the British invasion. Although the vessel was launched on August 25, it still required cannon locks (firing devices operating on the same principle as the flintlock on a musket) to enable the guns to fire. On September 1, Downie wrote to request cannon locks from the ordnance storekeeper at Quebec. He stressed the need for a rapid response to complete the war-worthiness of the *Confiance*: "In a few days, she will be before the Enemy, and the want of locks may be seriously injurious in the Action."[12] In addition to the *Confiance*, the British naval squadron consisted of a brig, two sloops, and between twelve and fourteen gunboats.

Facing them, under the command of Lieutenant Thomas Macdonough, was an American squadron outfitted with the 734-ton *Saratoga*, classed as a heavy corvette; the schooner *Ticonderoga*, whose guns had to be fired by flashing the lock of a pistol at the touch holes; the small sloop *Preble*; and ten gunboats. Launched to further strengthen this force was a large brig, the *Eagle*.[13]

By September 5, Prevost's force was thirteen kilometres from Plattsburgh. The slow advance gave the inhabitants of the area plenty of warning, and most of them decamped. Seven hundred New York militiamen destroyed bridges and skirmished with the enemy's advance units. On the evening of September 6, the British reached Plattsburgh. The town was deserted, but the invaders soon came under fire from the American vessels in Plattsburgh Bay.

To deal with Macdonough's harassment of Prevost's army, Downie needed to position his squadron in the bay to attack the American vessels. With the 1,200-ton *Confiance* and its crew of 325 men, Downie was confident of victory.

The British planned a simultaneous attack on land and water. Prevost would push across the Saranac River just south of Plattsburgh, where he would attack the much inferior U.S. force commanded by Brigadier General Alexander Macomb, which consisted of about three thousand regulars and militia, only half of whom were fit for duty. While the British were attacking Macomb's troops, Downie's fleet was to sail into Plattsburgh Bay from the north to challenge Macdonough's squadron.

In his book on the naval struggles during the war, Theodore Roosevelt tallied the guns available on each of the ships involved in the Battle of Plattsburgh to determine which side had the advantage in firepower. He concluded that while the British and American sides had almost equivalent overall firepower, the British had more long guns while the Americans had more carronades. This meant that the British had the edge on the lake when firing at long range, while the Americans had the advantage at close range.[14]

Macdonough took advantage of the natural defensive position offered him by the bay, which was about three kilometres wide. He set up his line just inside the mouth of the bay, positioning his ships between Crab Island in the southwest and Cumberland Head in the northeast.[15] A key question about the battle is why Prevost insisted that Downie sail into the bay to assault the strong American position. Why didn't he use his huge edge in manpower to assault the Americans south of Saranac River? Having then secured the shoreline, he could have set up his guns to mount a barrage on the American squadron, forcing them into the wider waters of the lake, where Downie would have been better placed to take them on. Later, Sir James Yeo, who served as commodore in the defence of British North America, expressed the opinion that Prevost put the British squadron at a serious disadvantage when he pressed Downie to attack the Americans at their anchorage in the bay.[16]

On the evening of September 9, Downie wrote that he would launch his attack on the American ships in Plattsburgh Bay the following day. Contrary winds, however, did not make this possible, and his attack was mounted on September 11. He brought *Confiance* as near as possible to *Saratoga*, but three hundred yards was the closest he could get. As soon as *Confiance* anchored, the guns on *Saratoga* opened fire. Then the 350-ton *Linnet* went after the *Eagle*, the northernmost vessel in the U.S. line. *Finch* and most of the British gunboats challenged *Ticonderoga*, *Preble*, and the U.S. gunboats.

The battle went badly for the British. A cannon was knocked loose from its carriage and crushed Downie to death. The 110-ton *Finch* was hit and drifted onto Crab Island, and the two British sloops were sunk. The 112-ton *Chubb* was disabled. British gunboats did manage to drive the U.S.'s *Preble* inshore, and *Saratoga* and *Confiance*

were both heavily damaged but the Americans had the better of the
fight. With a wealth of experience fighting on ships of this kind,
Macdonough was able to wind the *Saratoga* around on an anchor
and hawsers so that he could bring his undamaged larboard guns to
bear on the enemy vessel. The American gunners fired a volley of
hand spikes into the mass of British sailors on board the *Confiance*,
who were desperately trying to turn their vessel so they could fire.
Royal Navy Lieutenant James Robertson, who had taken command
following the death of Downie, ordered the ship's colours to be
struck.[17] By the time the *Confiance* surrendered, the ship had taken
105 shot holes in her hull.[18]

The U.S. naval victory not only set the stage for the crucial land
battle at Plattsburgh, it would also determine the American view of
the whole war.

While the British naval squadron was entering the bay, the armed
forces went on the offensive on land. The column was commanded by
Sir Frederick Robinson, an American-born officer who had fought
for the British during the Revolutionary War and migrated to
England at the end of the war. Robinson started off in the wrong
direction, which delayed his advance for an hour. Then four of his
battalions successfully crossed the river and drove back the defenders. Just before commanding a final assault on the American
positions, Robinson abruptly received the order to break off the
engagement and withdraw. Some of his men, having advanced too
far forward to receive the order, were forced to lay down their arms
and surrender.

Prevost had issued the sudden command to retire when he
learned that the British had lost the naval engagement, leaving a portion of his own force in a hopeless position. The large British force
turned in the opposite direction and headed north with alacrity. In
his report to Bathurst, the secretary of state for war and the colonies,
Prevost blamed the entire defeat on the British failure on the lake. He

continued: "Under the circumstances I had to determine whether I should consider my own fame in gratifying the ardor of the troops in persevering in the attack, or consult the more substantial interests of my country by withdrawing the Army which was yet uncrippled for the security of the provinces."[19]

Theodore Roosevelt concluded that the U.S. naval victory at Plattsburgh caused Prevost's army to flee "in great haste and confusion back to Canada, leaving our northern frontier clear for the remainder of the war; while the victory had a very great effect on the negotiations for peace." Of American leadership in the battle, he wrote, "Macdonough in this battle won a higher fame than any other commander of the war, British or American. He had a decidedly superior force to contend against, the officers and men of the two sides being about on a par in every respect; and it was solely owing to his foresight and resource that we won the victory . . . Down to the time of the Civil War he is the greatest figure in our naval history."[20] Almost a century after the battle was fought, the esteemed naval authority Alfred Thayer Mahan wrote that "the battle of Lake Champlain, more nearly than any other incident of the War of 1812, merits the epithet *decisive*."[21] Decades later, Winston Churchill declared that the results of the fighting at Plattsburgh made it "a decisive battle of the war."

Concluding his treatment of the battle, American historian Walter R. Borneman, in what can only be described as a surfeit of overstatement, contended that "had not Macomb and Macdonough made their stand, a British general less defensively inclined than Sir George Prevost may well have ended up spending the following winter in Albany if not New York City."[22]

While the American victors at Plattsburgh were celebrated in Washington, the fate of Sir George Prevost was very different. Prevost's time at the head of affairs in Lower Canada had always been controversial, as much for political as for military reasons. The influential English-speaking minority in Lower Canada resented Prevost, charging him with being too favourable to the province's francophone majority. The military debacle at Plattsburgh allowed the critics to carve up his reputation. In the *Montreal Herald*, a series of anonymous articles derided him, accusing him of both military and political mismanagement. The articles were subsequently published as a pamphlet titled *The Letters of Veritas and Nerva*.[23]

On March 2, 1815, the day after Prevost learned that the peace treaty at Ghent had been ratified, he was replaced as governor by Sir George Murray, who brought with him the news that Prevost had been ordered to return to London at once to account for his handling of the military expedition to Plattsburgh. When he arrived in England, Prevost was ordered by the Prince Regent to appear at a court martial. The trial was to begin on January 15, 1816, but Prevost died ten days beforehand. At the age of forty-nine, he ended his life a humiliated man.

Americans celebrated the victory on Lake Champlain, but Andrew Jackson's massive victory at New Orleans a few months later was the one they truly relished, the one they have savoured ever since. As American historian Walter R. Borneman put it, "Jackson had assembled a tattered force of army regulars, backwoods militia, and bayou pirates and bested the pride of British regulars."[24]

The battle was made famous for the baby-boom generation of Americans by country-and-western singer Johnny Horton's patriotic song. "In eighteen-fourteen we took a little trip," chanted Johnny, "along with Colonel Jackson down the mighty Mississipp' / we took a little bacon and we took a little beans / and we caught the bloody British in the town of New Orleans."[25]

It doesn't matter that Jackson did not reach the scene of the battle by travelling down the Mississippi. Nor has it mattered over the generations that the battle was fought after the Treaty of Ghent was signed between the warring parties, on Christmas Eve 1814. The fight at New Orleans had no effect on the outcome of the war, but it had got the pulse of Americans racing and helped Jackson win two terms as president of the United States.

The Battle of New Orleans grew out of the grand British strategy of 1814, which was to use the might of the Royal Navy and veteran personnel from the war against Napoleon to drive the Americans to end the war and to sign a treaty on terms favourable to the British. The punch to the centre at Washington and Baltimore in the summer of 1814 had been one campaign in the British strategy. Another, which had gone disastrously wrong, had been the invasion of U.S. territory south of Montreal and the battles at Plattsburgh. New Orleans had been the third planned blow, which, as it turned out, was not needed to bring the Americans to peace.

To attack New Orleans, the British planned to use a veteran army led by a veteran commander. Transported to the city by the Royal Navy, the troops would seize the port and the goods stored there, shutting down Mississippi commerce. On December 10, 1814, British troops landed from the ships of Vice Admiral Cochrane on the east bank of the Mississippi, not far from the mouth of the river. By December 23, the British had pushed to within 14.5 kilometres of the city.

The opportunity for a quick seizure of New Orleans was lost, however. It was only on Christmas Day that the commander of the British expedition, Major General Sir Edward Pakenham, arrived to take command. By that time, Andrew Jackson's troops and a labour force made up of slaves had used sugar barrels and earth to build a formidable breastwork behind a wide ditch. This barricade stretched for about a kilometre from the bank of the river to the edge of a swamp. Behind it, Jackson housed his regulars and militiamen. The troops were supported by four cannon and a naval battery on the west bank, which could provide additional firepower.

On January 8, 1815, Pakenham tried a two-pronged attack on this position. While his force attacked Jackson directly, fifteen hundred British regulars under the command of Colonel William Thornton were to cross the river and turn the flank of the U.S. position. The timing went horribly wrong. Thornton's force did get across the river, drive off a force of Kentucky militiamen, and seize the naval guns, but they were far too late. By then, the Americans had massacred

Pakenham's attack force, pounding the dense columns of men, who were mired in the mud. Pakenham died and the British suffered two thousand casualties; the Americans lost only seventy-one men.

The Americans had won gloriously. The still-powerful British force managed to retreat down the river and seize Fort Bowyer, at the entrance to Mobile Bay.[26] But by then, news that the war was over had reached New York, and from there it spread across the United States.

The legend that the United States won the War of 1812 soared after the Battle of New Orleans. It has remained aloft to this day.

Chapter 19

The Treaty of Ghent

O N CHRISTMAS EVE, 1814, the British and American commissioners came together to sign the Treaty of Ghent. Weighing on the political leadership of both countries was the sheer cost of the war. Over the course of the great war in Europe and the lesser conflict in North America, Britain had been accumulating an enormous national debt. The budget presented in June 1812 planned for additional borrowing of 22.4 million pounds. In 1813, the British treasury borrowed an additional 46.8 million pounds, and in 1814 it added 40.5 million pounds. The war with the United States over its full duration added about 25 million pounds to the national debt. This heavy burden was not fully paid off for decades to come. In the U.S., the overall cost of the war was 105 million dollars. The American national debt soared from 45 million dollars in 1812 to 127 million a year after the conclusion of the conflict.[1]

In addition, about 1,600 British soldiers were killed in action, nearly 3,700 were wounded, and about 3,300 died from disease. These figures do not include casualties among the Canadian militia or native allies. The Americans lost 2,260 men, and about 4,500 men were wounded. While there is no reliable figure for the number of American soldiers who died of disease, it is generally reckoned that about 15,000 Americans perished from all causes during the War of 1812.

Under the treaty, the borders between the United States and British North America reverted to those that existed at the start of the conflict. The exception to this clause, and it was an important one, was the islands in Passamaquoddy Bay, off the coasts of New Brunswick and Maine (still part of Massachusetts at the time), which were claimed by both parties. Each of these islands was to remain in the possession of the side occupying it at the end of the conflict. An article in the treaty outlined the procedure to be followed to resolve this territorial dispute through the appointment of commissioners. As it turned out, this set of issues came close to provoking another war between Britain and the U.S. in future decades. The dispute was resolved only through the signing of the Webster-Ashburton Treaty in 1842.

Under Article 9, both the United States and Great Britain agreed to end hostilities with native tribes and "forthwith to restore to such tribes or nations, respectively, all the possessions, rights and privileges, which they may have enjoyed or been entitled to in one thousand eight hundred and eleven, previous to such hostilities: provided always, that such tribes or nations shall agree to desist from all hostilities against [the United States or Britain in the respective sections referring to each side], their citizens and subjects ["subjects" only in the case of Britain], upon the ratification of the present treaty being notified to such tribes or nations, and shall so desist accordingly."[2] Simply put, this clause resolved that native tribes on both sides of the border were to be accorded the status they had enjoyed prior to the war, with the understanding that they would desist from undertaking any hostile acts against either the United States or Britain.

Article 9 was all that remained of Britain's pledge to Tecumseh to stand with the native confederacy in the struggle to regain lands lost to the United States. In the negotiations, the British had abandoned the concept of a native state in the Ohio country. Instead, all the native people were left with was lands not yet signed away in treaties with the U.S. government or claimed by American settlers.

Effectively, this did nothing to block the western tide of settlement, and it allowed the United States to deal with native tribes exactly as it pleased.

Tecumseh lived and died as a warrior in the Endless War, which began in North America nearly two centuries before his birth and continued well after his death. The quest on which he had staked everything, for a native state in North America, expired on Christmas Eve 1814, when American and British diplomats signed the Treaty of Ghent.

Epilogue

Two Mysteries

THE ALLIANCE BETWEEN the impetuous British general and the Shooting Star did not endure long. Two months after they met, Brock was dead. Tecumseh never found another British commander willing to take the fight to the enemy with the same élan. A year after Brock was killed on Queenston Heights, Tecumseh died on the battlefield at Moraviantown.

Had Brock and Tecumseh lived, it is reasonable to speculate that Brock would have used whatever influence he had to win the deal for Tecumseh to which he had committed himself. But how much influence would he have had? The diplomats who negotiated the peace treaty with the United States in Ghent were acting on the instructions of the government at Westminster. And the British cared above all about their broad imperial interests.

Tecumseh's confederacy was the final occasion in history when native forces played a crucial role in determining the outcome of a geostrategic struggle in North America. The inspired concept of a native state reached the peak of its influence in the years prior to the War of 1812 and during the first year of the conflict. With the Treaty of Ghent in 1814, the concept became a lost cause.

The British were glad to put the War of 1812 behind them. They regarded it as a strategic annoyance imposed on them by the

Americans. In their view, its outcome was satisfactory: no imperial territory was lost, and the British did not even have to concede to the United States on the issue of impressment. While British diplomats argued for a time in favour of a native state in North America, they quite easily shelved the concept when it became a barrier to achieving peace. On June 18, 1815, three years to the day after the American declaration of war, the British and their allies fought and won the decisive Battle of Waterloo. Napoleon was defeated and exiled to St. Helena, a small, windswept island in the South Atlantic. The year 1815 marked the dawn of Pax Britannica, the century in which Britain was the world's leading imperial power, a period of dominance that ended only with the outbreak of the First World War in August 1914.

Americans look back on the War of 1812 as a decisive trial through which the nation passed, emerging stronger and more united. American historians have depicted the conflict as the country's second war of independence, or as the war that forged a nation.[1]

Were it not for the repeated American claim in books, songs, and films that the United States won the War of 1812, the assertion would seem self-evidently absurd. After all, the U.S. initiated the conflict and gained no territory as a result. There is no question, though, that the young republic held its own on the battlefield against the world's greatest power and put an end to British intervention in American–Native affairs.

The war also pushed the Americans to overcome the dangerous ideological division that had plagued the country since the 1780s. The split between Republicans and Federalists reflected the great ideological-philosophical conflicts of the age of the French Revolution and the succeeding Napoleonic era. During these volatile decades, Americans, like Europeans, positioned themselves along a spectrum that extended from those who identified with the French Revolution to those who feared the Revolution and sided with the British resistance to France. By the end of the war, Americans had left behind the preoccupations of the Enlightenment, the French Revolution, and the Napoleonic age to embark on a more exclusively American journey.

For the French Canadians, the war was the latest in a long history of invasions from the south. During the Patriot invasion of Quebec in 1775, Americans had managed to occupy Montreal for a time, but no major regions or towns in Lower Canada were taken and held by U.S. forces in the War of 1812. The most noteworthy episode of the war for French Canadians was the Battle of Chateauguay in 1813, when Lieutenant Colonel de Salaberry led a small, largely French-Canadian militia unit to rout a much larger American force. De Salaberry emerged as a French-Canadian folk hero. His statue can be seen today at the National Assembly in Quebec City, sword in hand, beckoning his men to follow him.

The War of 1812 was Upper Canada's War of Independence. Upper Canadians emerged from the conflict with a North American sensibility and a conservative political culture. Loyalty to the Crown became the highest expression of public virtue. Those who refused to proclaim their loyalty were tainted with the double sin of being both overtly or covertly republican and pro-American. In sharp contrast to the Americans, Upper Canadians believed that maintaining strong ties to the British Crown was the route to independence — not within the Empire, but from the United States. The fact that they developed their unique character by clinging to an empire has always made the Upper Canadian identity perplexing.

The unpopular war did have one enduring historical consequence: north of Mexico, there were to be two great continental states, one of them much more populous and powerful than the other, to be sure. Against all odds, a transcontinental Canada, embracing many cultures and adopting two official languages, would take its place alongside the rising global power to the south. That Tecumseh and Brock, neither of whom was Canadian, are among the country's immortals attests to the enigma that is Canada.

A testament to the enduring legacy of these towering figures is the fact that two mysteries, one concerning Brock and the other Tecumseh, linger still today.

General Isaac Brock took to his grave the answer to a question about which observers remain divided: did he have an unacknowledged romance with a young woman by the name of Sophia Shaw?

To outward appearances, Brock appears to have been singularly devoted to his military career and his advancement in the army. He never married, and it is generally accepted that there is no evidence he ever established a relationship with a woman. But ever since his death, some have claimed that General Brock was engaged to Miss Sophia Shaw, a young woman who lived in York with her family. According to one story, as Brock set out on his horse Alfred en route to Queenston on the morning of his death, he encountered Sophia, dismounted briefly to accept a beverage from her, and then resumed his journey to the battle. Some claim, although the evidence is slight, that when Brock fell in battle at Queenston Heights in 1813, he muttered the name "Sophia" as he died. Years after the end of the war, Miss Shaw, heavily veiled and dressed in mourning clothes, appeared at a garden party at Government House in York.

If the stories about Miss Shaw are true, why did the general keep it a secret? There is evidence that Brock's friends in England would have regarded a marriage to any Canadian as beneath him. In April 1811, from Hampton Court Park in England, Colonel J. A. Vesey wrote to the general to tell him that he wished he "had a daughter old enough for you, as I would give her to you with pleasure. You should be married, particularly as fate seems to detain you so long in Canada — but pray do not marry there."[2] A month later, the colonel wrote again to Brock to commiserate with him about "the stupid and uninteresting time you must have passed in Upper Canada."[3]

Given the large age gap between the two — Sophia Shaw was in her late teens and Brock was forty-three when he died at Queenston — some historical analysts, among them Gillian Lenfestey in Guernsey, believe that Sophia was infatuated with the general and developed the delusional idea after his death that she and Brock had been betrothed.

The second mystery concerns the death of the great Shawnee chief and his subsequent resting place.

After it was known that Tecumseh had fallen on the battlefield in October 1813, Kentucky soldiers found a corpse they believed to be his and cut slices of flesh from the body to take home as souvenirs. Later it was believed that the body of the decoratively attired warrior was not that of Tecumseh, whose custom was to wear simple clothes into battle. The day after the fight, William Henry Harrison was taken to see the body of the warrior believed to be Tecumseh, but he did not recognize the swollen and disfigured remains as those of his old foe.

From there, the mystery goes in three directions. Some have insisted that Tecumseh was buried near the place where he fell — of this faction, some believe his bones have since been dug up and moved elsewhere, while others say that the great chief still lies in a grave on the battlefield and that someday his bones will be unearthed and his broken thigh bone will reveal his identity. Another theory holds that Tecumseh's body was removed from the field of battle to be buried in a grave in what is now the east end of London, Ontario. Yet another view is that Tecumseh's body was taken from the battle-field by native warriors and was transported for burial to the native territory of St. Anne Island, located on the Ontario side of the St. Clair River, across from the state of Michigan and adjacent to Walpole Island.

In 1931, when Wilson Knaggs and his family moved into the home of the elderly Sarah White on Walpole Island, Knaggs poked around in the attic, where he discovered a burlap bag containing human bones. When informed of the find, Mrs. White was not at all surprised. She told Knaggs that her late husband, Chief Joseph White, had placed the bones there, and that their presence was to remain a secret. Knaggs pressed further for an explanation, and Mrs. White finally told him that the bones were those of Tecumseh.[4]

According to the story, Chief White had acquired the bones from a Dr. Mitchell, who had himself obtained them from a burial site on St. Anne Island. Fearing that various parties would want to take possession of the remains, Chief White hid them around his property in a number of locations. Mrs. White had intended to go to her death without revealing her husband's secret.

Feeling the weight of responsibility for the find, Knaggs decided to tell the Walpole Island Soldiers' Club, consisting of native veterans of the First World War. The veterans acted quickly. They called in experts and shared their discovery with others, some of whom were skeptical. Dr. W. B. Rutherford of Sarnia, Ontario, was called in to examine the bones and managed to assemble the skeleton of a medium-sized male. What was missing was the critical piece of evidence: the thigh bone.

The veterans of Walpole Island held to their claim that Tecumseh had been found. Frustrated by the absence of any effort to honour Tecumseh with a monument and burial place on the island, they held a ceremony on a sunny day in August 1934. Guests from both Canada and the United States convened on Walpole Island to commemorate the life of the great leader, the discovery of his bones, and the plan to establish a burial site.

Progress toward establishing the site proceeded slowly. Finally, on August 25, 1941, several thousand people journeyed to Walpole Island to attend a ceremony in which the great Shawnee chief's bones were placed inside a casket made especially for the occasion. The casket was then sealed inside a stone cairn located on the northwest corner of the island, overlooking the St. Clair River.[5] As far as the veterans on Walpole Island were concerned, Tecumseh had found a resting place on native soil.

Notes

CHAPTER 1: TECUMSEH, THE SHOOTING STAR

1. Richard White, *The Middle Ground: Indians, Empires, and Republics in the Great Lakes Region, 1650–1815* (New York: Cambridge University Press, 2011), 269.
2. John Sugden, *Tecumseh: A Life* (New York: Henry Holt, 1997), 215.
3. Stephen Ruddell, *Reminiscences of Tecumseh's Youth* (Wisconsin Historical Society, 2003), 120; online facsimile edition at http://www.americanjourneys.org/aj-155.
4. John Sugden, *Tecumseh: A Life* (New York: Henry Holt, 1997), 23.
5. Benjamin Drake, *Life of Tecumseh, and of His Brother the Prophet; with a Historical Sketch of the Shawanoe Indians* (Cincinnati: E. Morgan, 1841), 9.
6. Ibid.
7. Albert Gallatin, *A Synopsis of the Indian Tribes within the United States East of the Rocky Mountains, and in the British and Russian Possessions in North America* (Cambridge: Cambridge University Press, 1836), 65–68.
8. Benjamin Drake, *Life of Tecumseh, and of His Brother the Prophet; with a Historical Sketch of the Shawanoe Indians* (Cincinnati: E. Morgan, 1841), 61–65.
9. E. B. O'Callaghan, ed., *Documents Relative to the Colonial History of the State of New York*, vol. 8 (Albany: Weed, Parsons, 1857), 111–37.
10. Benjamin Drake, *Life of Tecumseh, and of His Brother the Prophet; with a Historical Sketch of the Shawanoe Indians* (Cincinnati: E. Morgan, 1841), 34.
11. Stephen Ruddell, *Reminiscences of Tecumseh's Youth* (Wisconsin Historical Society, 2003), 121; online facsimile edition at http://www.americanjourneys.org/aj-155.
12. Benjamin Drake, *Life of Tecumseh, and of His Brother the Prophet; with a Historical Sketch of the Shawanoe Indians* (Cincinnati: E. Morgan, 1841), 47–49.
13. Ibid., 67.
14. John S. C. Abbott, *Daniel Boone: The Pioneer of Kentucky* (New York: Dodd and Mead, 1872), 194–209.
15. Ibid., 224.

16. Ibid., 244.

17. Colin G. Calloway, *One Vast Winter Count: The Native American West Before Lewis and Clark* (Lincoln: University of Nebraska Press, 2003), 369–70.

18. John Sugden, *Tecumseh: A Life* (New York: Henry Holt, 1997), 4–5.

19. Ibid., 36.

20. Adam Shortt and Arthur G. Doughty, *Canada and Its Provinces*, vol. 4 (Toronto: Publishers' Association of Canada, 1914), 712–13.

21. Colin G. Calloway, *One Vast Winter Count: The Native American West Before Lewis and Clark* (Lincoln: University of Nebraska Press, 2003), 372–73.

22. John Sugden, *Tecumseh: A Life* (New York: Henry Holt, 1997), 45–46.

23. Ibid., 44–45.

24. Benjamin Drake, *Life of Tecumseh, and of His Brother the Prophet; with a Historical Sketch of the Shawanoe Indians* (Cincinnati: E. Morgan, 1841), 67–68.

25. John Sugden, *Tecumseh: A Life* (New York: Henry Holt, 1997), 39–40.

26. Stephen Ruddell, *Reminiscences of Tecumseh's Youth* (Wisconsin Historical Society, 2003), 124; online facsimile edition at www.americanjourneys.org/aj-155.

27. Benjamin Drake, *Life of Tecumseh, and of His Brother the Prophet; with a Historical Sketch of the Shawanoe Indians* (Cincinnati: E. Morgan, 1841), 68.

Chapter 2: A Warrior's Odyssey

1. John Sugden, *Tecumseh: A Life* (New York: Henry Holt, 1997), 46–47, 49.

2. Henry A. Ford, A. M. and Mrs. Kate B. Ford. *History of Hamilton County, Ohio, with Illustrations and Biographical Sketches* (Cleveland: L. A. Williams, 1881), 56–65.

3. *Dictionary of Canadian Biography Online*, http://www.biographi.ca.

4. Stephen Ruddell, *Reminiscences of Tecumseh's Youth* (Wisconsin Historical Society, 2003), 125–26; online facsimile edition at http://www.americanjourneys.org/aj-155.

5. Ibid., 123.

6. Benjamin Drake, *Life of Tecumseh, and of His Brother the Prophet; with a Historical Sketch of the Shawanoe Indians* (Cincinnati: E. Morgan, 1841), 69.

7. Stephen Ruddell, *Reminiscences of Tecumseh's Youth* (Wisconsin Historical Society, 2003), 126; online facsimile edition at http://www.americanjourneys.org/aj-155.

8. John Sugden, *Tecumseh: A Life* (New York: Henry Holt, 1997), 61.

9. S. P. Hildreth, *Pioneer History: Being an Account of the First Examinations of the Ohio Valley, and the Early Settlement of the Northwest Territory* (Cincinnati: H. W. Derby; New York: A. B. Barnes, 1848), 222–25.

10. Benjamin Drake, *Life of Tecumseh, and of His Brother the Prophet; with a His-torical Sketch of the Shawanoe Indians* (Cincinnati: E. Morgan, 1841), 37.

11. William B. Kessel and Robert Wooster, eds., *Encyclopedia of Native American Wars and Warfare* (New York: Facts on File, 2005), 280.

12. Stephen Ruddell, *Reminiscences of Tecumseh's Youth* (Wisconsin Historical Society, 2003), 126–27; online facsimile edition at http://www.americanjourneys.org/aj-155.

13. Jim Poling, Sr., *Tecumseh: Shooting Star, Crouching Panther* (Toronto: Dundurn Press, 2009), 45.

14. Benjamin Drake, *Life of Tecumseh, and of His Brother the Prophet; with a His-torical Sketch of the Shawanoe Indians* (Cincinnati: E. Morgan, 1841), 71, 72.

15. Adam Shortt and Arthur G. Doughty, *Canada and Its Provinces*, vol. 3 (Toronto: Publishers' Association of Canada, 1914), 149.

16. Benjamin Drake, *Life of Tecumseh, and of His Brother the Prophet; with a His-torical Sketch of the Shawanoe Indians* (Cincinnati: E. Morgan, 1841), 81.

17. Wayne Moquin with Charles Van Doren, eds., *Great Documents in American Indian History* (New York: Praeger, 1973), 132.

18. Benjamin Drake, *Life of Tecumseh, and of His Brother the Prophet; with a His-torical Sketch of the Shawanoe Indians* (Cincinnati: E. Morgan, 1841), 83.

CHAPTER 3: A NEW POWER

1. Samuel Eliot Morison and Henry Steele Commager, *The Growth of the American Republic*, 7th ed., vol. 1 (New York: Oxford University Press, 1962), 380–81.

2. John M. Murrin, Paul E. Johnson, James M. McPherson, Gary Gerstle, and Emily S. Rosenberg, *Liberty, Equality, Power: A History of the American People*, 6th ed., vol. 1 (Beverly, MA: Wadsworth, 2012), 217.

3. James Madison, Secretary of State of the United States, to James Monroe and William Pinkney, United States Ministers to Great Britain, Department of State, 20 May 1807, in *Diplomatic Correspondence of the United States: Canadian Relations, 1784–1860*, vol. 1, 1784–1820, ed. William R. Manning (Washington: Carnegie Endowment for International Peace, 1940), 177–78.

4. John M. Murrin, Paul E. Johnson, James M. McPherson, Gary Gerstle, and Emily S. Rosenberg, *Liberty, Equality, Power: A History of the American People*, 6th ed., vol. 1 (Beverly, MA: Wadsworth, 2012), 217.

5. David S. Heidler and Jeanne T. Heidler, eds., *Encyclopedia of the War of 1812*, (Annapolis, MD: Naval Institute Press, 2004), 156.

6. Ibid., 168.

7. Theodore Roosevelt, *The Naval War of 1812* (n.p.: Seven Treasures Publications, 1999; first published 1882 by G. Putnam's Sons), 23.

8. N. A. M. Rodger, *The Command of the Ocean: A Naval History of Britain, 1649–1815* (London: Penguin, 2004), 566.

9. William James, *The Naval History of Great Britain*, new edition by Captain Chamier, R. N., vol. 4 [London, 1837], 324, cited in Theodore Roosevelt, *The Naval War of 1812* (n.p.: Seven Treasures Publications, 2009; first published 1882 by G. Putnam's Sons), 21.

10. Theodore Roosevelt, *The Naval War of 1812* (n.p.: Seven Treasures Publications, 2009; first published 1882 by G. Putnam's Sons), 21–22.

11. Robert V. Remini, *Henry Clay: Statesman for the Union* (New York: W. W. Norton, 1991), 29.

12. Ibid., 61.

13. Jay Feldman, *When the Mississippi Ran Backwards: Empire, Intrigue, Murder, and the New Madrid Earthquakes* (New York: Free Press, 2005), 197.

14. "Speech on the Resolution of the Committee on Foreign Relations, December 12, 1811," in *Union and Liberty: The Political Philosophy of John C. Calhoun*, ed. Ross M. Lence (Indianapolis: Liberty Fund, 1992), The Online Library of Liberty, 192. PDF copy available at http://oll.libertyfund.org.

15. Robert V. Remini, *Henry Clay: Statesman for the Union* (New York: W. W. Norton, 1991), 60.

16. A. J. Langguth, *Union 1812: The Americans Who Fought the Second War of Independence*, paperback edition (New York: Simon and Schuster, 2006), 151.

17. Jon Latimer, *1812: War with America* (Cambridge, MA: Harvard University Press, 2007), 31.

18. "Speech on the Resolution of the Committee on Foreign Relations, December 12, 1811," in *Union and Liberty: The Political Philosophy of John C. Calhoun*, ed. Ross M. Lence (Indianapolis: Liberty Fund, 1992), The Online Library of Liberty, 192. PDF copy available at http://oll.libertyfund.org.

19. Walter Borneman, *1812: The War that Forged a Nation* (New York: HarperCollins, 2004), 29.

Chapter 4: Isaac Brock and the Defence of the Canadas

1. N. A. M. Rodger, *The Command of the Ocean: A Naval History of Britain, 1649–1815* (London: Penguin, 2004), 608.

2. Gregory Fremont-Barnes, *The Royal Navy, 1793–1815* (Oxford: Osprey, 2007), 32.

3. Ibid., 44.

4. Ibid., 46.

5. Ibid., 10.

6. John Keegan, *Battle at Sea: From Man-of-War to Submarine* (London: Pimlico, 2004), 7–8.

7. Wesley B. Turner, *British Generals in the War of 1812: High Command in the Canadas* (Montreal: McGill-Queen's University Press, 1999), 11–12.

8. Ferdinand Brock Tupper, Esq., ed., *The Life and Correspondence of Major-General Sir Isaac Brock, K.B.* (London: Simpkin, Marshall, 1847), 4–5.

9. Ibid., 18.

10. Ibid., 8, 11–13.

11. Brock to Lieutenant-Colonel John Brock, 81st Regiment, at the Cape of Good Hope, London, 26 November 1799, in *The Life and Correspondence of Major-General Sir Isaac Brock, K.B.*, ed. Ferdinand Brock Tupper, Esq. (London: Simpkin, Marshall, 1847), 13.

12. Ferdinand Brock Tupper, Esq., ed., *The Life and Correspondence of Major-General Sir Isaac Brock, K.B.* (London: Simpkin, Marshall, 1847), 16–17.

13. Adam Shortt and Arthur G. Doughty, *Canada and Its Provinces*, vol. 3 (Toronto: Publishers' Association of Canada, 1914), 150–51.

14. Ferdinand Brock Tupper, Esq., ed., *The Life and Correspondence of Major-General Sir Isaac Brock, K.B.* (London: Simpkin, Marshall, 1847), 25–32.

15. Wesley B. Turner, *British Generals in the War of 1812: High Command in the Canadas* (Montreal: McGill-Queen's University Press, 1999), 61.

16. Jon Latimer, *1812: War with America* (Cambridge, MA: Harvard University Press, 2007), 37–38.

17. Brock to his brothers, Quebec, 19 November 1808, in *The Life and Correspondence of Major-General Sir Isaac Brock, K.B.*, ed. Ferdinand Brock Tupper, Esq. (London: Simpkin, Marshall, 1847), 73–74.

18. Brock to his brother Irving, Niagara, 10 January 1811, in *The Life and Correspondence of Major-General Sir Isaac Brock, K.B.*, ed. Ferdinand Brock Tupper, Esq. (London: Simpkin, Marshall, 1847), 87.

19. Brock to his sister-in-law, Mrs. W. Brock, Quebec, 8 June 1810, in *The Life and Correspondence of Major-General Sir Isaac Brock, K.B.*, ed. Ferdinand Brock Tupper, Esq. (London: Simpkin, Marshall, 1847), 76–77.

20. Ibid.

21. Colonel Baynes to Brigadier Brock, at Fort George, Quebec, 4 March 1811, in *The Life and Correspondence of Major-General Sir Isaac Brock, K.B.*, ed. Ferdinand Brock Tupper, Esq. (London: Simpkin, Marshall, 1847), 99.

CHAPTER 5: SHOWDOWN

1. Richard White, *The Middle Ground: Indians, Empires, and Republics in the Great Lakes Region, 1650–1815* (New York: Cambridge University Press, 2011), 474.

2. John Sugden, *Tecumseh: A Life* (New York: Henry Holt, 1997), 105–6.

3. Benjamin Drake, *Life of Tecumseh, and of His Brother the Prophet; with a Historical Sketch of the Shawanoe Indians* (Cincinnati: E. Morgan, 1841), 125–26.

4. John Sugden, *Tecumseh: A Life* (New York: Henry Holt, 1997), 183–85.

5. Benjamin Drake, *Life of Tecumseh, and of His Brother the Prophet; with a Historical Sketch of the Shawanoe Indians* (Cincinnati: E. Morgan, 1841), 125, 126.

6. Edward Egglestone and Lillie Egglestone Seelye, *The Shawnee People, or The Story of Tecumseh* (London, 1880), 182–86, cited in Carl F. Klinck, ed., *Tecumseh: Fact and Fiction in Early Records* (Ottawa: Tecumseh Press, 1978), 71–72.

7. Benjamin Drake, *Life of Tecumseh, and of His Brother the Prophet; with a Historical Sketch of the Shawanoe Indians* (Cincinnati: E. Morgan, 1841), 127, 128.

8. Ibid., 128–29.

9. Ibid., 129.

10. Ibid., 142.

11. Ibid., 138.

12. Gilbert Collins, *Guidebook to the Historic Sites of the War of 1812* (Toronto: Dundurn Press, 2006), 41.

13. John Sugden, *Tecumseh: A Life* (New York: Henry Holt, 1997), 212–13.

14. Ibid.

15. Ibid., 248–57.

16. Sean Michael O'Brien, *In Bitterness and in Tears: Andrew Jackson's Destruction of the Creeks and Seminoles* (Guilford, CT: Lyons Press, 2005), 21–22.

17. Ibid., 9, 11.

18. Gregory Evans Dowd, *A Spirited Resistance: The North American Indian Struggle for Unity, 1745–1815* (Baltimore: Johns Hopkins University Press, 1993), 152–54.

19. Michael D. Green, *The Politics of Indian Removal: Creek Government and Society in Crisis* (Lincoln: University of Nebraska Press, 1985), 39.

20. Sean Michael O'Brien, *In Bitterness and in Tears: Andrew Jackson's Destruction of the Creeks and Seminoles* (Guilford, CT: Lyons Press, 2005), 1.

21. Gregory Evans Dowd, *A Spirited Resistance: The North American Indian Struggle for Unity, 1745–1815* (Baltimore: Johns Hopkins University Press, 1993), 152.

22. Sean Michael O'Brien, *In Bitterness and in Tears: Andrew Jackson's Destruction of the Creeks and Seminoles* (Guilford, CT: Lyons Press, 2005), 13.

23. Michael D. Green, *The Politics of Indian Removal: Creek Government and Society in Crisis* (Lincoln: University of Nebraska Press, 1985), 39.

24. Gregory Evans Dowd, *A Spirited Resistance: The North American Indian Struggle for Unity, 1745–1815* (Baltimore: Johns Hopkins University Press, 1993), 146–47.

25. Everett T. Tomlinson, *Tecumseh's Young Braves: A Story of the Creek War* (Boston: Lee and Shepard, 1897), 24.

26. Sean Michael O'Brien, *In Bitterness and in Tears: Andrew Jackson's Destruction of the Creeks and Seminoles* (Guilford, CT: Lyons Press, 2005), 19.

27. Ibid., 19–20, 23.

28. Benjamin Drake, *Life of Tecumseh, and of His Brother the Prophet; with a Historical Sketch of the Shawanoe Indians* (Cincinnati: E. Morgan, 1841), 226.

29. John Sugden, *Tecumseh: A Life* (New York: Henry Holt, 1997), 245–46.

30. Jay Feldman, *When the Mississippi Ran Backwards: Empire, Intrigue, Murder, and the New Madrid Earthquakes* (New York: Free Press, 2005), 5–6.

31. Anders Breidlid, Fredrik Chr. Brøgger, Øyvind T. Gulliksen, and Torbjorn Sirevag, eds., *American Culture: An Anthology of Civilization Texts* (London: Routledge, 1996), 10–13.

32. Sean Michael O'Brien, *In Bitterness and in Tears: Andrew Jackson's Destruction of the Creeks and Seminoles* (Guilford, CT: Lyons Press, 2005), 23.

33. Allan W. Eckert, *A Sorrow in Our Heart: The Life of Tecumseh* (New York: Bantam, 1993), 662.

34. Benjamin Drake, *Life of Tecumseh, and of His Brother the Prophet; with a Historical Sketch of the Shawanoe Indians* (Cincinnati: E. Morgan, 1841), 144.

35. Michael D. Green, *The Politics of Indian Removal: Creek Government and Society in Crisis* (Lincoln: University of Nebraska Press, 1985), 39.

36. Sean Michael O'Brien, *In Bitterness and in Tears: Andrew Jackson's Destruction of the Creeks and Seminoles* (Guilford, CT: Lyons Press, 2005), 23.

37. Benjamin Drake, *Life of Tecumseh, and of His Brother the Prophet; with a Historical Sketch of the Shawanoe Indians* (Cincinnati: E. Morgan, 1841), 145.

CHAPTER 6: THE PROPHET

1. Benjamin Drake, *Life of Tecumseh, and of His Brother the Prophet; with a Historical Sketch of the Shawanoe Indians* (Cincinnati: E. Morgan, 1841), 105.

2. Ibid., 63.

3. Ibid., 86.

4. Ibid., 86–88.

5. Ibid., 87.

6. Roger L. Di Silvestro, *In the Shadow of Wounded Knee* (New York: Walker, 2007), 65.

7. Benjamin Drake, *Life of Tecumseh, and of His Brother the Prophet; with a Historical Sketch of the Shawanoe Indians* (Cincinnati: E. Morgan, 1841), 88.

8. Arthur J. Leighton, "'Eyes on the Wabash': A History of Indiana's Indian People from Pre-Contact through Removal" (Ph.D thesis, Purdue University, 2007), 228.

9. John Sugden, *Tecumseh: A Life* (New York: Henry Holt, 1997), 122–23.

10. Benjamin Drake, *Life of Tecumseh, and of His Brother the Prophet; with a Historical Sketch of the Shawanoe Indians* (Cincinnati: E. Morgan, 1841), 88.

11. Ibid., 89.

12. Ibid., 89–90.

13. Ferdinand Brock Tupper, Esq., ed., *The Life and Correspondence of Major-General Sir Isaac Brock, K.B.* (London: Simpkin, Marshall, 1847), 243, 244.

14. R. David Edmunds, *The Shawnee Prophet* (Lincoln: University of Nebraska Press, 1985), 104.

15. Benjamin Drake, *Life of Tecumseh, and of His Brother the Prophet; with a Historical Sketch of the Shawanoe Indians* (Cincinnati: E. Morgan, 1841), 146.

16. Jay Feldman, *When the Mississippi Ran Backwards: Empire, Intrigue, Murder, and the New Madrid Earthquakes* (New York: Free Press, 2005), 77.

17. Ibid., 77–78.

18. Ibid., 78.

19. Ibid., 197.

20. Ibid., 79–80.

21. Ibid., 81–82.

22. Colonel H. R. Gordon, *Tecumseh, Chief of the Shawanoes: A Tale of the War of 1812* (New York: E. P. Dutton, 1898), 66.

23. Jay Feldman, *When the Mississippi Ran Backwards: Empire, Intrigue, Murder, and the New Madrid Earthquakes* (New York: Free Press, 2005), 83.

CHAPTER 7: BROCK ON THE EVE OF WAR

1. Adam Shortt and Arthur G. Doughty, *Canada and Its Provinces*, vol. 4 (Toronto: Publishers' Association of Canada, 1914), 209.

2. Jac Weller, *Wellington at Waterloo* (Barnsley, UK: Greenhill Books, 1992), 24.

3. Jon Latimer, *1812: War with America* (Cambridge, MA: Harvard University Press, 2007), 8–9.

4. Stuart Reid, *British Redcoat, 1793–1815* (Oxford: Osprey, 1997), 18–21.

5. Ibid., 24.

6. Gregory Fremont-Barnes, *The Royal Navy, 1793–1815* (Oxford: Osprey, 2007), 54–57.

7. Jon Latimer, *1812: War with America* (Cambridge, MA: Harvard University Press, 2007), 8.

8. John Keegan, *Battle at Sea: From Man-of-War to Submarine* (London: Pimlico, 2004), 6.

9. Ferdinand Brock Tupper, Esq., *The Life and Correspondence of Major-General Sir Isaac Brock, K.B.* (London: Simpkin, Marshall, 1847), 123–24.

10. Brock to Colonel Baynes, the Adj.-General, York, 12 February 1812, in *The Life and Correspondence of Major-General Sir Isaac Brock, K.B.*, ed. Ferdinand Brock Tupper, Esq. (London: Simpkin, Marshall, 1847), 150.

11. Brock to Sir George Prevost, York, 16 May 1812, in T*he Life and Correspondence of Major-General Sir Isaac Brock, K.B.*, ed. Ferdinand Brock Tupper, Esq. (London: Simpkin, Marshall, 1847), 174.

12. Brock to Lieut.-General Sir G. Prevost, Bart., at Quebec, York, 2 December 1811, in *The Life and Correspondence of Major-General Sir Isaac Brock, K.B.*, ed. Ferdinand Brock Tupper, Esq. (London: Simpkin, Marshall, 1847), 127–28.

13. Ibid., 128.

14. Ibid., 129.

15. Ibid., 124.

16. Ibid., 123–24.

17. Ibid., 124.

18. Ferdinand Brock Tupper, Esq., ed., *The Life and Correspondence of Major-General Sir Isaac Brock*, K.B. (London: Simpkin, Marshall, 1847), 144, 145.

19. Brock to Sir George Prevost, York, February 1812, in *The Life and Correspondence of Major-General Sir Isaac Brock, K.B.*, ed. Ferdinand Brock Tupper, Esq. (London: Simpkin, Marshall, 1847), 153.

20. Sir Isaac Brock Papers, M.G. 24, A1, vol. 1, 26–27, National Archives of Canada.

21. Prevost to Brock, 30 April 1812, Sir Isaac Brock Papers, M.G. 24, A1, vol. 1, NAC Reel C-4621, National Archives of Canada.

22. Prevost to Brock, 27 May 1812, Sir Isaac Brock Papers, M.G. 24, A1, vol. 1, 26–27, National Archives of Canada.

CHAPTER 8: THE UNITED STATES DECLARES WAR ON GREAT BRITAIN

1. *Official Letters of the Military and Naval Officers of the United States, during the War with Great Britain in the Years 1812, 13, 14 & 15*, collected and annotated by John Brannan (Washington, 1823), 12–14.

2. Ibid., 12–15.

3. Walter Borneman, *1812: The War that Forged a Nation* (New York: HarperCollins, 2004), 49, 50.

4. D. B. Read, Q.C., *Life and Times of Major-General Sir Isaac Brock, K.B.* (Toronto: William Briggs, 1894), 121–24.

5. Ibid., 127–28.

6. Ferdinand Brock Tupper, Esq., ed., *The Life and Correspondence of Major-General Sir Isaac Brock, K.B.* (London: Simpkin, Marshall, 1847), 197, 198.

7. Brock to Prevost, 3 July 1812, Sir Isaac Brock Papers, M.G. 24, A1, vol. 1, NAC Reel C-4621, National Archives of Canada.

8. Prevost to Brock, 7 July 1812, Sir Isaac Brock Papers, M.G. 24, A1, vol. 1, 26–27, National Archives of Canada.

9. Prevost to Brock, 10 July 1812, Sir Isaac Brock Papers, M.G. 24, A1, vol. 1, NAC Reel C-4621, National Archives of Canada.

10. Walter Borneman, *1812: The War that Forged a Nation* (New York: HarperCollins, 2004), 57.

11. William James, *A Full and Correct Account of The Military Occurrences of the Late War Between Great Britain and The United States Of America, with an Appendix and Plates*, vol. 1 (London, 1818), 77.

12. Donald R. Hickey, *The War of 1812: A Forgotten Conflict* (Champaign, IL: University of Illinois Press, 1995), 74.

13. Jefferson to General Thaddeus Kosciusko, 28 June 1812, Monticello, in *The Works of Thomas Jefferson*, 12 vols., federal edition (New York: G. P. Putnam's Sons, 1904–5), 258.

14. Hickey, Donald R., *The War of 1812: A Forgotten Conflict* (Champaign, IL: University of Illinois Press, 1995), 88.

15. David S. Heidler and Jeanne T. Heidler, eds., *Encyclopedia of the War of 1812*, paperback edition (Annapolis, MD: Naval Institute Press, 2004), 247–49, 417–18.

16. A. J. Langguth, *Union 1812: The Americans Who Fought the Second War of Independence*, paperback edition (New York: Simon and Schuster, 2006), 178.

17. William Hull, *Memoirs of the Campaign of the North Western Army of the United States, A. D. 1812: In a Series of Letters Addressed to the Citizens of the United States* (Boston: True and Greene, 1824), 40–41.

18. *Official Letters of the Military and Naval Officers of the United States, during the War with Great Britain in the Years 1812, 13, 14 & 15*, collected and annotated by John Brannan (Washington, 1823), 30, 31.

19. William Hull, *Memoirs of the Campaign of the North Western Army of the United States, A. D. 1812: In a Series of Letters Addressed to the Citizens of the United States* (Boston: True and Greene, 1824), 47.

20. Ibid., 44.

21. Gilbert Collins, *Guidebook to the Historic Sites of the War of 1812* (Toronto: Dundurn Press, 2006), 47.

22. Ibid.

23. Ferdinand Brock Tupper, Esq., ed., *The Life and Correspondence of Major-General Sir Isaac Brock, K.B.* (London: Simpkin, Marshall, 1847), 209–11.

24. Brock to Sir George Prevost, York, 4 August 1812, in *The Life and Correspondence of Major-General Sir Isaac Brock, K.B.*, ed. Ferdinand Brock Tupper, Esq. (London: Simpkin, Marshall, 1847), 232–33.

25. Prevost to Brock, 31 July 1812, Sir Isaac Brock Papers, M.G. 24, A1, vol. 1, NAC Reel C-4621, National Archives of Canada.

26. *Official Letters of the Military and Naval Officers of the United States, during the War with Great Britain in the Years 1812, 13, 14 & 15*, collected and annotated by John Brannan (Washington, 1823), 34–35.

27. A. T. Mahan, *The Sea War of 1812: A History of the Maritime Conflict*, vol. 2 (n.p.: Leonaur, 2008), 409.

28. Prevost to Brock, Quebec, 31 July 1812, Sir Isaac Brock papers, M.G. 24, A1, vol. 1, National Archives of Canada.

29. Prevost to Brock, Quebec, 2 August 1812, Sir Isaac Brock papers, M.G. 24, A1, vol. 1, National Archives of Canada.

30. David S. Heidler and Jeanne T. Heidler, eds., *Encyclopedia of the War of 1812*, paperback edition (Annapolis, MD: Naval Institute Press, 2004), 248.

31. Samuel Williams, *Two Western Campaigns in the War of 1812–13* (Cincinnati: Robert Clarke, 1870), 29.

CHAPTER 9: TWO WARRIORS

1. Ferdinand Brock Tupper, Esq., ed., *The Life and Correspondence of Major-General Sir Isaac Brock, K.B.* (London: Simpkin, Marshall, 1847), 241.

2. Ibid., 243, 244.

3. Ethel T. Raymond, *Tecumseh: A Chronicle of the Last Great Leader of His People* (Gutenberg Project Ebook 24147, 2008; originally published in Toronto as vol. 17 of Chronicles of Canada, 1915), 14.

4. Benjamin Drake, *Life of Tecumseh, and of His Brother the Prophet; with a Historical Sketch of the Shawanoe Indians* (Cincinnati: E. Morgan, 1841), 224.

5. Ethel T. Raymond, *Tecumseh: A Chronicle of the Last Great Leader of His People* (Gutenberg Project Ebook 24147, 2008; originally published in Toronto as vol. 17 of Chronicles of Canada, 1915), 14.

6. Ibid., 15.

7. Ferdinand Brock Tupper, Esq., ed., *The Life and Correspondence of Major-General Sir Isaac Brock, K.B.* (London: Simpkin, Marshall, 1847), 308.

8. A. J. Langguth, *Union 1812: The Americans Who Fought the Second War of Independence*, paperback edition (New York: Simon and Schuster, 2006), 188.

CHAPTER 10: THE CAPTURE OF FORT DETROIT

1. A. J. Langguth, *Union 1812: The Americans Who Fought the Second War of Independence*, paperback edition (New York: Simon and Schuster, 2006), 191.

2. *Official Letters of the Military and Naval Officers of the United States, during*

the War with Great Britain in the Years 1812, 13, 14 & 15, collected and annotated by John Brannan (Washington, 1823), 41.

3.   Ibid.

4.   A. J. Langguth, *Union 1812: The Americans Who Fought the Second War of Independence*, paperback edition (New York: Simon and Schuster, 2006), 191–92.

5.   Jon Latimer, *1812: War with America* (Cambridge, MA: Harvard University
Press, 2007), 66.

6.   Ibid.

7.   Duncan Campbell Scott and Lady Matilda Edgar. *John Graves Simcoe and
General Brock* (Toronto: Morang, 1910), 253–54.

8.   Hull to Hon. W. Eustis, Secretary of the Department of War, Fort George, 26
August 1812, in *Official Letters of the Military and Naval Officers of the United
States, during the War with Great Britain in the Years 1812, 13, 14 & 15*, col-
lected and annotated by John Brannan (Washington, 1823), 44–49.

9.   Brock to Sir George Prevost, Head Quarters, Detroit, 16 August 1812, in *The
Life and Correspondence of Major-General Sir Isaac Brock, K.B.*, ed. Ferdinand
Brock Tupper, Esq. (London: Simpkin, Marshall, 1847), 269.

10.   Lewis Cass, Col. 3d reg. Ohio volunteers to The Hon. William Eustis, Secretary of
War, Washington, September 10, 1812, in *Official Letters of the Military and Naval
Officers of the United States, during the War with Great Britain in the Years 1812,
13, 14 & 15*, collected and annotated by John Brannan (Washington, 1823), 56–60.

11.   Adam Shortt and Arthur G. Doughty, *Canada and Its Provinces*, vol. 3 (Toronto: Publishers' Association of Canada, 1914), 224.

12.   Jon Latimer, *1812: War with America* (Cambridge, MA: Harvard University
Press, 2007), 68; and A. J. Langguth, *Union 1812: The Americans Who Fought
the Second War of Independence*, paperback edition (New York: Simon and
Schuster, 2006), 194.

13.   Jon Latimer, *1812: War with America* (Cambridge, MA: Harvard University
Press, 2007), 68.

14.   A. J. Langguth, *Union 1812: The Americans Who Fought the Second War of
Independence*, paperback edition (New York: Simon and Schuster, 2006), 194.

15.   Brock to the Earl of Liverpool, York, Upper Canada, 29 August, 1812, Colonial
Office Records, Indian Affairs Canada. RG 10, vol. 10017, Canada Q. 315,
Library and Archives Canada, 118.

16.   Stephen Ruddell, *Reminiscences of Tecumseh's Youth* (Wisconsin Historical Society, 2003), 123; online facsimile edition at http://www.americanjourneys.org/aj-155.

17.   A. J. Langguth, *Union 1812: The Americans Who Fought the Second War of Independence*, paperback edition (New York: Simon and Schuster, 2006), 195–96.

18.   Ibid., 198.

19.   Ibid., 273.

CHAPTER 11: DEATH OF THE GENERAL

1. A. J. Langguth, *Union 1812: The Americans Who Fought the Second War of Independence,* paperback edition (New York: Simon and Schuster, 2006), 211.
2. Solomon Van Rensselaer, *A Narrative of the Affair of Queenstown: In the War of 1812* (New York: Leavitt, Lord, 1836), 9.
3. Ibid., 10–14.
4. Ibid., 13.
5. Ibid., 30.
6. Ibid., 10–12.
7. Ibid., 41–42.
8. Jon Latimer, *1812: War with America* (Cambridge, MA: Harvard University Press, 2007), 75.
9. Solomon Van Rensselaer, *A Narrative of the Affair of Queenstown: In the War of 1812* (New York: Leavitt, Lord, 1836), 18–19.
10. Ibid., 72–73.
11. William James, *A Full and Correct Account of The Military Occurrences of the Late War Between Great Britain and The United States Of America, with an Appendix and Plates,* vol. 1 (London, 1818), 87.
12. Carl Benn, *The Iroquois in the War of 1812* (Toronto: University of Toronto Press, 1998), 89.
13. Ibid., 36, 37, 39–41.
14. Solomon Van Rensselaer, *A Narrative of the Affair of Queenstown: In the War of 1812,* appendix (New York: Leavitt, Lord, 1836), 72.
15. Ibid.
16. Ibid., appendix, 64.
17. Jon Latimer, *1812: War with America* (Cambridge, MA: Harvard University Press, 2007), 77–79.
18. Adam Shortt and Arthur G. Doughty, *Canada and Its Provinces,* vol. 3 (Toronto: Publishers' Association of Canada, 1914), 232.
19. Ibid., 233.
20. Jon Latimer, *1812: War with America* (Cambridge, MA: Harvard University Press, 2007), 79–80.
21. Carl Benn, *The Iroquois in the War of 1812* (Toronto: University of Toronto Press, 1998), 8, 47, 91.
22. Jon Latimer, *1812: War with America* (Cambridge, MA: Harvard University Press, 2007), 81; and Carl Benn, *The Iroquois in the War of 1812* (Toronto: University of Toronto Press, 1998), 91.
23. Adam Shortt and Arthur G. Doughty, *Canada and Its Provinces,* vol. 3 (Toronto: Publishers' Association of Canada, 1914), 234–35.

24. Carl Benn, *The Iroquois in the War of 1812* (Toronto: University of Toronto Press, 1998), 94–96.

25. Ibid., 96.

26. Ibid., 94–96.

27. Ibid., 103.

28. Solomon Van Rensselaer, *A Narrative of the Affair of Queenstown: In the War of 1812* (New York: Leavitt, Lord, 1836), 62–67.

29. A. J. Langguth, *Union 1812: The Americans Who Fought the Second War of Independence*, paperback edition (New York: Simon and Schuster, 2006), 217–18.

Chapter 12: York in Flames

1. Jefferson to Madison, 6 November 1812, in Thomas Jefferson, *The Works of Thomas Jefferson: Vol. XI Correspondence and Papers 1808–1816* (New York: Cosimo Inc., 2009), 270–71.

2. Henry Adams, *History of the United States of America During the Administrations of James Madison* (New York: The Library of America, 1986), 593.

3. Jon Latimer, *1812: War with America* (Cambridge, MA: Harvard University Press, 2007), 113.

4. David S. Heidler and Jeanne T. Heidler, eds., *Encyclopedia of the War of 1812*, paperback edition (Annapolis, MD: Naval Institute Press, 2004), 6.

5. *Official Letters of the Military and Naval Officers of the United States, during the War with Great Britain in the Years 1812, 13, 14 & 15*, collected and annotated by John Brannan (Washington, 1823), 133–34.

6. Ibid.

7. David S. Heidler and Jeanne T. Heidler, eds., *Encyclopedia of the War of 1812*, paperback edition (Annapolis, MD: Naval Institute Press, 2004), 90–91, 223–24.

8. Ibid., 223–224.

9. *Official Letters of the Military and Naval Officers of the United States, during the War with Great Britain in the Years 1812, 13, 14 & 15*, collected and annotated by John Brannan (Washington, 1823), 90–91.

10. A. T. Mahan, *The Sea War of 1812: A History of the Maritime Conflict*, vol. 2 (n.p.: Leonaur, 2008), 39.

11. Jon Latimer, *1812: War with America* (Cambridge, MA: Harvard University Press, 2007), 128–30.

12. G. Auchinleck, *The War of 1812: A History of the War Between Great Britain and the United States of America, During the Years 1812, 1813, and 1814* (Toronto: C. Chewett, 1862), 151–52.

13. Walter Borneman, *1812: The War that Forged a Nation* (New York: HarperCollins, 2004), 103.

14. William James, *A Full and Correct Account of The Military Occurrences of the Late War Between Great Britain and The United States Of America, with an Appendix and Plates*, vol. 1 (London, 1818), 142.

15. Ibid., vol. 1, 145.

16. Jon Latimer, *1812: War with America* (Cambridge, MA: Harvard University Press, 2007), 132.

17. G. Auchinleck, *The War of 1812: A History of the War Between Great Britain and the United States of America, During the Years 1812, 1813, and 1814* (Toronto: C. Chewett, 1862), 153.

18. Jon Latimer, *1812: War with America* (Cambridge, MA: Harvard University Press, 2007), 132.

19. Ibid.

20. G. Auchinleck, *The War of 1812: A History of the War Between Great Britain and the United States of America, During the Years 1812, 1813, and 1814* (Toronto: C. Chewett, 1862), 152.

21. Franklin D. Roosevelt, "Message to Congress Requesting Authority to Return a Mace to Canada," May 4, 1934.

22. Jon Latimer, *1812: War with America* (Cambridge, MA: Harvard University Press, 2007), 133.

23. Strachan to Dr. James Brown, 26 April 1813, Strachan Papers, Reel 10, MS 35-10, Ontario Department of Public Records and Archives.

24. Jon Latimer, *1812: War with America* (Cambridge, MA: Harvard University Press, 2007), 133.

25. G. Auchinleck, *The War of 1812: A History of the War Between Great Britain and the United States of America, During the Years 1812, 1813, and 1814* (Toronto: C. Chewett, 1862), 155.

26. Ibid., 133.

27. Wesley B. Turner, *British Generals in the War of 1812: High Command in the Canadas* (Montreal: McGill-Queen's University Press, 1999), 37.

28. G. Auchinleck, *The War of 1812: A History of the War Between Great Britain and the United States of America, During the Years 1812, 1813, and 1814* (Toronto: C. Chewett, 1862), 166.

29. William James, *A Full and Correct Account of The Military Occurrences of the Late War Between Great Britain and The United States Of America, with an Appendix and Plates*, vol. 1 (London, 1818), 170–71.

30. G. Auchinleck, *The War of 1812: A History of the War Between Great Britain and the United States of America, During the Years 1812, 1813, and 1814* (Toronto: C. Chewett, 1862), 156.

31. Ibid.

32. Ibid., 157.

33. William James, *A Full and Correct Account of the Military Occurrences of the Late War Between Great Britain and The United States Of America, with an Appendix and Plates* (London, 1818), 160.

34. J. Mackay Hitsman, *The Incredible War of 1812: A Military History*, updated by Donald E. Graves (Cap-Saint-Ignace, QC: Robin Brass Studio, 1999), 149.

35. G. Auchinleck, *The War of 1812: A History of the War Between Great Britain and the United States of America, During the Years 1812, 1813, and 1814* (Toronto: C. Chewett, 1862), 168–70.

36. J. Mackay Hitsman, *The Incredible War of 1812: A Military History*, updated by Donald E. Graves (Cap-Saint-Ignace, QC: Robin Brass Studio, 1999), 149–51.

37. Ibid., 154–55.

38. Carl Benn, *The Iroquois in the War of 1812* (Toronto: University of Toronto Press, 1998), 115–20.

Chapter 13: Tecumseh's Last Days

1. Benjamin Drake, *Life of Tecumseh, and of His Brother the Prophet; with a Historical Sketch of the Shawanoe Indians* (Cincinnati: E. Morgan, 1841), 182.

2. Stephen Budiansky, *Perilous Fight: America's Intrepid War with Britain on the High Seas, 1812–1815* (New York: Alfred A. Knopf, 2010), 253–54.

3. Benjamin Drake, *Life of Tecumseh, and of His Brother the Prophet; with a Historical Sketch of the Shawanoe Indians* (Cincinnati: E. Morgan, 1841), 188.

4. *Official Letters of the Military and Naval Officers of the United States, during the War with Great Britain in the Years 1812, 13, 14 & 15*, collected and annotated by John Brannan (Washington, 1823), 240–41.

5. A. J. Langguth, *Union 1812: The Americans Who Fought the Second War of Independence*, paperback edition (New York: Simon and Schuster, 2006), 261.

6. *Lucubrations of Humphrey Ravelin* (London, 1823), 355–56, cited in Carl F. Klinck, ed., *Tecumseh: Fact and Fiction in Early Records* (Ottawa: Tecumseh Press, 1978), 186.

7. Benjamin Drake, *Life of Tecumseh, and of His Brother the Prophet; with a Historical Sketch of the Shawanoe Indians* (Cincinnati: E. Morgan, 1841), 191.

8. William F. Coffin, *1812, the War, and Its Moral: A Canadian Chronicle* (Montreal, 1864), 226, cited in Carl F. Klinck, ed., *Tecumseh: Fact and Fiction in Early Records* (Ottawa: Tecumseh Press, 1978), 188.

9. Christopher B. Coleman, "The Ohio and the War of 1812," *Mississippi Valley Historical Review* 7, no. 1 (June 1920): 41.

10. A. J. Langguth, *Union 1812: The Americans Who Fought the Second War of Independence*, paperback edition (New York: Simon and Schuster, 2006), 262.

11. John Sugden, *Tecumseh: A Life* (New York: Henry Holt, 1997), 363.

12. Ibid., 122.

13. Ibid., 374.

14. Jon Latimer, *1812: War with America* (Cambridge, MA: Harvard University Press, 2007), 188–89.

15. *Time* Specials, August 21, 2008, "America's Worst Vice Presidents."

16. Theodore Roosevelt, *The Naval War of 1812* (n.p.: Seven Treasures Publications, 2009; first published 1882 by G. Putnam's Sons), 15.

CHAPTER 14: THE CREEK WAR

1. Gregory Evans Dowd, *A Spirited Resistance: The North American Indian Struggle for Unity, 1745–1815* (Baltimore: Johns Hopkins University Press, 1993), 157.

2. Sean Michael O'Brien, *In Bitterness and in Tears: Andrew Jackson's Destruction of the Creeks and Seminoles* (Guilford, CT: Lyons Press, 2005), 24–25.

3. Gregory Evans Dowd, *A Spirited Resistance: The North American Indian Struggle for Unity, 1745–1815* (Baltimore: Johns Hopkins University Press, 1993), 156.

4. J. F. Watts and Fred L. Israel, eds., *Presidential Documents: The Speeches, Proclamations, and Policies that Have Shaped the Nation from Washington to Clinton* (New York: Routledge, 2000), 41.

5. Sean Michael O'Brien, *In Bitterness and in Tears: Andrew Jackson's Destruction of the Creeks and Seminoles* (Guilford, CT: Lyons Press, 2005), 37–38.

6. Gregory Evans Dowd, *A Spirited Resistance: The North American Indian Struggle for Unity, 1745–1815* (Baltimore: Johns Hopkins University Press, 1993), 185.

7. Sean Michael O'Brien, *In Bitterness and in Tears: Andrew Jackson's Destruction of the Creeks and Seminoles* (Guilford, CT: Lyons Press, 2005), 39–40.

8. Gregory Evans Dowd, *A Spirited Resistance: The North American Indian Struggle for Unity, 1745–1815* (Baltimore: Johns Hopkins University Press, 1993), 185.

9. James Parton, *The Life of Andrew Jackson*, vol. 1 (New York: Mason Brothers, 1861), 418.

10. Ibid., vol. 1, 423–27.

11. A. J. Langguth, *Union 1812: The Americans Who Fought the Second War of Independence*, paperback edition (New York: Simon and Schuster, 2006), 276.

12. Sean Michael O'Brien, *In Bitterness and in Tears: Andrew Jackson's Destruction of the Creeks and Seminoles* (Guilford, CT: Lyons Press, 2005), 71.

13. David Crockett, *A Narrative of the Life of David Crockett, of the State of Tennessee* (Baltimore: E. L. Cary and A. Hart, 1834), 64.

14. Ibid., 81.

15. Ibid., 82.

16. James Parton, *The Life of Andrew Jackson*, vol. 1 (New York: Mason Brothers, 1861), 439.

17. A. J. Langguth, *Union 1812: The Americans Who Fought the Second War of Independence*, paperback edition (New York: Simon and Schuster, 2006), 279.

18. David Crockett, *A Narrative of the Life of David Crockett, of the State of Tennessee* (Baltimore: E. L. Cary and A. Hart, 1834), 84–85.

19. Sean Michael O'Brien, *In Bitterness and in Tears: Andrew Jackson's Destruction of the Creeks and Seminoles* (Guilford, CT: Lyons Press, 2005), 79.

20. Ibid., 60.

21. James Parton, *The Life of Andrew Jackson*, vol. 1 (New York: Mason Brothers, 1861), 453.

22. David Crockett, *A Narrative of the Life of David Crockett, of the State of Tennessee* (Baltimore: E. L. Cary and A. Hart, 1834), 88–89.

23. Sean Michael O'Brien, *In Bitterness and in Tears: Andrew Jackson's Destruction of the Creeks and Seminoles* (Guilford, CT: Lyons Press, 2005), 84–85.

24. Walter Borneman, *1812: The War that Forged a Nation* (New York: HarperCollins, 2004), 148.

25. Sean Michael O'Brien, *In Bitterness and in Tears: Andrew Jackson's Destruction of the Creeks and Seminoles* (Guilford, CT: Lyons Press, 2005), 98–99.

26. Ibid., 100–101.

27. Walter Borneman, *1812: The War that Forged a Nation* (New York: HarperCollins, 2004), 149.

28. Sean Michael O'Brien, *In Bitterness and in Tears: Andrew Jackson's Destruction of the Creeks and Seminoles* (Guilford, CT: Lyons Press, 2005), 149.

29. James Parton, *The Life of Andrew Jackson*, vol. 1 (New York: Mason Brothers, 1861), 524.

30. Michael D. Green, *The Politics of Indian Removal: Creek Government and Society in Crisis* (Lincoln: University of Nebraska Press, 1985), 43.

31. Sean Michael O'Brien, *In Bitterness and in Tears: Andrew Jackson's Destruction of the Creeks and Seminoles* (Guilford, CT: Lyons Press, 2005), 162–63.

CHAPTER 15: OUT OF THE FURNACE OF WAR, AN UPPER CANADIAN IDENTITY

1. Adam Shortt and Arthur G. Doughty, *Canada and Its Provinces*, vol. 3 (Toronto: Publishers' Association of Canada, 1914), 213.

2. Ibid., 210.

3. Ibid., 209–10.

4. Strachan to Richardson, 30 September 1812, Strachan Papers, Reel 10, MS 35-10, Ontario Department of Public Records and Archives.

5. Strachan to Wilberforce, 1 November 1812, Strachan Papers, Reel 10, MS 35-10, Ontario Department of Public Records and Archives.

6. Strachan to Richardson, November 1812, Strachan Papers, Reel 10, MS 35-10, Ontario Department of Public Records and Archives.

7. Strachan to Wellesley, 1 November 1812, Strachan Papers, Reel 10, MS 35-10, Ontario Department of Public Records and Archives.

8. David S. Heidler and Jeanne T. Heidler, eds., *Encyclopedia of the War of 1812*, paperback edition (Annapolis, MD: Naval Institute Press, 2004), 226.

9. Prevost to Bathurst, 8 October 1813, State Papers — Lower Canada, No. 91.

10. Donald E. Graves, *Field of Glory: The Battle of Crysler's Farm, 1813* (Toronto: Robin Brass Studio, 1999), xv.

11. James Ripley Jacobs, *Tarnished Warrior: Major-General James Wilkinson* (New York: Macmillan, 1938), 268–69, 274, 277.

12. J. Mackay Hitsman, *The Incredible War of 1812: A Military History*, updated by Donald E. Graves (Cap-Saint-Ignace, QC: Robin Brass Studio, 1999), 181.

13. Ibid., 183.

14. Ibid., 185–87.

15. *Official Letters of the Military and Naval Officers of the United States, during the War with Great Britain in the Years 1812, 13, 14 & 15*, collected and annotated by John Brannan (Washington, 1823), 249–52.

16. J. Mackay Hitsman, *The Incredible War of 1812: A Military History*, updated by Donald E. Graves (Cap-Saint-Ignace, QC: Robin Brass Studio, 1999), 187–88.

17. Ibid., 187.

18. James Ripley Jacobs, *Tarnished Warrior: Major-General James Wilkinson* (New York: Macmillan, 1938), 289.

19. J. Mackay Hitsman, *The Incredible War of 1812: A Military History*, updated by Donald E. Graves (Cap-Saint-Ignace, QC: Robin Brass Studio, 1999), 188.

20. Ibid., 189.

21. Jon Latimer, *1812: War with America* (Cambridge, MA: Harvard University Press, 2007), 211, 212; and J. Mackay Hitsman, *The Incredible War of 1812: A Military History*, updated by Donald E. Graves (Cap-Saint-Ignace, QC: Robin Brass Studio, 1999), 189–90.

22. James Ripley Jacobs, *Tarnished Warrior: Major-General James Wilkinson* (New York: Macmillan, 1938), 296.

23. James Wilkinson, *Wilkinson: Soldier and Pioneer* (New Orleans: Rogers, 1935), 231.

24. J. Mackay Hitsman, *The Incredible War of 1812: A Military History*, updated by Donald E. Graves (Cap-Saint-Ignace, QC: Robin Brass Studio, 1999), 192.

25. James Ripley Jacobs, *Tarnished Warrior: Major-General James Wilkinson* (New York: Macmillan, 1938), 298–99.

26. David S. Heidler and Jeanne T. Heidler, eds., *Encyclopedia of the War of 1812*, paperback edition (Annapolis, MD: Naval Institute Press, 2004), 331–32.

Chapter 16: Bloody Niagara

1. David S. Heidler and Jeanne T. Heidler, eds., *Encyclopedia of the War of 1812*, paperback edition (Annapolis, MD: Naval Institute Press, 2004), 331–32.

2. A. T. Mahan, *The Sea War of 1812: A History of the Maritime Conflict*, vol. 2 (n.p.: Leonaur, 2008), 411.

3. David S. Heidler and Jeanne T. Heidler, eds., *Encyclopedia of the War of 1812*, paperback edition (Annapolis, MD: Naval Institute Press, 2004), 3.

4. Walter Borneman, *1812: The War that Forged a Nation* (New York: HarperCollins, 2004), 264.

5. Ibid., 265.

6. Ibid., 265–66.

7. J. Mackay Hitsman, *The Incredible War of 1812: A Military History*, updated by Donald E. Graves (Cap-Saint-Ignace, QC: Robin Brass Studio, 1999), 213–14.

8. Donald E. Graves, *Where Right and Glory Lead! The Battle of Lundy's Lane, 1814* (Cap-Saint-Ignace, Quebec: Robin Brass Studio, 1993), 75–76.

9. Duncan Clark Fonds, 11, Microfilm Reel MS 572, Archives of Ontario.

10. J. Mackay Hitsman, *The Incredible War of 1812: A Military History*, updated by Donald E. Graves (Cap-Saint-Ignace, QC: Robin Brass Studio, 1999), 221–23.

11. Donald E. Graves, *Where Right and Glory Lead! The Battle of Lundy's Lane, 1814* (Cap-Saint-Ignace, Quebec: Robin Brass Studio, 1993), 89.

12. Ibid., 195–96.

13. Ibid., 197–99.

14. Louis L. Babcock, *The Siege of Fort Erie: An Episode of the War of 1812* (Buffalo: Peter Paul, 1899), 26.

Chapter 17: Rockets' Red Glare

1. Christopher T. George, *Terror on the Chesapeake: The War of 1812 on the Bay* (Shippensburg, PA: White Mane, 2000), 27.

2. Anthony S. Pitch, *The Burning of Washington: The British Invasion of 1814* (Annapolis, MD: Blue Jacket Books, Naval Institute Press, 2000), 17.

3. Ibid., 29.

4. Ibid., 18.

5. David S. Heidler and Jeanne T. Heidler, eds., *Encyclopedia of the War of 1812*, paperback edition (Annapolis, MD: Naval Institute Press, 2004), 558–59.

6. Wm. H. Winder, Brig. Gen. Comdg. 10th M.D., to Hon. John Armstrong, Secretary of War, Baltimore, 27 August 1814, in *Official Letters of the Military and Naval Officers of the United States during the War with Great Britain in the Years 1812, 13, 14 & 15*, collected and annotated by John Brannan (Washington, 1823), 400.

7. Anthony S. Pitch, *The Burning of Washington: The British Invasion of 1814* (Annapolis, MD: Blue Jacket Books, Naval Institute Press, 2000), 19.

8. Ibid.

9. *Niles' National Register* 4 (1813): 402.

10. A. J. Langguth, *Union 1812: The Americans Who Fought the Second War of Independence*, paperback edition (New York: Simon and Schuster, 2006), 294–95.

11. Anthony S. Pitch, *The Burning of Washington: The British Invasion of 1814* (Annapolis, MD: Blue Jacket Books, Naval Institute Press, 2000), 20.

12. Ibid.

13. Christopher T. George, *Terror on the Chesapeake: The War of 1812 on the Bay* (Shippensburg, PA: White Mane, 2000), 65–66.

14. Anthony S. Pitch, *The Burning of Washington: The British Invasion of 1814* (Annapolis, MD: Blue Jacket Books, Naval Institute Press, 2000), 22.

15. A. T. Mahan, *The Sea War of 1812: A History of the Maritime Conflict*, vol. 2 (n.p.: Leonaur, 2008), 338–39.

16. Ibid., 340–41.

17. David S. Heidler and Jeanne T. Heidler, eds., *Encyclopedia of the War of 1812*, paperback edition (Annapolis, MD: Naval Institute Press, 2004), 213.

18. Anthony S. Pitch, *The Burning of Washington: The British Invasion of 1814* (Annapolis, MD: Blue Jacket Books, Naval Institute Press, 2000), 30–31.

19. Jon Latimer, *1812: War with America* (Cambridge, MA: Harvard University Press, 2007), 309.

20. A. J. Langguth, *Union 1812: The Americans Who Fought the Second War of Independence*, paperback edition (New York: Simon and Schuster, 2006), 300.

21. Anthony S. Pitch, *The Burning of Washington: The British Invasion of 1814* (Annapolis, MD: Blue Jacket Books, Naval Institute Press, 2000), 67, 71.

22. A. T. Mahan, *The Sea War of 1812: A History of the Maritime Conflict*, vol. 2 (n.p.: Leonaur, 2008), 347.

23. Wm. H. Winder, Brig. Gen. Comdg. 10th M.D., to Hon. John Armstrong, Secretary of War, Baltimore, 27 August 1814, in *Official Letters of the Military and Naval Officers of the United States during the War with Great Britain in the Years 1812, 13, 14 & 15*, collected and annotated by John Brannan (Washington, 1823), 401.

24. Wm. H. Winder, Brig. Gen. Comdg. 10th M.D., to Hon. John Armstrong, Secretary of War, Baltimore, 27 August 1814, in *Official Letters of the Military and Naval Officers of the United States during the War with Great Britain in the Years 1812, 13, 14 & 15*, collected and annotated by John Brannan (Washington, 1823), 401.

25. Walter Borneman, *1812: The War that Forged a Nation* (New York: HarperCollins, 2004), 226–27.

26. Joshua Barney to Hon. W. Jones, Secretary of the Navy, Farm at Elk Ridge, 29 August 1814, in *Official Letters of the Military and Naval Officers of the United States during the War with Great Britain in the Years 1812, 13, 14 & 15*, collected and annotated by John Brannan (Washington, 1823), 406–7.

27. Jon Latimer, *1812: War with America* (Cambridge, MA: Harvard University Press, 2007), 315.

28. Ibid., 316.

29. Anthony S. Pitch, *The Burning of Washington: The British Invasion of 1814* (Annapolis, MD: Blue Jacket Books, Naval Institute Press, 2000), 87.

30. Alan Lloyd, *The Scorching of Washington: The War of 1812* (London: David and Charles, 1974), 171.

31. Jon Latimer, *1812: War with America* (Cambridge, MA: Harvard University Press, 2007), 316.

32. Christopher T. George, *Terror on the Chesapeake: The War of 1812 on the Bay* (Shippensburg, PA: White Mane, 2000), 107.

33. Anthony S. Pitch, *The Burning of Washington: The British Invasion of 1814* (Annapolis, MD: Blue Jacket Books, Naval Institute Press, 2000), 108.

34. Thomas Tingey to Hon. W. Jones, Secretary of the Navy, Navy Yard, Washington, 27 August 1814, in *Official Letters of the Military and Naval Officers of the United States during the War with Great Britain in the Years 1812, 13, 14 & 15*, collected and annotated by John Brannan (Washington, 1823), 402–3.

35. Anthony S. Pitch, *The Burning of Washington: The British Invasion of 1814* (Annapolis, MD: Blue Jacket Books, Naval Institute Press, 2000), 114.

36. Jon Latimer, *1812: War with America* (Cambridge, MA: Harvard University Press, 2007), 318.

37. Christopher T. George, *Terror on the Chesapeake: The War of 1812 on the Bay* (Shippensburg, PA: White Mane, 2000), 107–9.

38. Jon Latimer, *1812: War with America* (Cambridge, MA: Harvard University Press, 2007), 312, 320–22.

39. Thomas Jefferson, *The Papers of Thomas Jefferson*, Retirement Series, Vol. 8 (New Jersey: Princeton University Press, 2011), 215–16.

40. Jon Latimer, *1812: War with America* (Cambridge, MA: Harvard University Press, 2007), 322.

41. Anthony S. Pitch, *The Burning of Washington: The British Invasion of 1814* (Annapolis, MD: Blue Jacket Books, Naval Institute Press, 2000), 167–68.

42. Ibid., 168–69.

43. Ibid., 170–73.

44. A. T. Mahan, *The Sea War of 1812: A History of the Maritime Conflict*, vol. 2 (n.p.: Leonaur, 2008), 350.

45. Anthony S. Pitch, *The Burning of Washington: The British Invasion of 1814* (Annapolis, MD: Blue Jacket Books, Naval Institute Press, 2000), 178–79.

46. Ibid., 183–84, 194.

47. Christopher T. George, *Terror on the Chesapeake: The War of 1812 on the Bay* (Shippensburg, PA: White Mane, 2000), 138.

48. Jon Latimer, *1812: War with America* (Cambridge, MA: Harvard University Press, 2007), 328.

49. Anthony S. Pitch, *The Burning of Washington: The British Invasion of 1814* (Annapolis, MD: Blue Jacket Books, Naval Institute Press, 2000), 203–5.

50. Ibid., 203, 206.

51. Jon Latimer, *1812: War with America* (Cambridge, MA: Harvard University Press, 2007), 329.

52. Ibid., 330.

53. Anthony S. Pitch, *The Burning of Washington: The British Invasion of 1814* (Annapolis, MD: Blue Jacket Books, Naval Institute Press, 2000), 210–11.

54. Jon Latimer, *1812: War with America* (Cambridge, MA: Harvard University Press, 2007), 330.

55. Ibid., 333.

56. Anthony S. Pitch, *The Burning of Washington: The British Invasion of 1814* (Annapolis, MD: Blue Jacket Books, Naval Institute Press, 2000), 191–92.

57. Ibid., 218–19.

Chapter 18: American Victories at
Lake Champlain and New Orleans

1. Walter Borneman, *1812: The War that Forged a Nation* (New York: HarperCollins, 2004), 266.

2. James Monroe, Secretary of State of the United States, to Albert Gallatin, John Quincy Adams and James A. Bayard, United States Ministers to negotiate peace with Great Britain, Department of State, June 23, 1813, in *Diplomatic Correspondence of the United States: Canadian Relations, 1784–1860*, vol. 1, 1784–1820, ed. William R. Manning (Washington: Carnegie Endowment for International Peace, 1940), 219.

3. *Official Letters of the Military and Naval Officers of the United States during*

the War with Great Britain in the Years 1812, 13, 14 & 15, collected and annotated by John Brannan (Washington, 1823), 431–35.

4.   James Monroe, Secretary of State of the United States, to John Quincy Adams,
     James A. Bayard, Henry Clay and Jonathan Russell, United States Ministers
     to negotiate peace with Great Britain, Department of State, January 28, 1814,
     in *Diplomatic Correspondence of the United States: Canadian Relations,
     1784–1860*, vol. 1, 1784–1820, ed. William R. Manning (Washington: Carnegie
     Endowment for International Peace, 1940), 217.

5.   A. T. Mahan, *The Sea War of 1812: A History of the Maritime Conflict*, vol. 2
     (n.p.: Leonaur, 2008), 273.

6.   John Quincy Adams, James A. Bayard, Henry Clay and Jonathan Russell,
     United States Ministers to negotiate peace with Great Britain, to James Monroe,
     Secretary of State of the United States, Ghent, August 12, 1814, in *Diplomatic
     Correspondence of the United States: Canadian Relations, 1784–1860*, vol. 1,
     1784–1820, ed. William R. Manning (Washington: Carnegie Endowment for
     International Peace, 1940), 618.

7.   Jon Latimer, *1812: War with America* (Cambridge, MA: Harvard University
     Press, 2007), 31.

8.   A. T. Mahan, *The Sea War of 1812: A History of the Maritime Conflict*, vol. 2
     (n.p.: Leonaur, 2008), 354.

9.   Jon Latimer, *1812: War with America* (Cambridge, MA: Harvard University
     Press, 2007), 347–48.

10. Ibid., 333, 350.

11. A. J. Langguth, *Union 1812: The Americans Who Fought the Second War of
     Independence*, paperback edition (New York: Simon and Schuster, 2006), 331.

12. Keith A. Herkalo, *September Eleventh 1814: The Battles at Plattsburgh* (limited
     1st ed. available from http://www.battleofplattsburgh.org, 2007), 117.

13. Theodore Roosevelt, *The Naval War of 1812* (n.p.: Seven Treasures Publica-
     tions, 2009; first published 1882 by G. Putnam's Sons), 184.

14. Ibid., 186–89.

15. A. T. Mahan, *The Sea War of 1812: A History of the Maritime Conflict*, vol. 2
     (n.p.: Leonaur, 2008), 377–79.

16. Ibid., 383.

17. Ibid., 381–83.

18. Theodore Roosevelt, *The Naval War of 1812* (n.p.: Seven Treasures Publica-
     tions, 1999; first published 1882 by G. Putnam's Sons), 194.

19. Jon Latimer, *1812: War with America* (Cambridge, MA: Harvard University
     Press, 2007), 358, 359.

20. Theodore Roosevelt, *The Naval War of 1812* (n.p.: Seven Treasures Publica-
     tions, 1999; first published 1882 by G. Putnam's Sons), 195.

21. A. T. Mahan, *The Sea War of 1812: A History of the Maritime Conflict*, vol. 2 (n.p.: Leonaur, 2008), 383.

22. Walter Borneman, *1812: The War that Forged a Nation* (New York: HarperCollins, 2004), 213.

23. Jon Latimer, *1812: War with America* (Cambridge, MA: Harvard University Press, 2007), 358, 359.

24. Walter Borneman, *1812: The War that Forged a Nation* (New York: HarperCollins, 2004), 2.

25. Ibid., 271.

26. A. T. Mahan, *The Sea War of 1812: A History of the Maritime Conflict*, vol. 2 (n.p.: Leonaur, 2008), 398.

CHAPTER 19: THE TREATY OF GHENT

1. Jon Latimer, *1812: War with America* (Cambridge, MA: Harvard University Press, 2007), 389.

2. *Official Letters of the Military and Naval Officers of the United States during the War with Great Britain in the Years 1812, 13, 14 & 15*, collected and annotated by John Brannan (Washington, 1823), 504–10.

EPILOGUE: TWO MYSTERIES

1. Walter Borneman, *1812: The War that Forged a Nation* (New York: HarperCollins, 2004); and A. J. Langguth, *Union 1812: The Americans Who Fought the Second War of Independence*, paperback edition (New York: Simon and Schuster, 2006).

2. Colonel J. A. Vesey to Brigadier Brock, 9 April 1811, in *The Life and Correspondence of Major-General Sir Isaac Brock, K.B.*, ed. Ferdinand Brock Tupper, Esq. (London: Simpkin, Marshall, 1847), 100.

3. Colonel J. A. Vesey to Brigadier Brock, 9 May 1811, in *The Life and Correspondence of Major-General Sir Isaac Brock, K.B.*, ed. Ferdinand Brock Tupper, Esq. (London: Simpkin, Marshall, 1847), 100.

4. Guy St-Denis, *Tecumseh's Bones* (Montreal: McGill-Queen's University Press, 2005), 101.

5. Ibid., 161.

Select Bibliography

Abbott, John S. C. *Daniel Boone: The Pioneer of Kentucky.* New York: Dodd and Mead, 1872.

Adams, Henry. *History of the United States of America During the Administrations of James Madison.* New York: Library of America, 1986.

Albright, Harry. *New Orleans: The Battle of the Bayous.* New York: Hippocrene Books, 1990.

Allen, Robert S. *The Battle of Moraviantown, October 3, 1813.* Ottawa: Canadian War Museum, 1994.

Allen, Robert S. *His Majesty's Indian Allies: British Indian Policy in the Defence of Canada, 1774–1815.* Toronto: Dundurn Press, 1999.

Anson, Bert. *The Miami Indians.* Norman: University of Oklahoma Press, 1970.

Antal, Sandy. *A Wampum Denied: Procter's War of 1812.* Ottawa: Carleton University Press, 1997.

Armstrong, Frederick H. *Handbook of Upper Canadian Chronology.* Toronto: Dundurn Press, 1985.

Armstrong, John. *Notices of the War of 1812.* 2 vols. New York: Wiley and Putnam, 1840.

Auchinleck, G. *The War of 1812: A History of the War Between Great Britain and the United States Of America, During The Years 1812, 1813, and 1814.* Toronto: C. Chewett, 1862.

Averill, James P. *Fort Meigs: A Condensed History.* Toledo, OH: Blade Printing and Paper, 1886.

Babcock, Louis L. *The Siege of Fort Erie: An Episode of the War of 1812.* Buffalo: Peter Paul, 1899.

Babcock, Louis L. *The War of 1812 on the Niagara Frontier.* Buffalo: Buffalo Historical Society, 1927.

Bailey, John R. *Mackinac, Formerly Michilimackinac.* Lansing, MI: Darius D. Thorp and Son, 1895.

Bannister, J. A. "The Burning of Dover." *Western Ontario Historical Notes* 21 (March 1965).

Bayles, G. H. "Tecumseh and the Bayles Family Tradition." *Register of the Kentucky Historical Society* 46, no. 157 (1948).

Beasley, David R. *The Canadian Don Quixote: The Life and Works of Major John Richardson, Canada's First Novelist.* Erin, ON: Porcupine's Quill, 1977.

Beirne, Francis F. *The War of 1812.* New York: Dutton, 1949.

Benn, Carl. *The Battle of York.* Belleville, ON: Mika, 1984.

Benn, Carl. *The Iroquois in the War of 1812.* Toronto: University of Toronto Press, 1998.

Berger, Carl. *The Sense of Power: Studies in the Ideas of Canadian Imperialism, 1867–1914.* Toronto: University of Toronto Press, 1970.

Berton, Pierre. *War of 1812: The Invasion of Canada and Flames across the Border.* Toronto: Anchor Canada, 2011.

Borneman, Walter. *1812: The War that Forged a Nation.* New York: HarperCollins, 2004.

Brant, Irving. *James Madison: Commander in Chief, 1812–1836.* New York: Bobbs-Merrill, 1961.

Breidlid, Anders, Fredrik Chr. Brøgger, Øyvind T. Gulliksen, and Torbjorn Sirevag, eds. *American Culture: An Anthology of Civilization Texts.* New York: Routledge, 1996.

Briggs, John H. *Naval Administrations, 1827–1892.* London: Sampson Low, 1897.

Brooks, Charles B. *The Siege of New Orleans.* Seattle: University of Washington Press, 1961.

Brown, Dee. *Bury My Heart at Wounded Knee: An Indian History of the American West.* New York: Holt, Rinehart and Winston, 1970.

Brown, Roger H. *The Republic in Peril: 1812.* New York: W. W. Norton, 1971.

Budiansky, Stephen. *Perilous Fight: America's Intrepid War with Britain on the High Seas, 1812–1815.* New York: Alfred A. Knopf, 2010.

Burk, Kathleen. *Old World, New World: Great Britain and America from the Beginning.* New York: Atlantic Monthly Press, 2007.

Burr, Samuel Jones. *The Life and Times of William Henry Harrison.* New York: L. W. Ransom, 1840.

Byron, Gilbert. *The War of 1812 on the Chesapeake Bay.* Baltimore: Maryland Historical Society, 1964.

Caffrey, Kate. *The Lion and the Union: The Anglo-American War, 1812–1815.* London: Andre Deutsch, 1978.

Caffrey, Kate. *The Twilight's Last Gleaming: The British Against America, 1812–1815.* New York: Stein and Day, 1977.

Calhoun, John C. "Speech on the Resolution of the Committee on Foreign Relations, December 12, 1811." In *Union and Liberty: The Political Philosophy of John C. Calhoun.* Edited by Ross M. Lence. Indianapolis: Liberty Fund, 1992. Pdf copy available at the Online Library of Liberty, http://oll.libertyfund.org.

Calloway, Colin G. *Crown and Calumet: British-Indian Relations, 1783–1815.* Norman: University of Oklahoma Press, 1987.

Calloway, Colin G. *One Vast Winter Count: The Native American West before Lewis and Clark.* Lincoln: University of Nebraska Press, 2003.

Casselman, Alexander Clark. *Richardson's War of 1812.* Toronto: Historical Publishing, 1902.

Cleaves, Freeman. *Old Tippecanoe: William Henry Harrison and His Time.* New York: Kennikat Press, 1969. First published 1939 by Charles Scribner's Sons.

Coffin, William F. *1812; the War, and Its Moral: A Canadian Chronicle.* Montreal: John Lovell, 1864.

Coleman, Christopher B. "The Ohio Valley in the Preliminaries of the War of 1812." *Mississippi Valley Historical Review* 7, no. 1 (1920).

Colley, Linda. *Britons: Forging the Nation, 1707–1837.* New Haven: Yale University Press, 1992.

Collins, Gilbert. *Guidebook to the Historic Sites of the War of 1812.* Toronto: Dundurn Press, 2006.

Cookson, J. E. *The British Armed Nation, 1793–1815.* Oxford: Clarendon Press, 1997.

Crockett, David. *A Narrative of the Life of David Crockett, of the State of Tennessee.* Baltimore: E. L. Cary and A. Hart, 1834.

Cruikshank, E. A. "The Battle of Fort George." *Niagara Historical Society Publications,* 1 (1896).

Cruikshank, E. A. "Harrison and Procter: The River Raisin." *Royal Society of Canada Proceedings,* ser. 3, sect. 2, vol. 4 (1910).

Cruikshank, E. A. "John Beverly Robinson and the Trials for Treason." *Ontario Historical Society Papers and Records* 25 (1929).

Cruikshank, E. A. "The Siege of Fort Erie." *Lundy's Lane Historical Society Publications* 1, part 14 (1905).

Cruikshank, E.A. "A Study of Disaffection in Upper Canada." *Royal Society of Canada Transactions,* ser. 3, sect. 2, vol. 6 (1912).

Cumberland, Barlow. *The Battle of York.* Toronto: William Briggs, 1913.

Cushing, Daniel Lewis. *Captain Cushing in the War of 1812.* Edited by H. Lindley. Columbus: Ohio State Archaeological and Historical Society, 1944.

Dale, Ronald J. *The Invasion of Canada: Battles of the War of 1812.* Toronto: James Lorimer, 2001.

Dickason, Olive Patricia, and David T. McNab. *Canada's First Nations: A History of Founding Peoples from Earliest Times.* 4th ed. Toronto: Oxford University Press, 2009.

Dictionary of Canadian Biography Online. http://www.biographi.ca.

Di Silvestro, Roger L. *In the Shadow of Wounded Knee.* New York: Walker, 2007.

Dodge, Robert. *The Battle of Lake Erie.* Fostoria, OH: Gray Printing, 1967.

Douglas, R. Alan. "Weapons of the War of 1812." *Michigan History* 47 (1963).

Dowd, Gregory Evans. *A Spirited Resistance: The North American Indian Struggle for Unity, 1745–1815*. Baltimore: Johns Hopkins University Press, 1993.

Drake, Benjamin. *Life of Tecumseh, and of His Brother the Prophet; with a Historical Sketch of the Shawanoe Indians*. Cincinnati: E. Morgan, 1841.

Eaton, Clement. *Henry Clay and the Art of American Politics*. Boston: Little, Brown, 1957.

Eckert, Allan W. *A Sorrow in Our Heart: The Life of Tecumseh*. New York: Bantam, 1993.

Eckert, Edward K. *The Navy Department in the War of 1812*. Gainesville: University of Florida Press, 1973.

Edgar, Matilda. *General Brock*. Revised by E. A. Cruikshank. London: Oxford University Press, 1926.

Edmunds, R. David. *The Shawnee Prophet*. Lincoln: University of Nebraska Press, 1985.

Edmunds, R. David. *Tecumseh and the Quest for Indian Leadership*. Boston: Little, Brown, 1984.

Egglestone, Edward, and Lillie Eggelstone Seelye. *The Shawnee People, or The Story of Tecumseh*. London, 1880.

Ehle, John. *Trail of Tears: The Rise and Fall of the Cherokee Nation*. New York: Doubleday, 1988.

Elting, John R. *Amateurs to Arms! A Military History of the War of 1812*. New York: Da Capo, 1991.

Emsley, Clive. *British Society and the French Wars, 1793–1815*. London: Macmillan, 1979.

Erney, Richard Alton. *The Public Life of Henry Dearborn*. New York: Arno, 1979.

Feldman, Jay. *When the Mississippi Ran Backwards: Empire, Intrigue, Murder, and the New Madrid Earthquakes*. New York: Free Press, 2005.

Fitzgibbon, Mary A. *A Veteran of 1812: The Life of James Fitzgibbon*. Toronto: William Briggs, 1894.

Ford, Henry A., A.M. Ford, and Mrs. Kate B. Ford. *History of Hamilton County, Ohio, with Illustrations and Biographical Sketches*. Cleveland: L. A. William, 1881.

Forester, C. S. *The Naval War of 1812*. London: Landsborough, 1958.

Fraser, John. *Canadian Pen and Ink Sketches*. Montreal: Gazette, 1890.

Fremont-Barnes, Gregory. *The Royal Navy, 1793–1815*. Oxford: Osprey, 2007.

Gallatin, Albert. *A Synopsis of the Indian Tribes within the United States East of the Rocky Mountains, and in the British and Russian Possessions in North America*. Cambridge: Cambridge University Press, 1836.

Garner, John. *The Franchise and Politics in British North America*. Toronto: University of Toronto Press, 1969.

Gellner, John, ed. *Recollections of the War of 1812: Three Eyewitness Accounts.* Toronto: Baxter, 1964.

George, Christopher T. *Terror on the Chesapeake: The War of 1812 on the Bay.* Shippensburg, PA: White Mane, 2000.

Gerson, Noel B. *Mr. Madison's War, 1812: The Second War for Independence.* New York: Julian Messner, 1966.

Goebel, Dorothy B. *William Henry Harrison: A Political Biography.* Philadelphia: Porcupine, 1974. First published 1926 by Historical Bureau of the Indiana Library and Historical Department.

Gordon, Colonel H. R. *Tecumseh, Chief of the Shawanoes: A Tale of the War of 1812.* New York: E. P. Dutton, 1898.

Gough, Barry M. *Fighting Sail on Lake Huron and Georgian Bay: The War of 1812 and Its Aftermath.* Annapolis, MD: Naval Institute Press, 2002.

Graves, Donald E. "The Canadian Volunteers, 1813–1815." *Military Collector and Historian* 31 (Fall 1979).

Graves, Donald E. *Field of Glory: The Battle of Crysler's Farm, 1813.* Toronto: Robin Brass Studio, 1999.

Graves, Donald E. *Where Right and Glory Lead! The Battle of Lundy's Lane, 1814.* Cap-Saint-Ignace, QC: Robin Brass Studio, 1993.

Green, Ernest. *Lincoln at Bay: A Sketch of 1814.* Welland, ON: Tribune-Telegraph Press, 1923.

Green, Michael D. *The Politics of Indian Removal: Creek Government and Society in Crisis.* Lincoln: University of Nebraska Press, 1985.

Gurd, Norman S. *The Story of Tecumseh.* Toronto: W. Briggs, 1912.

Hallaman, E. *The British Invasions of Ohio: 1813.* Columbus: Anthony Wayne Parkway Board, Ohio Historical Society, 1958.

Hamil, Fred Coyne. *The Valley of the Lower Thames, 1640–1850.* Toronto: University of Toronto Press, 1951.

Hare, John S. "Military Punishments in the War of 1812." *Journal of the American Military Institute* 4 (Winter 1940).

Heidler, David S., and Jeanne T. Heidler, eds. *Encyclopedia of the War of 1812.* Annapolis, MD: Naval Institute Press, 2004.

Henderson, J. L. H. *John Strachan.* Toronto: University of Toronto Press, 1969.

Herkalo, Keith A. *September Eleventh 1814: The Battles at Plattsburgh.* Limited 1st ed., 2007. Available from www.battleofplattsburg.org.

Hickey, Donald R. *The War of 1812: A Forgotten Conflict.* Champaign: University of Illinois Press, 1995.

Hildreth, S. P. *Pioneer History: Being an Account of the First Examinations of the Ohio Valley, and the Early Settlement of the Northwest Territory.* Cincinnati: H. W. Derby; New York: A. B. Barnes, 1848.

Hitsman, J. MacKay. *The Incredible War of 1812: A Military History*. Updated by Donald E. Graves. Cap-Saint-Ignace, QC: Robin Brass Studio, 1999.

Hitsman, J. MacKay. "Sir George Prevost's Conduct of the Canadian War of 1812." *Canadian Historical Association Report* 41, no. 1 (1962).

Holland, James W. *Andrew Jackson and the Creek War: Victory at the Horseshoe*. Tuscaloosa: University of Alabama Press, 1968.

Ingersoll, Charles J. *Historical Sketch of the Second War between the United States of America and Great Britain*. 3 vols. Philadelphia: Lea and Blanchard, 1845–49.

Ingraham, Edward. *A Sketch of the Events Which Preceded the Capture of Washington by the British*. Philadelphia: Carey and Hart, 1849.

Irving, L. Homfray. *Officers of the British Forces in Canada during the War of 1812–15*. Welland, ON: Tribune, for the Canadian Military Institute, 1908.

Jacobs, James R. *Tarnished Warrior: Major-General James Wilkinson*. New York: Macmillan, 1938.

James, William. *A Full and Correct Account of the Military Occurrences of the Late War Between Great Britain and the United States of America*. London: Printed for the author and sold by Black, Kingsbury, Parbury, and Allen, 1818.

James, William. *The Naval History of Great Britain*. New edition by Captain Chamier, R.N., London, 1837. Cited in Theodore Roosevelt, *The Naval War of 1812*. N.p.: Seven Treasures Publications, 2009; first published 1882 by G. P. Putnam's Sons.

Jefferson, Thomas. *The Works of Thomas Jefferson*, federal edition. 12 vols. New York: G. P. Putnam's Sons, 1904–5.

Jefferson, Thomas. *The Works of Thomas Jefferson: Vol. XI Correspondence and Papers 1808–1816*. New York: Cosimo Inc., 2009.

Jonasson, E., ed. *Canadian Veterans of the War of 1812*. Winnipeg: Wheatfield Press, 1981.

Jones, Maldwyn. *The Limits of Liberty: American History, 1607–1980*. Oxford: Oxford University Press, 1983.

Keegan, John. *Battle at Sea: From Man-of-War to Submarine*. London: Pimlico, 2004.

Kellogg, Louise P. *The British Regime in Wisconsin and the Northwest*. Madison: State Historical Society of Wisconsin, 1935.

Kennedy, Paul M. *The Rise and Fall of the Great Powers: Economic Change and Military Conflict from 1500 to 2000*. London: Unwin Hyman, 1988.

Kerr, W. B. "The Occupation of York." *Canadian Historical Review* 5, no. 1 (1924).

Kessel, William B., and Robert Wooster, eds. *Encyclopedia of Native American Wars and Warfare*. New York: Facts on File, 2005.

Langguth, A. J. *Union 1812: The Americans Who Fought the Second War of Independence*. New York: Simon and Schuster, 2006.

Latimer, Jon. *1812: War with America*. Cambridge, MA: Harvard University Press, 2007.

Lauriston, Victor. *Romantic Kent: The Story of a County*. Chatham, ON: Shepherd, 1952.

Lawson, Don. *The War of 1812: America's Second War for Independence*. London: Abelard-Schuman, 1966.

Lees, James. *The Masting and Rigging of English Ships of War, 1625–1860*. London: Conway Maritime Press, 1984.

Leighton, Arthur J. "'Eyes on the Wabash': A History of Indiana's Indian People from Pre-Contact through Removal." Ph.D. thesis, Purdue University, 2007.

Lloyd, Alan. *The Scorching of Washington: The War of 1812*. London: David and Charles, 1974.

Lower, Arthur R. M. *Canadians in the Making: A Social History of Canada*. Toronto: Longmans, Green, 1958.

Mahan, A. T. *The Sea War of 1812: A History of the Maritime Conflict*. Vol. 2. N.p.: Leonaur, 2008.

Mahon, John K. *The War of 1812*. Gainesville: University of Florida Press, 1972.

Marine, William M. *The British Invasion of Maryland, 1812–15*. Hatboro, PA: Tradition Press, 1965.

Mayo, Bernard. *Henry Clay, Spokesman of the New West*. Boston: Houghton Mifflin, 1937.

McAfee, Robert. *History of the Late War in the Western Country*. Lexington, KY: Worsley and Smith, 1816.

McKenzie, Ruth. *Laura Secord: The Legend and the Lady*. Toronto: McClelland and Stewart, 1971.

Morison, Samuel Eliot, and Henry Steele Commager. *The Growth of the American Republic*. 7th ed. New York: Oxford University Press, 1962.

Moquin, Wayne, with Charles Van Doren, eds. *Great Documents in American Indian History*. New York: Praeger, 1973.

Murrin, John M., Paul E. Johnson, James M. McPherson, Gary Gerstle, and Emily S. Rosenberg. *Liberty, Equality, Power: A History of the American People*. 6th ed. Beverly, MA: Wadsworth, 2011.

Niles, Hezekiah. *Niles' National Register*. Vol. 4. Philadelphia, 1813.

Nursey, Walter R. *The Story of Isaac Brock, Hero, Defender and Saviour of Upper Canada, 1812*. Toronto: William Briggs, 1908.

O'Brien, Sean Michael. *In Bitterness and in Tears: Andrew Jackson's Destruction of the Creeks and Seminoles*. Guilford, CT: Lyons Press, 2005.

O'Callaghan, E. B. *Documents Relative to the Colonial History of the State of New York*. Albany: Weed, Parsons, 1857.

Oman, Charles. *Wellington's Army, 1809–1814*. London: Edward Arnold, 1913.

Parton, James. *Life of Andrew Jackson*. Vol. 1. New York: Mason Brothers, 1861.

Pitch, Anthony S. *The Burning of Washington: The British Invasion of 1814*. Annapolis, MD: Blue Jacket Books, Naval Institute Press, 2000.

Poling, Jim, Sr. *Tecumseh: Shooting Star, Crouching Panther.* Toronto: Dundurn Press, 2009.

Randall, E. O. "Tecumseh, the Shawnee Chief." *Ohio Archaeological and Historical Society Publications* 15 (December 1906).

Read, D. B., *Life and Times of Major-General Sir Isaac Brock, K.B.* Toronto: William Briggs, 1894.

Reid, Stuart. *British Redcoat, 1793–1815.* Oxford: Osprey, 1997.

Remini, Robert V. *Henry Clay: Statesman for the Union.* New York: W. W. Norton, 1991.

Rodger, N. A. M. *The Command of the Ocean: A Naval History of Britain, 1649–1815.* London: Penguin, 2004.

Roosevelt, Theodore. *The Naval War of 1812.* N.p.: Seven Treasures Publications, 2009. First published 1882 by G. Putnam's Sons.

Rowland, D. *Andrew Jackson's Campaign against the British, or the Mississippi Territory in The War of 1812.* New York: Macmillan, 1926.

Ryerson, Adolphus Egerton. *The Loyalists of America and Their Times, from 1620 to 1816.* 2nd ed. 2 vols. Toronto: William Briggs, 1880.

Schmalz, Peter S. *The Ojibwa of Southern Ontario.* Toronto: University of Toronto Press, 1991.

Scott, Duncan Campbell, and Lady Edgar. *John Graves Simcoe and General Brock.* Toronto: Morang, 1910.

Shortt, Adam, and Doughty, Arthur G. *Canada and Its Provinces.* 23 vols. Toronto: Publishers' Association of Canada, 1914–17.

Skaggs, David Curtis, and Larry L. Nelson, eds. *The Sixty Years' War for the Great Lakes, 1754–1814.* East Lansing: Michigan State University Press, 2001.

Skeen, C. Edward. "Mr. Madison's Secretary of War." *Pennsylvania Magazine of History and Biography* 100, no. 4 (1976).

Smelser, Marshall. "Tecumseh, Harrison and the War of 1812." *Indiana Magazine of History* 65, no. 1 (1969).

Smith, Alison. "John Strachan and Early Upper Canada, 1799–1814." *Ontario History* 52 (1960).

Smith, J. H. "The Battle of Stoney Creek." *Journal and Proceedings of the Hamilton Association* 13 (1896–97).

Snow, Richard. "The Battle of Lake Erie." *American Heritage* 27, no. 2 (1976).

Stacey, C. P. "Another Look at the Battle of Lake Erie." *Canadian Historical Review* 39, no. 1 (1958).

Stacey, C. P. *The Battle of Little York.* Toronto: Toronto Historical Board, 1963.

Stacey, C. P. "The Ships of the British Squadron on Lake Ontario, 1812–14." *Canadian Historical Review* 34, no. 4 (1953).

St-Denis, Guy. *Tecumseh's Bones.* Montreal: McGill-Queen's University Press, 2005.

Sugden, John. *Blue Jacket: Warrior of the Shawnees.* Lincoln: University of Nebraska Press, 2000.

Sugden, John. *Tecumseh: A Life.* New York: Henry Holt, 1997.

Sugden, John. *Tecumseh's Last Stand.* Norman: University of Oklahoma Press, 1985.

Tanner, Helen Hornbeck, ed. *Atlas of Great Lakes Indian History.* Norman: University of Oklahoma Press, 1987.

Taylor, Alan. *The Civil War of 1812: American Citizens, British Subjects, Irish Rebels, and Indian Allies.* New York: Alfred A. Knopf, 2010.

Time Specials. "America's Worst Vice Presidents." August 21, 2008.

Tomlinson, Everett, T. *Tecumseh's Young Braves: A Story of The Creek War.* Boston: Lee and Shepard, 1897.

Turner, Wesley B. *British Generals in the War of 1812.* Montreal: McGill-Queen's University Press, 1999.

Watson, O. K. "Moraviantown." *Ontario Historical Society Papers and Records* 28 (1932).

Watts, J. F., and Fred L. Israel, eds. *Presidential Documents: The Speeches, Proclamations and Policies That Have Shaped the Nation from Washington to Clinton.* New York: Routledge, 2000.

Way, Ronald. "The Day of Crysler's Farm." *Canadian Geographical Journal* 62 (1961).

Weller, Jac. *Wellington at Waterloo.* Barnsley, UK: Greenhill Books, 1992.

White, Richard. *The Middle Ground: Indians, Empires, and Republics in the Great Lakes Region, 1650–1815.* New York: Cambridge University Press, 2011.

Williams, Samuel. *Two Western Campaigns in the War of 1812–13.* Cincinnati: Robert Clarke, 1870.

Willig, Timothy D. "Prophetstown on the Wabash: The Native Spiritual Defense of the Old Northwest." *Michigan Historical Review* 23, no. 2 (1997).

Willig, Timothy D. *Restoring the Chain of Friendship: British Policy and the Indians of the Great Lakes, 1783–1815.* Lincoln: University of Nebraska Press, 2008.

Wilkinson, James. *Wilkinson: Soldier and Pioneer.* New Orleans: Rogers Printing Co., 1935.

Wood, William. *The War with the United States.* Toronto: University of Toronto Press, 1967.

Wise, S. F., and Craig R. Brown. *Canada Views the United States: Nineteenth-Century Political Attitudes.* Toronto: Macmillan, 1967.

Yaple, R. L. "The Auxiliaries: Foreign and Miscellaneous Regiments in the British Army, 1802–1817." *Journal of the Society for Army Historical Research* 50 (1972).

Young, Bennett H. "The Battle of the Thames." *Filson Club Publications* 18 (1903).

Zacks, Richard. *The Pirate Coast: Thomas Jefferson, the First Marines, and the Secret Mission of 1805.* New York: Hyperion, 2005.

Zaslow, Morris, and Wesley B. Turner, eds. *The Defended Border: Upper Canada and the War of 1812.* Toronto: Macmillan, 1964.

Zimmerman, James Fulton. *Impressment of American Seamen*. New York: Kennikat Press, 1966.

Zuehlke, Mark. *For Honour's Sake: The War of 1812 and the Brokering of an Uneasy Peace*. Toronto: Alfred A. Knopf, 2006.

Primary Sources

Armstrong, John. *Hints to Young Generals, by an Old Soldier*. Kingston, NY, 1812.

Babcock, James L., ed. "The Campaign of 1814 on the Niagara Frontier." *Niagara Frontier* 10 (1963).

Brannan, John. *Collected and Annotated, Official Letters of the Military and Naval Officers of the United States during the War with Great Britain in the Years 1812, 13, 14 & 15*. Washington: Way & Gideon, 1823.

Brenton, E. B. *Some Account of the Public Life of the Late Lieutenant General Sir George Prevost, Bart., Particularly of His Services in the Canadas*. London: Cadell, 1823.

Chapin, Cyrenius. *Chapin's Review of Armstrong's Notices of the War of 1812*. Black Rock, NY: D. P. Adams, 1836.

Combs, Leslie. "Account of Fort Meigs." *American Historical Record* 1 (1872).

Cruikshank, E. A., ed. *The Documentary History of the Campaign upon the Niagara Frontier, 1812–1814*. 9 vols. Welland, ON: Lundy's Lane Historical Society, 1896–1908.

Cruikshank, E. A., ed. *Documents Relating to the Invasion of the Niagara Peninsula by the United States Army Commanded by General Jacob Brown in July and August 1814*. Niagara-on-the-Lake: Niagara Historical Society Publications 33 (1920).

Edgar, Matilda. *Ten Years of Upper Canada in Peace and War, 1805–1815; Being the Ridout Letters*. Toronto: William Briggs, 1890.

Hull, William. *The Memoirs of the Campaign of the North Western Army of the United States, A.D. 1812: In a Series of Letters Addressed to the Citizens of the United States*. Boston: True and Greene, 1824.

Jefferson, Thomas. *The Papers of Thomas Jefferson*. Retirement Series. Vol. 8. New Jersey: Princeton University Press, 2011.

Klinck, Carl F., ed. *Tecumseh: Fact and Fiction in Early Records*. Ottawa: Tecumseh Press, 1978.

Madison, James. *The Writings of James Madison*. Vol. 8, 1808–1819. Edited by Gaillard Hunt. New York: G. P. Putnam's Sons, 1908.

Manning, William R. *Diplomatic Correspondence of the United States: Canadian Relations, 1784–1860*. Vol. 1, 1784–1821. Washington: Carnegie Endowment for International Peace, 1940.

McClure, George. *Causes of the Destruction of the American Towns on the Niagara Frontier and Failure of the Campaign of the Fall of 1813*. Bath, NY, 1817.

Monroe, James. *The Writings of James Monroe: Including a Collection of His Public and Private Papers and Correspondence*. Vol. 5. Edited by Stanislaus Murray Hamilton. New York: G. P. Putnam's Sons, 1901.

Richardson, John. "A Canadian Campaign." *New Monthly Magazine*, 1827.

Richardson, John. *Richardson's War of 1812*. Edited by Alexander C. Casselman. Toronto: Historical Publishing, 1902.

Roach, Isaac. "Journal of Major Isaac Roach, 1812–1824." *Pennsylvania Magazine of History and Biography* 17 (1893).

Roosevelt, Franklin D. "Message to Congress Requesting Authority to Return a Mace to Canada." May 4, 1934.

Sheaffe, Roger Hale. "Documents Relating to the War of 1812: The Letterbook of Gen. Sir Roger Hale Sheaffe." *Buffalo Historical Society Publications* 17 (1913).

"The Siege of Fort Meigs." *Register of the Kentucky Historical Society* 19 (1929).

Strachan, John. *The John Strachan Letterbook, 1812–1834*. Edited by George Spragge. Toronto: Ontario Historical Society, 1946.

Tupper, Ferdinand Brock, ed. *The Life and Correspondence of Major-General Sir Isaac Brock, K.B.* London: Simpkin, Marshall, 1847.

United States Congress. *American State Papers: Foreign Relations*. Vol. 3. Washington: Gales and Seaton, 1832.

United States Congress. *American State Papers: Naval Affairs*. Vol. 1. Washington: Gales and Seaton, 1832.

Van Rensselaer, Solomon. *A Narrative of the Affair of Queenstown: In the War of 1812*. New York: Leavitt, Lord, 1836.

Wood, Eleazer. "Eleazer D. Wood's Journal of the Northwestern Campaign." In George Cullum, ed., *Campaigns of the War of 1812–15*. New York: J. Miller, 1879.

Wood, William C. H., ed. *Select British Documents of the Canadian War of 1812*. Vol. 13–15, 17. Toronto: Champlain Society, 1920–28.

York [Upper Canada] *Gazette*, 1812–13.

Unpublished Primary Sources

Strachan Papers. MS 35, Microfilm reels 1, 5 and 10. Archives of Ontario.

Prevost to Bathurst, 8 October 1813. F. B. Tupper Papers: State Papers of Lower Canada, no. 91, Microfilm reel MS 496. Archives of Ontario.

Duncan Clark Fonds [Duncan Clark was a lieutenant in the Volunteer Incorporated Militia Battalion of the Eastern and Johnston Districts, serving in the War of 1812]. Microfilm reel MS 572. Archives of Ontario.

Letters received by the Secretary of the Navy Commissioned Officers, 1802–1884.
RG 45, vol. 9–11, 15, 21–22. Archives of the United States, 1812–14.

Sir Isaac Brock Papers. M.G. 24, A1, vol. 1, NAC microfilm reel C-4621. Library and
Archives Canada.

Brock to the Earl of Liverpool, York, Upper Canada, 29 August 1812. Colonial
Office Records, Indian Affairs, Canada. RG 10, vol. 10017, Canada Q. 315
Library and Archives Canada.

Ruddell, Stephen. *Reminiscences of Tecumseh's Youth.* Wisconsin Historical
Society, Digital Library and Archives, 2003. Online facsimile edition http://
www.americanjourneys.org/aj-155.

Acknowledgements

I am grateful to the many people who have advised me, assisted me, worked with me, and offered encouragement in the realization of this book. I appreciate the support of everyone at Anansi, in particular Kate McQuaid, Trish Osuch, and Kelly Joseph. Thanks to Peter Norman for his thoughtful and precise copyedit of the manuscript.

I am especially grateful to Anansi publisher Sarah MacLachlan for her warm encouragement and constant backing over the past two years.

Many thanks to Nan Froman, Michael Solomon, and my good friend Patsy Aldana at Groundwood for their collaboration on the associated book for young readers, titled *Tecumseh*. Working with artist Richard Rudnicki on that project has been richly rewarding.

As always, my literary agent, Jackie Kaiser, did a great job with the book at the proposal stage and in making the link with House of Anansi.

My gratitude goes out to the people on the island of Guernsey who assisted me during my visit there in March 2011. I am grateful for the helpful input of Dr. Jason Monaghan, Director of the Guernsey Museum, and Amanda Bennett, Chief Librarian of the Priaulx Library. Thanks to my good friend Catharine Walter for hosting me and organizing my schedule. Many thanks to Liz Head, who helped so much in setting up meetings. I greatly enjoyed meeting and benefitting from the insights of historian Gillian Lenfestey. Olly Brock, a descendant of the family whose most illustrious member was Sir Isaac, welcomed me into his home. I am indebted to him for his generosity in offering stories, interpretation, and sources with respect to his famous namesake.

I am deeply grateful to my colleague Professor David T. McNab in the Department of Equity Studies at York University for reviewing the manuscript and offering advice. David's scholarship and published works on indigenous peoples have been a great source of knowledge and perspective for me.

Paul-Émile McNab, who has toiled with me for a year and a half, doing research and tracking down sources, has been absolutely critical to this book. Paul's ability to hunt down original documents and navigate archives is a wonder to behold. His work on aboriginal history and his knowledge of the field have made him indispensable. I have emerged from this working relationship with a friend and a colleague.

Words cannot capture my gratitude to Janie Yoon, my editor, for the way she has taken on this project. She developed an encompassing perspective on the book and its subject matter that has helped transform the work into an exploration of history "in the moment." At every point she pushed for more immediacy, better pacing, and a spotlight on the two principal figures that locates them against the backdrop of the critical historical developments on both sides of the Atlantic. She is indefatigable. Awesome.

Thanks so much to Sandy, who lived through the intensity of this project, always providing encouragement, while doing her own writing.

Index

JAMES LAXER is the bestselling and award-winning author of twenty-five books, including *Stalking the Elephant: My Discovery of America* (published by the New Press in New York as *Discovering America*), *The Border: Canada, the U.S. and Dispatches from the Forty-Ninth Parallel*, *The Acadians: In Search of a Homeland*, and *Tecumseh*, a book for young readers. He was a former columnist for the *Toronto Star*, and he was host of a public affairs show on TV Ontario for three seasons. He won a Gemini Award for screenwriting on *Reckoning*, a film series about Canada and the global economy, which was produced by the National Film Board of Canada. He is a professor of political science in the Department of Equity Studies at York University. He lives in Toronto.